HEART COUNTRY

Kerry McGinnis was twelve when her father decided to leave the city and go droving with his four children. The family roamed widely before eventually settling in the Queensland Gulf Country. Kerry has worked as a shepherd, droving hand, gardener, and a stock-camp and station cook. Together with her brother and sister she now operates the family property Bowthorn, which is also a tourist destination.

Kerry is the author of the best-selling *Pieces of Blue*, and has published articles and short stories in various publications, including the *Sydney Morning Herald*, the *Herald & Weekly Times*, *Meanjin* and the *Bulletin*.

ALSO BY KERRY MCGINNIS

Pieces of Blue

Heart Country

KERRY MCGINNIS

VIKING

Viking
Penguin Books Australia Ltd
487 Maroondah Highway, PO Box 257
Ringwood, Victoria 3134, Australia
Penguin Books Ltd
Harmondsworth, Middlesex, England
Penguin Putnam Inc.
375 Hudson Street, New York, New York 10014, USA
Penguin Books Canada Limited
10 Alcorn Avenue, Toronto, Ontario, Canada M4V 3B2
Penguin Books (NZ) Ltd
Cnr Rosedale and Airborne Roads, Albany, Auckland, New Zealand
Penguin Books (South Africa) (Pty) Ltd
5 Watkins Street, Denver Ext 4, 2094, South Africa
Penguin Books India (P) Ltd
11, Community Centre, Panchsheel Park, New Delhi 110 017, India

First published by Penguin Books Australia Ltd 2001

10 9 8 7 6 5 4 3 2 1

Cover design by Melissa Fraser, Penguin Design Studio
Text design by Marina Messiha, Penguin Design Studio
Front cover photograph by Nick Rains
Back cover photograph: author with Carmen, 1966
Typeset in 11.5/18 pt Granjon by Midland Typesetters, Maryborough, Victoria
Made and printed in Australia by Australian Print Group, Maryborough, Victoria

National Library of Australia
Cataloguing-in-Publication data:

McGinnis, Kerry.
Heart country.

ISBN 0 670 89921 6.

1. McGinnis, Kerry. 2. Country life – Australia –
Biography. 3. Australia – Rural conditions – Biography. I.
Title.

307.72092

This project has been assisted by the Commonwealth Government through the Australia Council, its arts funding and advisory body.

www. penguin.com.au

For Judith and Patrick John

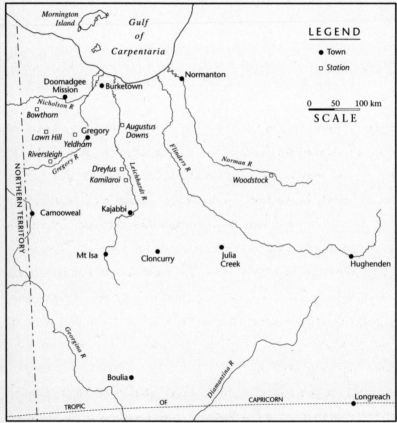

Map of key places mentioned in the text

ONE

I don't know when it was that I began to grow tired of droving. I was thinking about it that day we pulled off the road where the Lily Hole turnoff ran in across the stony ridge. Dad parked the Bedford under some scraggy whitewoods, and Red and Larry, the two dogs, jumped off the load and began to nose around. I sat for a moment staring about at the scrubby range country. The far side of the moon could not have been any rougher. The road slid and wound, angling steeply down into rocky creeks, clinging to narrow cuts on the shoulders of boulder-strewn slopes. It made your body ache just to contemplate bouncing over it.

'Well, are you gunna swing the billy?' Dad limped past, banging on the mudguard, and I sighed mutinously and thrust the cab door open. I was tired of that part of it – camp cooking was for boy scouts – but I got the billy off the load and threw down Dad's folding chair while I was at it.

Dad toed it open with a grunt and sat down. He was riding again, but his hip had never come right since his accident on Dreyfus Station. That was two years ago now. He had given up droving then, but twelve months pottering around the town common had driven him back. He was fifty-seven, too young to quit work, so he had thrown away his stick and stocked up on garlic tablets, which somebody had told him were good for arthritis. It was ironic that now he was ready to go droving again, I wanted to stop. We'd been living on the road for years – making a base camp at Redwater during the Wet season and spending the rest of the time on the stock routes droving cattle for a living. We hired men as needed, but mostly it was just Dad, my two brothers, my sister and myself – what Dad liked to call a reliable team.

It was very still in the shade. I could hear the tick of the cooling engine and the bubbling sound when the billy boiled. I made the tea, thinking of the thousands of times I had done so in every kind of camp and weather. I lifted off the billy with a fold of my hat brim, and Red, who had flopped down under the truck, put his head on one side and pricked his ears.

'Plant coming, boy?' Dad cocked his head. Red stalked into the open, growling softly, which brought Larry out to join him. They stared fixedly up the track and now I could hear it too, a hum in the air, a vehicle labouring through the range towards us. It was another drover's turnout, a white truck piled high with stores, swags, saddles and cooking gear. Watching it come was like seeing yourself in the mirror. This was the drab, workaday face we showed to others – fencing-wire handles on the billies and dust coating the swags. Spare hobbles strung along the tie rail, and ropes sticking out of dirty corn bags. Even the two figures that got out when the truck stopped were interchangeable with us – scuffed boots, sun-faded jeans, and cotton shirts (hand-washed in a bucket and spread over a bush to dry), topped off with sweat-stained hats. Their hands were as red and roughened as mine, their faces and arms as brown.

'Kevin.' Dad greeted and shook hands with the driver, the shorter of the two, a man of medium height with broad cheekbones and big freckled hands, the backs of them covered with ginger hair. He handled the Gregory Downs cattle and was the best rough-rider in the Gulf.

'Colin,' Kevin said, jabbing a thumb at his silent companion.

I murmured a greeting, but the stranger lidded his eyes and squatted off to one side, not willing to talk.

'See my plant?' Dad lowered himself onto his seat again.

'Few miles back. Young Pat said you're taking the Riversleighs. Good long trip?'

'Yep. Down to the Fort. Bit o' stone on the route, but that'll be no novelty, any road.' His gaze swept over the surrounding hills with their cladding of spinifex and stunted scrub. 'Anything can get a living here'll think anywhere else is Heaven. Where's your mob?'

'Rockland.' Kevin tapped his pannikin with a spoon to settle the leaves. 'Taking their bullocks to the Isa. And maybe a mob of spayers, later on. What about your other lad?' He blew on his tea. 'Still working a plant?'

'Sian? He's shifting bulls for Australian Estates. They sent up a trainload for Kamilaroi, and he's walking them out. Then he'll be breaking colts for 'em till the Dreyfus cattle go.' Dad lifted his head because the dogs were growling again. 'Popular spot today – 'nother motor car.'

The four of us listened intently to the reverberating surge of sound that gradually deepened.

'Gotta be a truck.' Kevin set his tea aside and rose. 'I'd better shift mine.'

'Grader.' Colin's voice made me start. He'd been so silent behind his pannikin I had almost forgotten he was there. He was right, though, and soon afterwards it appeared, crawling slowly up the slope towards us, blade high.

'We'll need a traffic cop next.' Dad looked over at the fire. 'Anything left in the billy?'

I got up to fill it, and while I was standing at the tap watching the great yellow machine, I caught a dazzle of sun on chrome behind it and heard the roar of a second diesel motor.

It was a truck, a massive red and silver thing with a slatted stock crate, towing a similar trailer behind, both of them loaded with cattle. Patches of red and white hide swayed inside it. I glimpsed muzzles and horns and suddenly the whole of a lower ear.

'Hey! They're Thorntons!' The stock from Thorntonia Station were notoriously hard to handle. We'd taken them twice and been lucky, but they weren't cattle you'd choose to drove.

'So they are.' Dad was on his feet staring too. 'Old Tom must be desperate. They'll never get 'em over this road.'

The truck roared through his words, battering at the slope above the grind of gears. I could see the driver hunched over the wheel, and the loose rubble on the road beginning to churn and spray beneath the great tyres. Then slowly, its diesel bellowing defeat, it began to roll back, bucking the trailer behind it.

'Hell's teeth, he'll jackknife the dog!' Hands on hips, Kevin watched with interest, but the grader driver was already paying out the coils of a steel cable to take the truck in tow.

The cattle in the stock crates lurched and crashed. Hooves thudded continually, and I caught a whiff of fresh dung as they pulled slowly past us. The grader stopped then, and the driver got down to unhook the cable before continuing on his way again with no more than a wave to the four of us watching there. The truck followed, crawling more carefully down the slope, its trailer swaying. Behind us the unwanted billy boiled quietly on the dying fire.

'Makes yer feel a bit redundant.' Dad glanced across at Kevin, but he appeared unworried.

'That? Huh! You see if they don't walk the next lot out. Old Tom musta lost his marbles to be trying to truck 'em through the range. They'll be bruised to buggery, let alone the cost of the grader. Why, you could lose a coupla hundred walking 'em and still come out in front.' He tilted his hat to scratch his head, eyeing the sun as he did so. 'We'd better be shoving off, Mac. Thanks for the tea, Kerry. See you down the road sometime.'

They were scarcely out of sight before the horses arrived, walking in long files as they picked their way through the stone.

Patrick sang out to them and Simon, who was leading, pulled up, the rest slowing around him. Judith rode Blackmagic up to the whitewoods and stepped down into the shade to tie him up.

'You see the roadtrain?' She filled a pannikin from the tap. 'It's stuck in a gully half a mile back. The driver's hopping mad – reckons it's the worst road he's ever seen. Said he's surprised they ever got a bullock wagon over it, never mind a truck.'

'And there're two more coming – roadtrains, I mean.' Patrick shook his head, amazed. 'Only they have to wait till the first one's through the hills so the grader can go back for them. Bunch of nutters, you ask me.'

'That's what Kevin thinks,' I began, then Dad jabbed his pipe stem in the direction of Gregory, the way the truck had gone.

'It's the writing on the wall, that is, for the entire industry. Jesus! How can you all be so blind?' He shook his head. 'It's happening right before your eyes and you still haven't grasped what it means.'

'Means they'll need a new clutch in the truck the way he's going through the gears.' Patrick was flippant but Dad silenced him with a look. I saw he wasn't just scoring points, he was in earnest.

'What'd yer see, eh? Eh? Well, I'll tell yer. You saw two men doing the work o' five of us and about fifty times as fast. And that's on a track like this! So ask yerselves – when the roads improve, what's gunna happen then?'

Judith shrugged. 'Who cares? That's twenty years off, at least.'

'It isn't. They'll have bitumen on the Normanton Beef Road inside two, or I'll eat me hat.' He tapped it for emphasis.

'Jeez.' Patrick stared at him. 'But are you saying trucks'll do us out o' business?' He thought about it. 'S'pose you could be right. It'd change everything if they were carting big numbers o' cattle – the selling points, the railhead. Without road mobs there wouldn't be half the work about for ringers – no call for plant horses either. Why, us and Kevin and old Doug . . .'

'Now you're getting the picture.' Dad nodded, satisfied. 'It's happening all over. There's mechanised harvesters and pickers already. The cattle industry'll go the way of the farms – there's no more cane-cutting gangs in the sugar country. Give it another ten years and there won't be a drover left on the roads.'

It was the cue I needed. 'Suits me. I've seen enough stock routes and watched enough cattle to last me the rest of my life. The road-trains are welcome to 'em.'

Judith said reasonably (because Dad was a bit inclined to believe that nothing this side of the fifties had any merit), 'Well, everything changes. I mean, it must've been like that for teamsters when trucks first came in. You can't stop it happening.'

'But you don't have to let it happen to you,' Dad snapped at her. 'That's the point. If you see it coming, you can get out. It's time we started thinking of doing just that.'

I might as well not have spoken. Neither of them had listened. I opened my mouth to enlarge on the theme, but Patrick, who seemed always to be hungry, wasn't going to let an epoch-making change interfere with his lunch. 'Are you gunna make that tea or not?' he demanded. 'I'm starving.'

'Oh, for heaven's sake!' I kicked the ends of the burnt sticks back round the billy and tossed a lidful of leaves in. The bay mare, Emily, was sneaking off camp – let her get away with it and they'd all go. Dad whistled Larry out to get her back, then everybody was eating and the moment to raise the matter had passed. The trouble was, I thought, watching them sitting about in the scrappy shade with pannikins in their hands, we were a team. How could I quit if the others didn't want to, and what would I do, anyway? Only a handful of girls worked on the stations, mostly as governesses, and a scant few, like Judith and me, in stock camps. But you needed to have a family in the game; it wasn't a career a single girl could undertake alone if she wanted to retain her reputation.

I thought about it all the rest of the way into Lily Hole, where we were to camp that night. Dad, who was driving, tucked the truck into the scrub behind a bit of a ridge which would shelter us from the wind. It was only the end of May but the nights were freezing. There were blue and white water lilies floating on the surface of the creek, and little stumpy-tailed kingfishers bobbing and diving from overhanging boughs. Pads criss-crossed the flat, and the dung of old cattle camps patterned the shade trees.

I had finished cooking the bread by the time the horses arrived, and once we'd hobbled up, Judith and I rolled a clean change of clothes into our towels and walked down along the creek for a bath. It was warm in the sun, sheltered from the wind by the high bank, but the water was icy.

'Gives you a good warm glow afterwards, though.' Judith, her hair pinned high, towelled herself vigorously.

'Yeah. Banging your head feels nice when you stop, too.' I hopped on one foot to keep my clean sock out of the dirt. 'I'm sick of cold baths and washing in a bucket. I wish we could give up this sort of life, do something different. Don't you get tired of it?'

'The watching and the cooking, yes, but in a way the horses make up for that. You don't want to live in town, do you?'

'No, but I don't want to be stuck in a camp for the rest of my life, either.'

'Well,' she perched on a rock and began to comb out her long hair, 'what do you want?'

I sat down to pull on my boots. 'Something like the house we had at Renmark.' I thought back on it, remembering the roses Dad had grown and the floors we'd all polished at weekends. We had only been kids then, for that had been in 1956 – I'd been eleven, Judith going on ten, Patrick only seven, and Sian thirteen. It was 1963 now, and a different world. Dad had worked in town back in those days, but he'd thrown up the job and the house after the big flood. We'd gone to Sydney next, then returned to the bush and had been on the road ever since. But really we'd been travelling in one way or another from the day my mother died, when I was six. I think movement had originally helped Dad to handle things – as if physical motion could distance him from grief. Nowadays shifting about went with the job. 'A proper house,' I said, 'not some old shack like at Redwater that we just camp in during the Wet. A chance to wear a dress occasionally and ...' I looked at her, daring her to laugh, 'some girlfriends. D'you realise that we don't know any girls at all? It's men, men, men everywhere, all of 'em rabbiting on about stockwork and their mates and the buck-jumpers they've ridden. They bore me to death.'

'I find stockwork interesting. But mustering's better than droving.' Judith tucked in her plait. 'Anyway, maybe you'll get married soon. Phil's pretty keen on you.'

'And get more of the same for breakfast, lunch and tea? No thanks.'

I picked up my clothes and glanced at the sun. 'Look at the time! I've gotta get back and start tea.'

It was next morning over a late breakfast – late for us because the sun was up, casting long shadows across the horse camp where the patient nags waited – that Dad made his announcement.

'What we've got to do,' he said, as if there had been no break in conversation, 'is get a property. Instead of droving other people's cattle, we'll start running our own.'

I stared at him. I had often thought of exactly that, but it seemed a dream far beyond our reach.

'What about Redwater?' Judith set her plate of curry aside.

'Put it on the market. With the work we've done on it – the yards and new fencing – we could ask more than we paid. Who needs a paddock if you've got your own station?'

'Where do we get the money?' I looked at the plant and the truck which, with a modest bank account, was the sum total of our worldly goods.

Patrick stared at me blankly as the enormity of the idea took hold. 'Jeez! A station. It'd have to cost . . .' He couldn't decide on a figure and finished lamely, 'Lots. Heaps of dough. The cattle alone –'

'Have a bit o' sense, boy.' Dad's fingers ferreted through his beard in a way he had when he thought out loud. 'We're not talking stock and machinery. Unimproved land is what we'd be looking at. We'd build it up slowly, sticking to the droving for a year or two yet. Soon as we had cattle of our own to sell, we could quit the road for good. What d'you think?'

Put like that it sounded great, and we said so.

Dad nodded, pleased with our enthusiasm. 'Leave the thinking to them with a natural gift for it,' he said, sounding smug. 'We'd all have to take a cut in wages, o'course, and go after every penny we can get. I'll talk to Sian, then start making a few enquiries. Who's taking the horses today?'

The steers weren't leaving until Friday, so we had a full day to kill at the station, or, more accurately, in the camp that we'd made beyond it, between the Gregory River and Verdun Creek. The manager didn't want our plant in his horse paddock.

'Wonder who Mr Verdun was.' It was tough-looking country to get your name on, I thought. 'One of those buried back by the road, d'you reckon?' We had passed three old graves there with neither stone nor marking, the railing about them shrunken and grey with age.

Dad looked pained. 'Don't show your ignorance to the world like that. Verdun's a place. In France. They fought a battle there in the 1914–18 war. I thought everybody knew that.'

I flushed, stung into anger. 'Well, I didn't. I wasn't around then, so how am I supposed to find out these things if I don't ask?'

He looked surprised. 'You can read, can't you? Quitting school needn't stop you learning. I taught meself. There's no reason you can't do the same. Anybody can educate 'emselves.'

'Right.' I swung on my heel, throwing the words over my shoulder: 'Well, as soon as we get rid of these cattle, I will!'

❧

We had camped by scores of rivers, from Alice Springs to Normanton, but except when it rained, none of them had flowed.

The Gregory did. Its spring-fed waters slid silkily between pandanus-encrusted banks, greeny-blue where the deep holes were, sparkling clear over the river pebbles lining the shallows. You would never think the barren hills and scrubby ridges beyond its banks belonged to the same world. Giant fig and paperbark crowded the flood channels, and cabbage palm shot, arrow-straight, into the clear sky.

I lay on my back in the shade staring up at their exotic splendour and seeing only castles of my own building. When we had our own station, we'd have a house – one of those kit homes, probably, that people used in the north – with wide verandahs and airy rooms. I would grow plants in big tubs, and shade trees, and we'd invite the neighbours over for barbecues. There'd be sheds for saddles and other gear, too – no more dragging them inside to keep them out of the weather, as we did at Redwater. The house would be a proper home, like the one we'd left so long ago in Renmark, with a stove and a fridge, and a bathroom with hot water permanently on tap. I imagined curtains and tablecloths and a breakfast set of white china. And I'd never wear jeans again, except to ride.

Something moved low down in the corner of my eye. I lifted my head, startled to see how far the sun had moved, and saw Judith's legs coming through the scrub. She walked across to where I lay and dropped the bucket of wet clothes she'd been carrying so close beside me I jerked out of the way.

'You!' She'd been crying. Her eyes were red and bitter. 'I yelled my head off and you're lying here sleeping.'

'I wasn't,' I said. 'But why? What were you yelling for?'

'Because Pom-Pom was drowning! Oh, don't bother,' she cried as I started to scramble up. 'She's well and truly dead by now, so don't disturb yourself.'

'But how? If I'd heard you I would've come. Of course I would. It's no good getting mad about it. Just tell me what happened.'

The chestnut filly had gone into the river where a break in the pandanus thickets lining the banks gave access to the water. But the river had undercut the bank, as so often happened in the deep channels of the fast-flowing Gregory, and with neither bottom nor bank for her hind feet to thrust against, Pom-Pom had been unable to hoist herself out. She must have fought the current until she was exhausted, because she'd been floating on her ribs with her lower nostril dipping under when Judith found her.

'I tried to push a stick under her, get her head up, but in the end she just sank and turned over. I saw her feet and a bit of her tail, then she vanished. If you'd heard me –'

'I probably couldn't have done anything.'

'You can swim, at least.' She sounded bleak.

'Yes, but ... And anyway, you could learn. It's not that hard.'

'You know I can't. I've tried and tried. I might've learned when I was little at Sedan, only I had bronchitis when the grade fours were going to the pool and Aunt Mary kept me back.' She brooded on the memory. 'Then I started learning at Renmark. But I just got to dog-paddle and Dad wouldn't let me go any more, so it's his fault as much as mine.'

'What d'you mean, wouldn't let you go any more? Why not?'

'It was when you were in hospital. He said I could go after school, but I had to be home by five or something. Only I hadn't learned to tell the time properly, and I got it wrong and was late. So that was that. End of lessons.'

I didn't ask why she hadn't explained. Dad had never been a listener and was impatient of excuses. 'I didn't know. And now that poor little filly's dead.'

I got up and walked across to the bank. The blue-green river no longer looked beautiful but sly and treacherous, the exotic tropical fronds of the vegetation an inimical spiny wall. I sighed and stared about me at the camp, wondering if life would ever change. Castles in the air were all very well, but reality was the drab clutter around me; it was money, and relationships, and things going wrong.

T W O

The hired man's name was Billy Noble. He was blond and taciturn, a bit older than Sian, and knew his work. Dad was pleased with him. He was like Judith, he said, in that he saw trouble coming and acted to stop it before it happened. You didn't catch either of them sitting watching the lead ring up, or the toey stuff on the wings split for the scrub. They'd be already moving to prevent it before the cattle had properly nutted out what they meant to do.

'You think they do that? Work it out, I mean.' I looked at Dad sitting across the fire from me, swigging coffee while the mob fed slowly up to the dinner-camp. We were out of the hills by then, on the black soil country past Top Water dam where the Mitchell grass grew thick as wheat. Tiny birds swayed on its stems, though I never found out exactly what they were after. You just saw them there, nodding with the moving grass in the windy sunlight.

'Too right,' Dad said. 'If cattle were any smarter, you wouldn't handle 'em. They leave a horse for dead when it comes to brains. Horses just react – cattle work things out.'

'Uh-uh, they panic.' I shook my head. 'They rush.'

'In a mob, yep. But if it's stuck in a bog, or tangled in a fence, which fares better, horse or beast?'

'The beast does.' I remembered Pom-Pom. Any cow in her position would have swum for it, even if it meant leaving her mates.

''s right.' Dad watched Judith trot up the wing to turn a steer in. She stood easily in the irons, seat clear of the polished saddle leather, hands resting on bay Joseph's neck. 'Pity your sister's not a man. She's got the sort o' talent you can't teach. Experience helps, but your true stockman's born, not made.' He got up to go as I stared indignantly at him.

'You think so? What this country needs, of course, is another stockman. Men are ten a penny already out here. I don't want to be the only girl in the country, thank you very much.'

Still, I thought later, if we had to have men, Billy wasn't so bad. It was his first time on the road. He'd worked on Thorntonia the year after we'd taken those cattle, and done a couple of seasons in the Cow camp at Dreyfus. Big properties ran more than one stock camp, and the one that handled the branding in the breeder paddocks was always known as the Cow camp. Billy had been in the downs country on Dalgonally for a few months too, but had soon pulled the pin to head back north.

'Why?' We were on another dinner-camp and Patrick spoke through a mouthful of bread and beef.

'Too many blokes giving orders,' Billy said. 'Never seen so many pannikin bosses in me life. The manager was Mister to everybody but the overseer – if he had a name, I never heard it.'

'Besides, you're crazy about bulldust and watching cattle, aren't you?' Judith had found a yellow cocky's feather and was fixing it to her hat.

For a moment he looked so puzzled that we all laughed. He grinned and bobbed upright to check the mob where they stood or lay in thick dark clusters of shade and sunlight across the dinner-camp. Dad, who'd been napping by the front wheel, sat up then and reached for the watch he carried in a pouch on his belt. It was the only timepiece in the camp because stockmen never wore wristwatches, which were vulnerable in falls.

'Time to go.' Patrick took the words out of Dad's mouth. They headed for their horses while I got the shovel to cover the crumbling coals of our fire. Then, tuckerbox closed, load secured, and the two dogs riding the swags, I nosed the Bedford back onto the stock-route, following then overtaking the feeding mob.

At Kamilaroi we camped in the Triangle, a three-sided paddock – I could never decide if it was the funniest-shaped watering lane I'd ever seen, or the weirdest-placed holding paddock. At any rate, it was open pebbly plain with a scatter of scrub towards the west. The full moon rose on the early dogwatch, slipping up out of the dark as big as a house. Just for a moment, when it first appeared, I reined to a stop and sat staring, convinced it was the glow of a fire. Then the whole of the circle swam up like a fat blood orange, and by the time Patrick rode out to start his watch it had risen higher and shrunk to its normal size, and shone like polished pewter in the east.

The night was cold and still. The little noises of the mob – the flap of a beast's ear, the gurgling rumble of its gut, a long exhaled sigh and grunt as a steer lay down – were as clear as shouts in my mind. I heard the flat slap of Rose's hooves as Patrick left the night-horse tree, and was pulling the scarf off (we only had the one and shared it) to hand to him as he reined up beside me.

'Sian's come,' he said. 'Rode in with his swag half an hour back. God, it's cold!' He hitched the woollen folds around his neck and thrust his chin into it. 'Says he'll give us a watch.'

'Good on him. Did somebody tell him about it – finding a place to buy, I mean? What'd he say?'

'He's all for it.' Patrick moved Rose on and I yawned and headed for camp, pleased and impatient afresh as I was each time I thought of the station we would buy.

Sian's mount was at the night-horse tree with a halter over its bridle. It snorted and pulled back at my approach, rolling a white eye, and I heard the halter-shank creak with the strain of the horse's weight.

'Come up!' I hissed. Its front feet snapped forward with a jerk and it snorted, a sound like a bag ripping. Station horses were a liability in a camp because they never got the handling that drovers' nags did, and consequently were never as quiet. This one stood like a poker, the line of its head and neck tense against the moon. I wouldn't have fancied riding it on watch.

Sian's swag was back in its old place by the front wheel, but he, like the rest of the camp, was asleep. I drank a pannikin of coffee from the billy standing by the fire, pulled my hat, coat, and boots off and rolled into bed.

Sian was gone again by daylight so that he wouldn't be late for work. He was drawing station wages and three pound a head for each colt he broke in, but it didn't cover watching other blokes' cattle, he said, through a mouthful of steak. I saw him only briefly because I did the dogwatch while the others had breakfast, and by the time I got back in to warm my numb hands at the dying fire, the light from the coming day was flooding behind me.

Patrick was squatting in the ashes drinking tea, his hair curling over the collar of his grimy shirt.

'Had breakfast?' he asked.

'What do you think? I hope you've left me some tea.'

'There's plenty.'

He pushed the billy closer to the coals and yawned. 'The watching's the worst thing about this job. When we're station owners, I'm gunna spend every night of my life in bed.'

'And I will never have sore knuckles again,' I said, wincing as I stuck my hands in the washing bowl. Doubt shook me then, and I looked from the withered greenery of the windbreak to the cluttered table and the towel hanging over the truck door – everything was where it should be. But it still looked a squalid mess in the growing light. 'It's a lot of money and years of work. D'you really think we can do it?'

'I don't see why not.' Patrick's light-coloured eyes were grave, older than his years. He'd never really had a childhood. 'They reckon old Tyson started with one horse, and we've got a lot more going for us than that.'

'The work's the easy part.' I forked cold steak from the camp oven onto a slice of bread. 'And Tyson was a millionaire, anyway.'

'Who started off a battler.' Patrick stood up to warm the back of his legs, letting the words drop over his shoulder. 'So we'd be pegging level there.' He sounded so confident about it that I forgot my disquiet and bit hungrily into the steak.

～

The steers ran up for the first time on the White Dog camp at the Gleeson boundary. I heard the rolling thunder of their hooves from deep in my sleep and sat bolt upright in a tangle of blankets just as it stopped. The sudden hush that gripped the night was nearly as unsettling as the noise had been. There was dust in the starlight and Judith's voice calling, 'Whoa, bullocks. Whoa, little fellas. Whoa, there,' and the beat of trotting hooves.

Dad was limping for the night-horse tree. Billy slipped by him, and I heard them both ride out whistling two different tunes. It was a thin noise, lonely as a curlew's call in the dark, and lost when the stillness was broken by the first bellow.

I pushed the fire together and stood the coffee billy closer to the coals. The steers were bawling and milling about, the dangerous moment over. In the dark a horse went by at a good clip, and the breeze brought the smell of dust and wet dung. It was my watch next. I pulled the blankets up again and tumbled back into sleep.

A couple of days later, while we were crossing Dreyfus Station, Billy got a ducking in the river when Sue, the bay mare he was riding, fell on the bank. The river channel there was steep and narrow, the flood-banks choked with scrub and shoulder-high burr some thirty feet above the actual water. The mob flowed down into it, splashing and wading, spreading out as they drank – a sea of horns and flat, thrusting faces amid the brown river water. When they were full they surged back, heading for the steep, churned-up bank. Billy, pressing to beat them up it, jumped Sue at its greasy slickness and landed them both upside down in the water.

The steers took off, galloping up the bank like mad things. Sue bolted too, straight into the burrs, where she took a header over the trailing reins. Billy had to swim for his hat, which he'd lost in the fall, then extricate Sue before rejoining the mob. He was blue with cold by then, so Dad sent him on ahead to the camp to change his clothes. But cleaning up Sue was another matter. She was a heavy-boned mare with a thick winter's coat that was now covered, from forelock to fetlocks, in Nagoora burr. Grape-size, the burrs clustered on her like ticks, only a good deal pricklier. Patrick and I picked determinedly at them for half an hour, until I remembered the old hand shears from our Territory days. I found them, still scabbarded, among the other tools. And without further ado we shore her.

'Jesus,' Dad said, stunned, when they rode into dinner-camp.

Judith gave a shriek of laughter. 'Where's her tail?'

Only the whiskered bone was left. Sue swished it, turning her shorn head and neck to lop an ear at us in the way she had, and the sight broke us all up.

I had trimmed her legs to the bone, the underside of her head, and her belly. Patrick had collar-roped her hind feet to get at them, and I had finished the job on her tail with my nail scissors.

'She looks like yer favourite nightmare,' Dad said. 'And I'm talking dreams, not droving.' He stooped for the tea billy. 'What'd yer do with the burrs?'

The question was so like him. I said sharply, 'I slung 'em all over the paddock, of course. D'you think I don't know a noxious weed when I meet it? Why did I go to the trouble of cleaning her up, if that was the case?'

He looked surprised. 'Keep your hair on, girl.'

'Well, stop treating me like a child.' Then Billy, coming in last, caught sight of the mare and started the others off again.

⌇

We turned east at Collulah Station, heading out through the red ridge country to the Dugald River and the Yambungan scrub. The bookkeeper at Collulah gave me the names of the next three stations along the route, and the following morning, before I left camp, I rigged the wireless and sat in the cab, writing out the telegrams of notice. Drovers had to inform property owners when they would be entering their country, and tell them the size of the mob, where they came from and who was in charge.

Wireless traffic sessions were always busy through the season. When my turn came I sent the first telegram, waited for the operator to confirm she had received it, then was almost blasted out of my seat by an agitated female voice cutting in.

'Urgent medical! This is Kamilaroi with an urgent medical. Can anybody hear me? I have an urgent medical.'

The operator said smoothly, 'Stand by, Kamilaroi. I'm getting the doctor for you now. All stations stand by. What is the nature of your medical, Kamilaroi?'

A rattle of sound came through the speaker – the woman had her mouth too close to the mike and was breathing into it. Her voice was high, teetering on the edge of panic. 'It's a young man, one of the station lads.' She gulped raggedly. 'He was, was riding a colt. My husband's just brought him back in the vehicle. Is the doctor there yet? Over.'

It was Dr Robinson who answered, his voice a soothing wave of sound. I could hear it but not the actual words, because my brain had frozen. My hands were suddenly cold and my heart seemed to be trying to slam through my chest wall. It had to be Sian. He was paid to ride colts, and the way the woman was carrying on, this wasn't a simple fall. She was crying now, and through my terror I itched to slap her. Words began to have meaning again, like vivid gouts of paint flung before my mind's eye.

'. . . hung up in the stirrup iron, my husband said. He's been dragged for – I don't know, miles! And kicked. He, his face has . . . gone, Doctor. There's so much blood, and we can't find a pulse.' Her voice was jagged, spiky as splintered glass. 'I don't know what to do. Tell me what to do.'

'I don't think there is anything you can do, by the sound of things,' Dr Robinson said calmly. 'Let me speak to your husband, please. Do you know if the patient had a family, or where they might be?'

The breath stopped in my throat. I clenched my eyes shut, waiting.

'Oh, no, he's not – he wasn't married, I mean. But his father runs a garage. In Winton, I think. Somewhere down there, but Trevor knows. Here he is now, Doctor.'

I snapped the switch off and sat there trembling, simultaneously wondering who it was and how I would have broken the news to Dad if it had been Sian. I wasn't surprised that his face had gone, as the woman put it. There was enough stone in that paddock to pave a highway, more than sufficient to kill some luckless ringer. In a little while I remembered the telegrams and switched back on but was ten minutes too late. The operator, getting no answer, had passed me by, and there was nothing for it but to sit and wait until the next traffic list was read.

I told the rest of them about it on the dinner-camp, but Patrick was the only one to link it, as I had, to us.

'Just as well it wasn't Sian.'

'Poor sod,' Billy muttered, and that was all.

I couldn't forget it, though, and riding my watch that night I kept thinking about the young man (a boy, perhaps someone like Charlie, a ringer back on Ardmore I had really liked), who had saddled a colt at daybreak and ridden unknowingly to his death. Accidents happened regularly in stock camps – someone was always being kicked, or trodden on, or thrown – but I had never known of anyone dying from one till now. It made me shiver to realise how fragile a thing life is, that the same thing could happen at any moment to any one of us.

It wasn't that I hadn't been aware of this, I thought, but it had always seemed no more than an unlikely possibility. No more real (and this despite Dad's accident on Dreyfus, which had been a bad one) than death in old age. I stared into the powdery blackness where the stars glittered above the sleeping mob, and it was as if the world lurched a little, changing everything forever. It was an eerie feeling, like knowing that you had but to step sideways for an instant to find nothing at all beneath your feet.

I slept fitfully that night, the hoofbeats of the night-horses weaving themselves into my dream where the accident at Kamilaroi replayed itself over and over, first with an unknown chestnut horse, and then with mad bay Dolly. I recognised her at once, and my heart began to pound with dread as I tried to catch the reins, knowing the rider would fall and that when it did a brown plait would swing out and it would be Judith. I shot upright in my blankets, gasping in horror, to stare around at the sleeping camp. The morning star was starting its climb and Dad's swag was empty, so dawn couldn't be far off. Shuddering, I lay down again, trying to blot out the images of death.

Dinner-camp next day was on the Dugald River. I pulled into the shade and unpacked, got the fire and billies ready and poked the heavy old coffee jug onto the coals. It would be noon before the cattle arrived, though Patrick would be along sooner with the plant. That was time enough. I got the wireless pad and biro out and began to write the story of the dead boy who had risen on an ordinary day, no different from this one, to do a job that hundreds of others were doing across the stations and stock routes of the north – only he had died and they still lived.

The sensation of walking a narrow plank across an abyss returned as I wrote. Perhaps something as simple as the flapping of a saddlecloth had started the horse – if so, had he ridden into the wind instead, might that not have saved him? And if it had, if he had come back to the yards and unsaddled and hosed the horse down as usual, how would he know that by so small a decision he had cheated death?

I had thought I would write the story in a morning, but I finished it a week later, two days before we were due to deliver the cattle, and even then the telling of it was easier than deciding on the spelling of the longer words. There was an old *Register* sliding around the floor of the truck with a page for submissions. I copied the address onto an envelope and licked it shut, knowing I could post it at the Fort. As a child I had wanted to write stories, and I was surprised to find I still did. But I would have to get a dictionary first.

Billy left us on delivery day, fed up with watching. He'd sleep for a week, he said, then look for another job – droving was a mug's game. Dad and Judith headed off to Dreyfus with the truck to line up supplies and men for the next trip, while Patrick and I walked the horses back, making about thirty miles a day.

It was cold going, and wet. The clear June skies had given way to streaky cloud, which by mid-afternoon of the second day had deepened into grey overcast.

'What's a south wind mean this time of year?' Patrick eyed the sullen sky, his coat collar pulled tight under his smooth jaw. He wasn't shaving yet, but he had been working so long we all tended to forget he was still only a kid.

'Who knows?' I grabbed at my hat, knocking my sore knuckles as I did so, and felt the skin split. The wind whined, blowing the horses' tails forward, along with the dust they kicked up. My hands, bleeding now, smarted in the cold. 'Rain, for a quid.'

'In June?'

'Why not? If it's inconvenient.'

And rain it did. Chill little showers tapering off into a persistent drizzle that blackened the scrub and whetted the edge of the wind. The road firmed, then softened, the sound of hooves changing from a clop to a squelchy tread. At midday we built a smoky fire under our hats and boiled the quart pots, using water that had run off into the table drain. The horses foraged while we ate, the wet glistening on their shaggy coats like translucent seed pearls.

That night we camped on the verandah of an empty mustering hut. There were seventy points of rain in the gauge set up on a post near the wood heap, and water still dripped from the lowering sky. Inside the hut was a kerosene fridge full of meat, and a scrubbed deal table. We helped ourselves to steak, and I left a note written in charcoal on one corner of the table so that they would know who had been through.

By noon bits of broken blue were showing through the overcast, and light ran and glinted on the water surface in the table drains. Our damp greatcoats sat on our shoulders like lead weights, but it was too cold to remove them. When the sun broke through, its light was pallid and without warmth. Our toes ached in our boots. Patrick cracked his whip to bring Lancer in and the sound cut through the cold air like a gunshot, shocking Pigeon, my one-eyed mount, into a sudden plunge that jarred my chattering teeth.

Shortly afterwards, a truck came churning towards us, cutting deep tracks through the red gravel. I turned the plant off the road to give the driver a clear run, but he stuck his head out the window instead and pulled up. It was Graeme, a Collulah jackeroo. Pigeon snorted and reared; he didn't like ten-ton trucks on his blind side. I hopped off and got hold of the reins close under the bit to turn him on the narrow shoulder, just as Graeme jumped out of the cab and slammed the door behind us. The grey's shoulder hit my back like a pile driver, and I went face down the slope into sloppy mud. His feet missed my head but trod squarely on my outflung hand, pressing it into the ooze.

'Jeez! You okay? What happened?' Graeme called from the top of the bank. Pigeon and the rest of the plant went bush, with Patrick after them.

'You did! You slammed the door, you idiot! Can't you see he's blind?' I wiped my face on the sleeve of my greatcoat and glared at him, cradling my throbbing hand. It was sore but undamaged, cushioned from most of Pigeon's weight by the mud.

Graeme was contrite. He tilted his water bottle for me to wash my face and offered a relatively clean grease-rag from the cab to dry it on. Then Patrick returned with the horses.

'Where're you going?' Graeme caught Pigeon and led him over to me, watching as I swung up.

'Back to Dreyfus.' I flipped my sore hand at him. The back of it was already swelling, and by the time we reached the station late next day it was bruised to the exact shape of a hoof.

Only Judith was there when we arrived. Dad and Sian had left that morning, she said, gone off to Quamby in the landrover to meet a man who had a property to sell.

THREE

'Who is he?' I pulled my saddle off, careful of my sore hand. 'And where's the country?'

'That's some bruise.' Judith inspected it. 'Something walk on you, did it?'

'Pigeon, but never mind that. Tell us about this fella Dad's with.'

His name, Judith said, was Lew somebody, and he was a gypsy. We'd got the packs off by then, hobbled up and were drinking tea in the camp. It wasn't too late, about mid-afternoon on a short winter's day. Judith had bread baking in the oven and was fussing with the coals, raking them off the lid onto the pile around the sides. They looked black in the sunlight but glowed red when the wind touched them.

'A gypsy?' I pictured a swarthy man with gold earrings and a hooked nose. 'Who says?'

'Mike, the mailman. He said he's been trying to sell the place for a coupla years now. They were talking about it yesterday – Dad and Mike, I mean. Then the boss came down this morning and told us the trucks had been put back two days, so the mob's not leaving till Friday. That's when Dad said he'd hunt up this Lew fella – he's got a store or something at Quamby.'

'Where's that?'

She pointed with her chin, blackfella fashion. 'South and east of the railhead on the Donors Hill road – just a pub and a racetrack, Mike says. They'll be back Thursday. And there's five mission boys coming on the plane tomorrow. Old Bindi, the camp cook, is gunna fetch 'em out to us.'

I groaned. 'Five! Think of the bread. I'd better make more.'

Dad got back late on Thursday night with George Jenkins, the fencing contractor. They'd done a wheel bearing on the 'rover a hundred yards short of the Quamby pub. Dad had ordered a new one out on the mail truck and Sian had stayed behind to put it in.

'He should be back Sunday arvo, at the latest.' Dad spread his hands to the fire, jerking his head at an idle carbide drum near the break. 'Have a siddown, George. There'll be a feed ready in a minute.'

I turned the steak in the oven lid and dropped chopped onions onto the hot metal. 'Did you see the gypsy?'

'Yep. All in good time. That billy ever gunna boil?' Which was hint enough that he didn't want to discuss it in front of a stranger. But once George's tail-lights had vanished into the night, Dad rubbed his hands together with satisfaction. 'Well,' he said, 'it could be what we're looking for.'

Judith and Patrick spoke together. 'Where is it?' 'What size is it?'

I had a different question. 'Hang on, start at the beginning with the gypsy. What did he look like – young, dark? Could you tell he was a gypsy? Did he look different, I mean?'

'Different how?' The question stymied Dad.

'Don't be dense. Did he have curly hair and look sort of, I dunno – Spanish? Dark and handsome. Just different. With earrings, maybe,' I added hopefully.

'For crying out loud!' Dad snorted. 'What gets into you girls? He might've had earrings, he might've been tattooed from his neck to his navel, I didn't notice. He was just an ordinary, middle-aged sort of bloke in dirty clothes. Oh, and a conchie during the war, on account of being a gypsy, because they don't believe in fighting.' Dad's tone was scathing. As a returned soldier he had no sympathy for conscientious objectors. 'But that's his business. What's ours is that he's keen to sell.' He rummaged a paper out of his pocket. 'I've got all the details here.'

The property was called Yeldham and lay west of the Gregory River, bounded by Gregory Downs, Lawn Hill Station and Kamarga. It covered a hundred and seventy-six square miles and was as God made it, according to Dad, except for a few miles of boundary fence on the Gregory side and a road traversing it from east to west. No stock and no improvements. I sighed at the last bit but wasn't really surprised. I had never believed we could buy land containing a ready-made home. That was something we would have to do ourselves.

'What about water?' Judith was more interested in the land.

31

'Nothing permanent. A creek, but it's dry by mid-year. Main reason he hasn't sold it yet, I'd say. He wants three and a half thousand quid for it.'

We gasped. In 1963 that was a lot of money. We got nine and sixpence for each Dreyfus bullock delivered to the railhead. I tried to work out how many we'd need to handle to make that much, but gave up. I'd never been any good at figures. 'But if the water's stopped other people buying,' I shrugged, 'well, we couldn't even run the plant on a dry block.'

'Bores,' Patrick said, and Dad nodded.

'If we take it – and I'm not going past "if" until we've had a pretty good look at it – that's the way to go. Dams run dry come a bad year, but we'll worry about that part once we've seen the country. Lot o' scrub, he said, but that might mean anything. I dunno what he's done for a crust all his life, but he's never worked stock.'

'Why would he buy it, then?' Patrick looked puzzled.

'Money. You buy cheap and sell dear. It's called speculatin'. Half the world does it.' Dad glanced over at the hatted shapes around the blackfellas' fire and got up, holding his hip. 'Better sort the boys out so they'll know who's going where tomorrow.'

Next morning he and Judith left with the mob, taking the truck, half the plant and three of the mission men. Patrick and I and the other two, whose names were Dick and Phil, stayed on in the boundary camp tailing the horses and waiting for Sian to return.

Dick was a Ganggalida man from the western Gulf country. He proved to be good with horses and a reliable worker. Phil had lost an eye, and the shrunken socket gave his black face a menacing look. He was Lardil, a man from the coast, but all the Aboriginals lived in the missions now and went out to work. On watch at night, Phil sang hymns in a deep bell of a voice, but Dick preferred Slim Dusty. He sang 'When The Golden Sliprails Go Down', 'The Pub With No Beer' and 'Trumby' with ear-bashing repetition. 'Trumby' was the saga of a boy who died because he couldn't read or write. Neither could Dick. He'd been 'grown up' on a station, he said, and never went to school. He signed his wages sheet with a thumb-print, inspecting the whorled impressions afresh each time as if he had never seen them before.

Sian, when he came, had little to add to Dad's account of the meeting with Lew, except his surname, which was Bennet – disappointingly ordinary. In books, gypsies were always called Carlo or Jess. They were lean, dark, exciting men with hair-trigger tempers and passionate natures. I hadn't really expected him to drive a painted caravan, but some remnant of romance should have hung about him. It didn't. Sian, like Dad, was dismissive.

'A bit of a slob,' he said. 'Kids everywhere and his so-called shop's falling down round his ears. Hard country that, round Quamby. Looks like it hasn't rained there for forty years.'

∽

The weeks slipped by as, one after another, the mobs went south to the railhead, plodding from camp to monotonously familiar camp: the Triangle, the Five Mile Plain, the White Dog and Stove camps. Other mobs moved ahead and behind us – bullocks, spayed cows, store cattle – pouring south along the river in a great sprawling tide. The bulldust rose in choking clouds on the track, tainting the wide sky pink, and everywhere you looked were the trampled, dung-spotted cattle camps, or the moving blur of the big mobs.

Sometimes, wrestling the landrover along the rutted, bulldusty route, past pea-bush swamps and stands of black-heart coolibah, with the river on my right hand and the sky sitting on the horizon like a monstrous inverted bowl, I was overwhelmed by the bigness of it. I would visualise the mobs before and behind us: fifteen hundred from Robinson River, a thousand bullocks from Planet, spayed cows from Armranald, fats from Nardoo, and old Fin coming down with the Lawn Hill mob. A vast moving pageant of which I was a part.

I could write about it someday, I thought. Capture in words the purpose and discipline of it all, because we were like an army on the move, each of us intent on earning a living, but beyond that still a part of the great annual rhythm of the cattle country which contained within it so many inconsequential things. Like the way the bullocks' tails flicked all together at daybreak, whisking above straight backs like drum majors' batons, or how, when the sun struck the dust just right, the mob seemed to drift within a nimbus of light. This effect was caused by the refraction of sunlight through dust particles, but it looked like a golden mist cloaking the drifting herd.

At such moments I wished I could paint, because although I had no desire to work cattle as Judith did, I did like them. For their shape and rich colouring, for the measured curve of their faces and the smooth sweep of creamy horns. I liked the way they stared with upthrust muzzle and steady ears: cattle rely more on scent than sight. Country without cattle, I thought, glancing through the dusty timber as I drove, looked empty somehow, like an untenanted house. It needed those dark, scattered shapes, feeding or stringing to water along the pads, to turn wilderness into a property. If we bought Yeldham, we would be buying nothing but land. Only stocking would make of it first a station and then a home.

Collulah homestead was on the river, approached by a winding drive through gum flats. The gate at the horse yards, where I usually filled my water drums, was open, and I drove through it without giving a thought to Larry, loose on the back. It was only as I neared the homestead and glimpsed him in the mirror, sailing over the side, that I remembered, and by then it was too late. Fighting was Larry's great pleasure and besetting sin. He cleaned up the station dogs as he met them, and stopping him was like trying to wrestle a bear.

I could hear the snarling roar of the fight the moment the engine stopped. Cursing, I jumped from the truck and ran.

Larry and his victim were under the loading platform of the station store, built so that trucks could back up to it and unload straight onto the apron. The top half of the platform supports had been boxed in for added strength, and behind this, amid a clutter of dead weeds and roly-poly, Larry was going at it like a Doberman unstuffing kittens. Amid the flying foam and blood, the other dog's snarls had changed to screams, and I saw that he wasn't even a cattle breed, but some sort of smooth-haired bitzer that Larry was going to kill. I scooted under and grabbed his collar, and we were wrestling in the dirt when Graeme's face bobbed into view below the boxing.

'What's going on?'

'I'm making a rice pudding.' I gave him the standard answer to stupid questions, but he didn't take offence.

'So let me give you a hand.'

'Get the chain off the side rail, then.' I was panting as I dragged the bristling dog towards the opening. 'Watch out, he's so stirred up he'll have you too. Who owns the pooch?'

Graeme's eyebrows wriggled expressively. 'The boss's wife.'

'Oh, great! It would be. Just when I've got a message for him, too.'

'Tell me. I'll pass it on.'

'Would you?' I was grateful for the offer. People were often funny about having their dogs minced up by our killing machine. Not a few had wanted to shoot him. 'Thanks. Tell him Sian's leaving a lame bullock in the Four Mile – he'll pick him up next trip.' I toed Larry none too gently in the ribs. 'Get yourself onto the load, you useless mutt, and let's get going before we're caught.'

Graeme waved as I reversed and drove off. I forgave him then for the incident with Pigeon, but catching sight of myself in the wing mirror I did wonder why it was I always finished up covered in dirt when he was around.

෴

At the end of the second-last trip, the five mission boys went back to Dreyfus to catch the mail plane home. We would do the final mob ourselves. It would be into August before we finished, but we might still pick up another trip before the season ended.

'What about Bennet's place?' Sian asked. 'Are we gunna look it over or not?'

'Soon as the last o' the bullocks have trucked, we'll take a week off.' Dad was expansive. 'Then paddock the horses and we'll all go. Unless something else comes up,' he added, suddenly prudent again. And of course something did.

It was a letter containing the offer of the Valerie Downs steers. Dad passed it round, then got the calendar out, muttering calculations as he did so. 'Let's see – leave on the tenth, last day o' the first quarter, so the moon'd be with us. Bit of a squeeze getting the horses there. That's seventy, ninety, then the turnoff and the last stretch – good three stages in that. Okay.' He turned to us. 'We can do it. And the extra money might make the difference if I'm going to the banks. We'll take 'em.'

'And Yeldham?' I was disappointed and sounded it.

'Your brother and I'll go take a look while the rest o' you are shifting the plant.'

'So when do we get to see it?'

'Later,' he said, and with this I had to be content.

It was just another trip, memorable only for Darky getting her jaw wedged through the off-side stirrup iron one night. I heard a heavy body thump onto the ground at the night-horse tree and jumped out of bed to hunt whichever horse it was back onto its feet before it rolled on the saddle.

Judith was there before me, bent over the mare, berating her in a sibilant whisper as she thrashed about. 'Here, kneel on her neck,' she said when she saw me. 'You wouldn't think it possible, but the stupid little hussy has got her face in the iron! I've gotta get the leather off.' Luckily she was saddled with my Giltrow poley, and once we'd gained an inch of slack the leather slipped easily off the stirrup hook. Darky surged to her feet then, the iron still hanging from her lower jaw, and Judith grabbed it and yanked it off. The mare snorted, then stood trembling and flopping her lips together to ease the smart.

'Comes of having no brains.' I rubbed my bare arms, listening for the mob, but the bullocks were quiet under the stars. The Cross had sunk to the horizon and the horsebells were still. The only sound was our breathing and the faint, popping hiss of the carbide light on the table. Judith slipped the leather back onto its hook and tilted her face to the sky.

'D'you think it'll still look the same when we're station owners? When the land we're standing on is ours, I mean. You know, town people never look at the sky and there's gotta be some reason. Maybe just living in a house makes you forget it's there.'

'I dunno. Hey! I've just thought – if we buy it, we'll have an address.' Letters were an infrequent occurrence, those that came sometimes taking weeks to catch up.

'Yeah.' She yawned. 'It'll be different. Do you think we'll miss all this, just a bit?'

'You'll still have your horses. I'll settle for a stove.' I was yawning too and shivering with cold. 'I'm going back to bed.'

The minute the last train pulled out from the trucking yards on delivery day, we started back, pegging away in reverse through the stages we had made with the cattle. We passed the Coppermine camp and the red ridges of the Dobbyn turnoff, clattered through the river pebbles at Collulah, and went on across Cemetery Flat where the bones of fifty horses were spread about on the claypan.

Dad and Sian left us there, heading off in the landrover while we turned east. They had arranged to meet Lew Bennet at the Gregory pub and go on out to Yeldham. They'd be at Valerie Downs waiting for us, Dad said, when we arrived. He had sketched Patrick a mud map showing the tracks and waters, so we pushed on, with Judith scribbling out a waybill en route. Nobody ever asked to see one, but theoretically any copper or station manager could.

At Bang-Bang I filled the water tanks from the bore. Just as I was leaving, a woman came out of the bare house-yard to stand by the gate, arm up to shade her eyes, a toddler clutching at her skirt.

'Would you like a cuppa?' She had a tentative voice, a young woman with a still, brown face and watchful eyes.

A paralysing shyness gripped me. I was unused to the company of my own sex and knew I would find nothing to say to her. I could see us both caught by sticky silence across a table, unable to escape, and rushed into speech.

'Oh, no thanks. I've got to meet the others. Thanks all the same.' But even as I babbled, part of me wanted to stay. I could have asked her about the child, I thought, driving away, and wished I was brave enough to return and accept her offer. It was easy enough to talk to men – why should women be so different?

The steers were leaving from the holding paddock at Three Tree Dam. We arrived at the appointed date with a couple of hours of daylight left and found the station stock camp there, flanked by our landrover. The yards, set about with prickly bushes, lay behind them, and the smoke of the campfire went up in a thin spiral through the golden light. Trees, many more than three, lined the back wall of the dam, but they were the only ones in sight. On all sides the plains spread to the horizon, broken only by the distant blobs of stock. If you could see daylight under them, they were horses. Cattle had blockier builds and shorter legs – their bodies merged with the grass.

Dad came over while I was throwing the swags off and began lifting the firewood down. There was nothing to burn on the plains, so you carried your own. I looked at him, but you could never guess anything from his face.

'Had no trouble, then?'

'No. The plant'll be here in an hour.' I stuck my hands on my hips. 'Well? Is it a state secret? Are we buying the place or not?'

'We are. Tried her with the stick and there's tons o' ground water. Means a boring plant, but I've seen the boss and I'm off to the Isa tomorrow to try the banks. I'll be meeting Lew in there to sign the papers, if I can raise the loan.'

'But the steers –'

'Sian'll take 'em.'

'Still leaves us a man short.'

'Nope. Picked up a bloke at Gregory.'

A bell tonged faintly, the deep-toned Condamine that Simon always wore – the plant was coming. I cocked my head to listen, my eyes picking up the thin skein of dust above the track. I was thinking that I would always remember this moment when the past and future met. We were adrift now, as rootless as blown roly-poly, but by next week (for I never doubted that Dad would secure the loan) we would have a place of our own.

'Better get the billy swung for 'em,' Dad prompted, and it didn't even irritate me. He could never stop himself from telling you your job. I snatched the billy out of its box and sprang recklessly off the load, happy enough to fly.

FOUR

I was riding Lady Meg when we entered the Yeldham country as owners. The others had gone ahead in the vehicles while Judith and I followed with the horses, coming in over the western ridges from the previous night's camp at Archie Creek. Judith rode Peronel, a raking yellow-bay that could walk at seven miles an hour. We called her Camel-legs, but nothing in the plant could equal her stride.

We had been dead lucky. Despite it being too early for proper rain, the country had copped a couple of good storms. Water lay warm and inky-black in the stony creek near the western boundary, and Big Sandy, the main watercourse, had its large holes filled. There was water enough for us and the horses to live off until the Wet, and by then we would have the bore.

Dad had found a drilling rig in Mt Isa, and towed it out while the rest of us waited for him at Lilydale Springs, tailing the plant in the long valley there.

'A bargain,' he'd said proudly, showing off the oil-stained structure with its folded derrick and gigantic walking beam. The cables looked rusty, and there were bits of timber bolted onto the frame here and there to strengthen it. One side of the trailer it rode on sagged beneath the weight of metal bars and pipes and pulleys.

'One thing we forgot,' I said. 'Who's going to work this thing?'

'Who d'you think?' Dad tamped his pipe as he checked the tyres. 'I'm a driller. I've still got my licence, and that's the identical rig I served me time on.'

'It looks like it, too.' Patrick eyed it critically, but I interrupted him before he could get into a slanging match with Dad.

'You were a driller?' I was surprised afresh at how little I really knew him. Only last summer he had taught Patrick morse code, and had once tried to interest Sian in building a wireless, which was when I had learned he'd been a signalman during the Second World War.

It seemed odd to have known someone for so long and yet so imperfectly. There were aspects of his life that he never talked about, like the war and his marriage. Oh, he told stories of his army days and his early life in the bush, to the point, sometimes, where their repetition maddened us, but thinking about it now I realised it was all just surface stuff, nothing of what he'd felt but only what he had done. It made him difficult to know, and for possibly the first time I wondered what it was that drove him.

Now, riding along the rough and narrow track that looped in over low ridges clad with broken rock, red termite mounds and the gnarled shapes of snappy gums, I saw that the gypsy had been right when he said it was scrub country. The turpentine bush spread before us like a green sea, broken by islands of swamp box and, where the soil changed, stretches of bauhinia, whitewood, and a red, flowering softwood we came to know as the cotton tree.

After that there was a flat, a sort of watershed between two ridges where the vehicle tracks had turned off, and I cantered over to have a look. There was an overgrown mound and the remains of an old windlass. I sat my saddle, examining Dad's tracks, while the plant jogged past. He had walked about here, cut a divining stick – the trimmed-off foliage lay withered beneath the tree – and tested for water, but couldn't have liked the results.

We went on, not caring how long it took, excitement kindling at each new discovery. I remembered a morning after rain long ago, when we'd first started travelling with the wagonette, and the world had seemed new, touched by change. It was like that. The yellow flowers of the bindi-eyes were jewels in the grass, the circles scribed in the sand by the tips of swaying tussocks as meaningful as words. We counted off the timber as we spotted it – ironwood, cabbage gum, bloodwood.

'There's some wattle.' Judith pointed, sunlight catching the cocky's feather in her hat. And five minutes later, 'Hey! A supple-jack.' Her mouth opened again as she turned to me across the narrow track, the climbing sun on her face, and my voice chimed with hers: 'Thou shalt not cut a supplejack for firewood, or any other purpose.'

'The gospel according to Mac,' I intoned. Then in quite a different voice, 'Ye gods! Will you look at the spiders.' The turpentine bushes had thinned, and every space between them seemed filled with the ropy strands of the Saint Andrew's Cross spider. They glittered in the sun – dozens, hundreds of them, everywhere I looked. I shuddered. 'I'm not riding through them!'

'Relax,' Judith said. Spiders didn't worry her. 'Soon as we put stock in, they'll thin out. The scrub too, I shouldn't wonder. You know, I could have my pony stud here, when we get paddocks. I'll have saved enough by then for a stallion and a few mares.' It had been her dream for years, and with the increasing interest in pony clubs around the country, it was now a practical one. 'Have to wait till we quit the road though – I'd want to be here with them. You've only got to turn your back on a horse and it's in trouble. Where's Cuddles going?'

The brown mare had swung off the road on my side. I sang out to her but she kept going, and when I cantered up she was still following the truck tracks which had turned off along the bank of a small creek. We came to where the vehicles had crossed it and then to a partly cleared line where somebody had stood a dozen fence posts before giving up on the job. The camp was further on, not far from the little creek. The horses stopped when they reached the vehicles, and I looked around at low-growing box scrub, at anthills crowding like tombstones, and the bright green of new shoots through old grass. A cotton tree was in blossom by the creek, and halfway between it and the camp lay a cleared area marked with a freshly cut peg. A tree I hadn't seen before grew beside it.

'Wild plum.' Dad saw me looking from the saddle and came over. 'I got a strong pull here, the water's not deep. We'll name the bore for the tree when we get it.'

'If,' Sian said.

'Jesus! Have a bit o' faith, will yer? Yer carp away like an old woman.'

That was the strange thing about Dad – you couldn't call him an optimist because he constantly foresaw obstacles and disasters in every project undertaken, but at the same time his imagination was skipping ahead to the certainty of its completion.

Sian was cautious by nature. He repeated, 'If. And *if* it's usable. Think of some of the bores we know – brackish, pure soda some-times – it might be shallow, it might be good. And there mightn't be enough of it to fill a tank even.'

'Then we'll try somewhere else.' I turned Meg in a slow circle, taking the country in again. 'I hope we don't have to, though; this'll be a nice spot for the house. Look over there. You can just see the hills.'

For the first few weeks we watered the plant in the shallow swamp lying between our camp and the road. A bit of a shed stood there, a crazy structure of rusted iron over termite-riddled rails, housing old junk. An ancient kerosene fridge, a portable post-hole borer – only both tyres being perished it wasn't very portable – and stuff like crosscut saws, old tow chains and packsaddle trees.

There was a spindly garden tree a couple of feet high in the yellow clay fronting the swamp, and back on the sand country under the bushes, safe from cockies and crows, a vine sporting two ripe watermelons.

'Well, that was worth the ride,' Dad said, wiping his beard off and tossing the rinds back into the scrub. 'Whatever its faults prove to be, we know the country'll grow good melons. What're you doing there?'

I'd found a shovel head in the shack and was scooping a watering trench around the little tree. 'Saving it. When we get the bore, I'm going to transplant it. Our first garden tree. What sort is it, do you think?'

'Something pretty tough or it wouldn't still be here. Swamp's dropping fast – better take the horses down to Big Sandy tomorrow. Well, let's get back. Time to get that diesel thumping again.'

The drilling was not going well. We'd been at it for weeks now and had had nothing but trouble. Every part of the rig was old, of course, and that caused mechanical problems. Dad and the boys had respliced the cable, built up the worn edges of the pulleys and strengthened the rig's frame. The diesel had seen better days too, about forty years' worth, Sian reckoned. He fiddled with the injectors for an hour, then kicked it disgustedly, yelling, 'What the hell did you buy this heap o' junk for, anyway?'

'You think you coulda done better for the money? Be my guest.' Dad was cutting the ends from two 44-gallon drums, which he had to take to Burketown to get welded up to make a water tank for the engine. Lacking a pump, we bucketed water out of Big Sandy into a temporary tank fixed to the truck bed, then transferred it by hand again to the engine-cooling tank.

The first twelve feet of hole were easy. It was only when we hit the yellow clay – called slippery-back – that the problems started. The clay had to be worked very wet if the sand pump was to pick it up, and it kept caving in, burying the sinker bar with which the actual drilling was done. We had to case it to stop the caving, then, halfway down, the casing jammed. Only the rig could shift it. And when it did the hole collapsed.

47

With jacks and rollers we moved the rig a few feet sideways and started again. This time the casing went without a hitch, until the lip of it jammed on a rock at a depth of thirty feet. There was no room to slide the casing past the rock, but there was too little rock protruding for the tool to bite. It simply glanced off sideways, taking the hole gradually out of line. One after another we took up the shiny tobacco tin lid that Dad used for a mirror, caught the sun on it and turned it down the hole to see for ourselves how crooked it was. There was nothing else for it, and for the third time we shifted the rig and started again.

It was baking hot by then, the days sliding dryly past. No further rain had fallen, and the green was fading from the grass. The derrick stood dark against the hurtful glitter of the empty sky, and willy-winds tore through the scrub with a noise like canvas ripping. The diesel thudded all day long, with either Dad or Sian on the tool string, and Patrick scampering up the derrick whenever the sand-pump line jumped off its pulley. Drilling was dirty work: skin, clothes, boots, the rig itself, everything was splashed with clay. Dad put his hat aside and wore a cap made from a trouser leg to catch the rain of liquid mud that squirted from the bottom of the sand pump every time it swooped up past him out of the hole.

Then we were through the slippery-back and into firmer ground. Things went better then. The tobacco tins, containing samples from the cuttings trench where the pump was emptied, multiplied. It took much longer now to run the tools down the hole. We screwed a third length of casing on and then a fourth, and heaved the next one into place, ready to be swung over and lowered the following day.

Dad tied bits of rag at measured lengths on the cable, to more easily gauge the depth of the hole, and when you let your hand ride up and down on it, feeling far below the shock of the bit hitting, you could sense the ease with which it was punching through towards the water. We never doubted it was there. Dad might say he didn't believe in the stick, but he also added that he wouldn't dream of drilling without checking it out by divination first.

Judith said, 'Huh?' but Patrick grasped his essential meaning.

'It's like, heads I win, tails you lose. Who's gunna help me with the horses?'

It was an hour or more past the usual time for watering the plant, but we had added casing twice today and had had a visit as well, from the manager of Gregory Downs. He didn't believe we'd get water and came periodically to tell us so. There was no shallow groundwater in the immediate district, he said. Gregory had dams, and Lawn Hill's bores were artesian, many hundreds of feet deep.

'Time'll tell,' was all Dad would say, but he said it pretty often.

Sian was drilling, so Judith and I took our bridles and followed Patrick after the horses. They were already shuffling their way to water, so it was just a matter of unhobbling them as we caught up and jogging the last mile bareback.

We had discovered another deep hole in Big Sandy, upstream from the road crossing and a little closer to the camp. Ebony and wild plum fringed the banks, which were pocked with yabby holes, and blue wildflowers massed in the damp hollows like patches of sky dropped down for a visit. When the light was right, you could see clear through the reflections to the fine gravel in the bottom.

The horses pushed forward until they stood shoulder-deep, the ripples widening around each gulping mouth. The reflections of ghost horses, brown, bay and pied, wavered beneath them, shivering to bits when they moved. The droplets ran in crystal streams from dark muzzles and distended bellies as they splashed their way out. I knew they would stand for a while in the shade before feeding off, leaving us plenty of time for a swim.

We did it every day, piling our boots, hats and belts on the bank before plunging into the delicious chill of the hole. Judith dog-paddled cautiously at the edge, and I swam underwater to get thoroughly wet all at once, then floated dreamily on my back, watching the way the sun limned the ebony leaves with light. Something brushed my shoulder and I floundered upright to fight off a ducking from Patrick, but it must have been a fish because he was out of sight. And so were most of the horses. I hung there indecisively for a moment, then stroked resignedly for the bank. Once they got a lead on, they wouldn't stop, and our swim would be over.

Grabbing my hat, I scrambled dripping onto bay Jody's back and went gingerly after them. Bare feet were not a good idea in the scrub. The lead was fanned out, feeding. I turned it back, cursing them all for a misbegotten bunch of mules, whacking my wet jeans with a handful of turpentine sticks to hurry them along.

While I was doing this, Judith got out of her depth, panicked, and sank to the bottom of the hole. She surfaced once, then went down again, and was drowning when Patrick reached her. She had collapsed retching under the ebony trees when I rode up. She looked white and shivery in the shadows – as did Patrick, with the same dark hair plastered to the shape of their skulls and their wet clothes clinging. I squatted beside them on the bank, and for a long time we just stayed there, not looking at one another, minds numb with the enormity of what had almost happened. It seemed too awful to talk about, and watching Judith from the corner of my eye my mind kept making images of daily life from which she was missing. Then Simon's bell rang vigorously as he rubbed his neck against a leaning bloodwood, and the sound broke the trance that held us.

Patrick spoke first. 'Look at Cuddles, bet yer she's in foal.'

Studying the brown mare, you could see he was right. There was a slight thickening of her girth, but mostly it was in the way she stood.

'It'll be the Dreyfus horse – what's-his-name, Ashanti,' Judith said. 'There were at least three mares in season when Johnny brought him into the yards that day, remember? Most likely they'll all have foals. Be worth keeping, too.'

Johnny was a dark-haired young ringer from the Cow camp. I thought Judith might be sweet on him. He certainly was on her. She'd got quite pretty in the last year, and Johnny wasn't the only man to notice. She reached for her boots and pulled them on, then combed her fingers through her wet hair and tossed Patrick his belt and knife.

'Let's get going.'

'You okay?' I asked.

'Yeah, but I'm through with creeks. C'mon, it's late.'

Even so, we didn't hurry. We didn't seem to be able to, but let Jody and the other two plod at their own pace. My clothes dried on me while I watched the sun dazzle on the moving manes of the chestnuts and greys and tried not to think of how we could have been coming home.

No driving was necessary. The plant knew as well as we did where it was going and simply followed the deep pads cut through the red soil by their constant toing and froing. Light glittered on the webs in the turpentine and the turning leaves of the swamp box, and there was a monstrous willy-wind loose in the scrub over Little Sandy. It was a hundred feet high at least, a twisting red column carrying a freight of twigs and leaves and gritty dust.

'Oh, God!' I moaned. 'It's heading straight for the camp.' But it swooped across the creek instead, and the leading horses put their tails up and took off, kicking and squealing in play.

We streamed into camp with a great shying and clangour of bells, to see Dad limping towards us, his mud-stained rag on his head.

'Well,' he said, 'we did it.'

'What? Whoa back there, Simon!' He was plunging after Widgie, teeth bared. Jody snorted, dancing sideways – from her shadow, I thought, until I noticed Sian hanging from the derrick about ten feet up, waving his hat like a maniac.

'Water!' he yelled. 'We hit water! We've got us a bore.'

We called it Trinity in the end, not Plum Tree as Dad had planned, because it was three in one. It was a hundred and twenty feet deep and, when measured, pumped almost two thousand gallons an hour. A good supply. The water would have to be analysed before we could use it, but we passed a dipperful round and agreed we had tasted worse.

'And a lot better,' Patrick said candidly. He spat his second mouthful out. 'Soda there, or something. So we've got the bore, what're we gunna do now?'

'Do, champ?' Dad repeated as if amazed he should ask. 'Equip it, o' course, and get some stock. I can see this place five years from now. Tank over there by the plum tree, thirty-foot tower on the mill, pads running in like spokes on a wheel. And over there,' he pointed, and so hypnotic was his vision our heads all swung to look, 'under the bauhinias, twenty, fifty, a hundred breeders – big, roomy-framed shorthorns with their calves at foot, just poking out to feed. Takes time. And work. But that's where this place is headed.'

'And what about the house?' Judith voiced my thoughts.

'That'll take longer,' he said. 'The cattle first, so they can keep us, but one day we'll have that, too.'

FIVE

The Wet was a light one that year and finished early. By March the roads were dry and the rivers back within their banks, the plant ready to go.

I viewed the new season with mixed feelings because, whether at Yeldham or on the road, we were still camping and for the time being we had done as much as we could at home. Empty days were boring ones; I missed the bustle of the travelling life as much as I disliked its discomforts. But life seemed to quicken as the air cooled and the floating thunderheads of summer gave way to wispy wind clouds scrawled like autumn messages across the pale sky. The sight of them fuelled a restlessness in me. I wished I could start work on a garden, but that was pointless – there would be nobody at home to care for it. Or that we would at least get the offer of a mob to somewhere different, somewhere we had never been. Then the Riversleigh manager called us, not with a job, but to enquire about our brand.

'It's "crank nine em" on the near thigh,' Dad said into the microphone. 'Mind telling me why you're asking?'

'She's yours then,' came the disembodied voice. 'Thought the crank was an ess. I've got a young chestnut mare here with that brand. Dunno where she came from. We mustered her outa the river paddock yestiddy.'

'We haven't lost anything down that way,' Dad said. 'Hang on, I'll ask me daughter.'

We all looked at Judith, who kept a roll-call of the plant and their brands in her head. She had her eyes screwed shut and spoke without opening them. 'Ask how many feet.'

'She'll have four, like most horses,' Patrick said.

'Idiot! How many *white* feet.'

'Near hind white and a very small star, just a few hairs,' came the answer.

Judith's eyes flew wide in amazement. 'It's gotta be Pom-Pom. She can't have drowned after all.'

Learning the filly was still alive was one thing, recovering her quite another, until a letter came the following Thursday from old Tom at Thorntonia. He must have had a sickener of trucks, as Kevin had foretold, because he offered Dad his bullocks, a thousand head, leaving in April.

'Thought we weren't gunna touch 'em ever again,' Sian said.

'Yeah.' Dad pushed his beard back and forth with the palm of his hand while he thought about it. 'It's work, and we know we can handle 'em. We could split the plant. Send half down to Dreyfus to wait for the bullocks – you and the young fella could do that. I could nip into the Isa for rations, then meet you at Dreyfus on me way back. Meantime, the girls could take the rest o' the horses round through Riversleigh to Thorntonia. Pick up the filly going past and get to the station with, oh, a week in hand. Give us time to shoe up.'

'Is it worth the risk?' Sian asked. 'There're other mobs.'

'There's other drovers, too,' Dad said. 'They're trucking some o' the cattle from the Barkly now. Which means the blokes who useta handle them will be looking for mobs to replace 'em. If we stock the place this year, we'll need extra money from somewhere. I reckon we should take them, but it's up to you lot. If you don't want to ...'

In the end we agreed, though with Sian still Jonahing on about pushing our luck. It took a couple of days to prepare things because we were to leave the second vehicle, loaded with its camp gear, at Gregory. So we rolled our swags, packed the tucker and cooking gear, and pulled down the tarpaulin that we had lived under through summer. There wasn't much left by then, just the steel pipe we'd used as a fly-rig and a bit of a boughshed we had built. Patrick had greased the pump-jack, and now Dad stowed the diesel belt in a cornbag which he hung in the plum tree, and we were ready to roll.

Because we had the furthest to go, Judith and I left first. We'd built a drafting yard over the summer, so with this, and the fence of the now completed horse paddock to help, we split the plant and got our half of it away, using Larry and the whips. We had the packs on Locket and Legs, which wasn't a good choice because

Legs was loony and Locket a homer. She kept going bush, and I wound up leading Legs – it was easier that way.

Judith had scribbled out the brands for Dad (some of our bought horses had half a day's reading burnt into their hides) so that he could pick up a permit from Gregory. The river by then was low enough to ford to reach the little township set on the edge of the blacksoil plains. It wasn't much, just a pub, hall, and police station manned by a constable. There was a racetrack up the road a bit and an old cemetery down towards the river. It was the centre of the district, with a population of eight, four of whom were kids.

My spirits rose as we rode and the unsettling restlessness I had felt left me.

'It's because we've always moved about so much,' Judith reflected when we talked about it. 'So we're like open-range cattle, really. You put them into paddocks and they never do any good – they've gotta have space, otherwise they just walk the fence and pine.'

'I'd rather be likened to a migratory bird or something than a cow, thanks very much. All the same ...' I sniffed at the air. It smelt of hot stone and horse sweat, and the vanilla sweetness of blossoming wattle. 'It's great, isn't it? You know, by the time we're old – forty or fifty, say – this'll all have changed. There'll be paddocks and grids, maybe even a bitumen road, and tons of litter and tourists buzzing around. And none of them will ever know it was like this.' I swept an arm around at the broken ridges where the short grass glowed gold against the red rock, then green where the hardier spinifex spread. There was water in the little creeks, dark pools lying lightless in the shade with dragonflies in powder-blue jackets hovering above them.

'And your grandkids'll think you were a tootin' shootin' cowgirl,' Judith said, and changed her voice to a high squeak. '"Tell us about when you were a pioneer, Granny, and rode horses all over, and how you met Grandpa."'

'Oh, yeah! *If*, you mean. Enough to turn you off, though, isn't it? Thinking of him as a future grandpa. And Great-aunt Judy, with her spurs still jingling, can tell 'em all about mustering on the big runs.'

'Yep. I'll get to be as big a bore as Dad on the Old Days. But it still beats cooking.'

A brown quail darted out of the grass under my horse's feet, sending him skittering sideways. Its wings beat frantically and I could see the liquid sheen of its eye. Larry, pacing at Boko's heels, had jumped when the horse did and now his jaws snapped together and crunched. We stared in horror, and he dropped the limp bundle of feathers as if wondering how it had got into his mouth in the first place.

'Murderer!' I cried, and Judith caught him on the jaw with the tip of the stick she threw. Larry yelped and lowered his ears, giving a deprecatory wag of his tail, but it didn't stop him wolfing his kill on the spot.

∽

It was a full moon the night we camped at Lilydale Springs. We came in along the pads, aiming for the green thicket at the cliff's base where the spring welled. The sandstone wall looked sheer but there were ledges and cracks you could climb by if you wanted a view of the valley. Under the overhang at the top where the wild goats camped were faded rock paintings, and below the trough beside the overflow two fruit trees grew, a mango and a lemon. The mango was bare, of course, in March, but the lemons were ripe. We ate them, dipped in sugar, until our teeth rebelled, then climbed up through the undergrowth to the spring and pulled off our clothes. It was nice to have the place to ourselves to bathe at leisure and wash our hair, secure in the privacy our isolation afforded.

Sitting on a sun-warmed rock scraping soapy lather from my legs, I said, 'It really bugs me the way we always have to be the ones to fit bathing and that around the men in the camp. I mean, if they want to undress, they just tell us to clear out – and they don't even look to see if we have. We're the ones who have to sneak around the bushes and freeze ourselves in creek-beds in the middle of the night to get a bit of privacy.'

'Well, it's a man's country, isn't it? So we're here on sufferance, anyway. And you don't see the half of it,' Judith said. 'When you're working with them, the older men aren't so bad. But the young ringers either want to claim you as their girl or sulk and ignore you, because having to work with a woman demeans them.'

'How can it?'

'I don't know. Tell me why there's a male rate for station cooks and a lower one for females, and we'll both be wiser. Same job, isn't it?'

Something pattered into the foliage beside me and I looked up as a little rain of pebbles bounced off the cliff. A black, wedge-shaped face peered down at me, its curved horns sharp against the sky.

'There's a goat up there.'

'Must be one of Tom's.'

A prospector called Tom Connolly had built and then abandoned the hut now crumbling into decay beside the fruit trees he had planted. There had once been bantams, too, but if the dingoes hadn't got them, they would have reverted to the wild by this time and gone back to the trees.

We made our fire well clear of the old hut, with its eerie creakings, and sat by it after our meal while the moon rose, listening to the bells spreading through the silver-leaf box that covered the valley floor. Nothing much would have changed in that valley over the last thousand years, I thought. Man had been there but his marks lay lightly on the land, the faded ochre paintings on the cliff behind me probably the oldest and most enduring example. If a willy-wind were to scoop up the trough and old hut, a few Wet seasons revegetate the sandy track, all would be as it once was. It was a vaguely depressing thought. I wondered whether in ten years time our own efforts at Yeldham could be so easily obliterated.

Something flittered at the edge of my vision. I tipped my head back to look at the cliff and a bat, soundless as feather-down, fled across the silver night. Another followed it out of a shadowy crack in the rock and then the sky was full of them, all swooping silently above us. I listened, but heard only the fire's soft flutter and the drip of water from the overflowing trough.

Judith had her head in a book, reading it by firelight.

'You'll ruin your eyes,' I said. 'Listen, can you hear the bats?'

She looked up. 'And of course you won't!'

I had my exercise book out to work on a poem I was writing

about the green time of colts – I had become a great fan of Will Ogilvie's poetry. 'Never mind that, can you? I remember them squeaking in the old sheds at Jervois, and now I can't hear a sound.'

'It's because you're too old, that's all.' She yawned. 'I read about it in the *Reader's Digest*. Only children hear them because the pitch is too high for adult ears. Did you hang the meat?'

'Yes. It's scary, isn't it? How quickly things change? Nothing seems to last any time –' But she wasn't listening and even as I was speaking there had come to me, sudden as the passing wink of light on a wet leaf, an idea for the poem, a distillation of the thoughts of growth and change I had had that evening.

Next morning, when we came to the Gregory, there was a large road camp at the river crossing: tents, vehicles, machinery, scattered untidily around as though dropped from the skies. The plant, trotting with ears erect through the river growth, wheeled snorting from the shape and noise of it. Men in shorts and navy Jacky Howe singlets were building a causeway across the spill of swift, shallow water. Charlie Steen's camp, I remembered then. I'd heard his call sign often enough on the wireless.

Judith rode in the lead, downstream of the construction work, coaxing the horses across. They went warily through the water, then burst up the bank in a rush, muscles rippling under shiny hides and tails curled high. She ignored the men who waved and chiacked us as we clattered past – they were always rowdier in a bunch than when encountered singly, I thought. I waved to Charlie, a big man with his belly hanging over his belt, and stuck my nose in the air when a wolf whistle sounded behind me.

Pom-Pom was in the yards. Judith walked up to her and patted her neck. 'You're one lucky little mare,' she said. 'Just shows – miracles do happen.'

'Either that or she's half cat.' I opened the gates and chased her out, and we pushed on through rougher country where the horses walked in two long files, picking their way through broken stone. Two days later we came out of the hills onto the sand country of the Seymour River where Dad and the boys were waiting. We shod up there, then moved camp to the familiar dusty flat beside the yards at the station.

'Can't tell you how I appreciate you taking these little fellas of mine, Mac,' old Tom the manager rumbled. He always spoke of his cattle that way, as if they were particularly dozy milkers' calves. If it was an act, it was a good one – he'd been known to sack a man for swearing at a bullock. 'You won't have any trouble with this mob.' He always said that, too. Then, as usual, he dropped his voice, casting a hunted look behind him at the cluster of station buildings. 'Thought I might grab a feed with you. I've got this terrible woman in the kitchen.'

He must have cornered the market on them, Sian observed caustically. Tom was speaking of his cook, a different one each time, but none escaped that description. And it seemed that culinary problems were catching, because the camp cook was on a bender. He'd been on the metho, Tom explained philosophically, and lay unconscious in the dirt on the broad of his back under the camp truck. He was an old man with sunken cheeks and white chest hair spilling from the neck of his dirty singlet. He lay sprawled as if dead, and smelt so much that I thought for a moment he was.

'That's metho, or white lightning.' Dad grimaced in disgust.

'You'd better knock up a feed for the boys – they won't be getting anything from him tonight.'

'Let them go up to the kitchen, then,' I protested, but I knew, even as I spoke, that it wouldn't work. Station cooks didn't follow the rules, they made them. They were a touchy, peculiar breed, both men and women. Tom would leave his stockmen to fend for themselves before he'd think of upsetting his latest terrible woman with extra mouths to feed.

Grumbling angrily, I cooked them a meal, but only the horse-tailer bothered to thank me. The rest took it as their due. There were four white men and two black ones, and it was one of these last that Larry took to as he walked boldly up to the table with his dirty plate. He was reaching to put it down when the dog came at him from under the truck with a snarl to freeze blood, his every hair on end. The blackfella let out a scream and simply rose in the air, gaining the truck bed in one bound. He stood there shaking, and in the half-light afforded by the carbide lamps I saw that the healthy gloss of his black cheeks had changed to a muddy grey.

Sian hoiked Larry away at the chain's end, while Dad cautioned all the men about walking into the camp as if they owned it.

'That dog'll have yer as quick as look at yer,' he said. 'I keep him to watch out for me girls.' It was news to me, but I held my peace, guessing him to be obliquely warning off one of them. You got all types in stock camps. Most of them were decent enough but, as Dad had told us when I was fifteen and we first started employing men, wearing ringer's boots wasn't an automatic guarantee of character.

The camp cook was groggy and sick next day, barely able to

stand, much less work, so we left without him. The Thorntonia men loaded their swags and packs onto our truck and we headed off into the ranges over the route we'd watched the road trains struggle with the previous year.

On the third morning, the station men rode out to help with a count before turning for home, all except the head stockman who stayed behind to load the packhorses. They were fat and fresh and hadn't been worked for years. He didn't hobble them – station men didn't use hobbles much, depending more on yards – and they had him all over the flat before he got the final swag positioned and the meter straps tightened. The last horse was the touchiest, a high-headed yellow-bay standing with ears back and tail at half cock, just waiting to explode. I could see the swag was rolled too short, and he'd left off the circingle. Amazed, I watched him loop the halter-shank round the horse's neck ready to release him.

'You, uh, short a circingle?' I could actually see where he'd draped it over his saddler's neck but felt I couldn't be more direct. Even though I had obviously seen more horses packed than he had, as camp boss he wasn't going to stand there and let a girl tell him he was wrong.

'Aah, don't need it. Besides, I've got my writing case in my swag and don't want to crush it. She'll be right.'

She'd be just about as wrong as that nag could make it, I thought. The man wasn't just an idiot but a congenital one. (I had a dictionary now and was making a point of using it.)

'Well, I'll get out of your way.' I looked at the scrub and gullies abutting the slope where the bullocks had camped. 'Don't want to start him off.' But I needn't have bothered, for the bay suddenly yanked away, roaring like a bull, with the swag round his ears and the packsaddle already starting to slip. He went straight for the scrub, shifting the saddle a little with every root. It would be under his belly any second, I knew, and everything that could smash would.

∽

There had been so little rain on the Police Creek watershed throughout the summer that the creek was already dry. We would have to walk the cattle through the night to make the water next day. So we camped on the flat amid the spindly box, where last year's pads still showed, and watched the bullocks till the moon rose. There was only a bit over half of it left by then, but Dad wouldn't chance moving the mob without the light it gave. Not with the scrub around, he said. When he stood them up in the weak grey light, the cattle seemed to drift through it like shadows, silent except for the click of hooves against stone.

Night cast a wild glamour over the rocky track, which was so steep in places that the headlights bored yellow tunnels into the sky. Treetops lunged at me out of the black pit where the track fell away to the creek bottoms below, and piles of bulldozed rocks loomed like broken walls half glimpsed on the edge of vision.

There was something wrong with the truck. I peered through the dust layer at the lighted dash, but there was nothing to account for the loss of power. I was only in second, because the gullies were sharp, the pinches steep, but I shifted down into first gear anyway.

There was a smell like burning rubber and the steering wheel seemed heavy, but everything was different at night.

'Nothing, I hope,' I muttered without much conviction, flattening the accelerator for the next climb. Almost immediately the speed dropped off, and two-thirds of the way up I knew I wasn't going to make it. Then the motor died. I stabbed for the brake pedal and felt it slide to the floor as we careered backwards down the slope. Desperately I hauled the wheel about, trying not to think of the fifteen-foot drop into the bottoms, and just when I thought I had made it there came a terrific crash behind and the truck rocked to a standstill.

I turned the lights off and just sat there shaking, until Patrick's head, bobbing suddenly into the window frame, frightened a scream from me.

'God! Don't do that!'

'Who'd you think it was? You know there's only a tree holding you outa the creek? And you've bust the tail-light.' He sniffed and his voice sharpened accusingly. 'You're not safe to let out. Can't you smell it? The bloody truck's on fire!'

Furious after my fright, I tumbled out of the cab. 'And a good thing too! If you want to drive it, you're welcome. It won't climb the hills; the rotten thing hasn't got enough power to pull the skin off a rice pudding.'

'What d'yer expect with the brakes locked on?' He looked up from where he crouched at the front end. 'The tyre's so hot it's smoking! I'll have to pull the wheel off. I dunno how the hell you can sit there and keep driving without realising there's something wrong.'

'Because I am not a mechanic.' I snatched Prudence's reins from him. 'You fix it. I'll take the horses on. That way everyone should be happy. And if Dad doesn't like it, he can find himself another cook!'

SIX

The bullocks, following their previous pattern, didn't rush until they reached the open country. Maybe they had a thing about plains, Sian said. And maybe, Judith retorted, they were just bloody-minded – you could get killed every bit as quick in the broken blacksoil as you could in the scrub. Dad, sitting twisted in the saddle to rest his hip while the mob fed, saw things differently.

'Ev'ryone o' these buggers is worth fifteen bob to us, delivered. Remember that and keep your spurs in when they jump.'

The stages and the moon wore away together. We turned south, heading out to the Four Mile and Cartridge Creek, and met the mailman near old Fiery Downs. The Flying Doctor had been into Augustas, he told us, to pick up somebody hurt on a bolter; the Armranald cattle were on the road; and Kevin, ahead of us with Territory steers, had seen a saltwater croc in the Twenty Mile crossing where the quicksand was bad this year. Patrick swore to seeing one there last year, too. It had followed him across behind the plant, he'd said, but we hadn't believed him – not a man-eater, not so far inland.

May came, bringing colder nights as the moon grew. The night-horses were nearly as jumpy as the cattle by then. You only had to twitch in the saddle and they were galloping, flinging dirt behind them in an effort to get space between themselves and the mob. The tally of broken and sleepless nights added up to a bone-deep weariness. Everything was an effort – getting up in the morning, loading firewood, the extra labour of butchering a beast for meat. I might like cattle, I thought, but it didn't include anything bred on Thorntonia.

'How's the trip going?' Mike the mailman had asked.

'Good,' I'd said, because what was the point of saying otherwise? And it was going well. We had only lost two bullocks – one dead, one missing in a rush – and crippled Marshall, a little bay horse that had come from the Thring country years ago. He would never gallop again, and thinking of him now, I remembered when he was a colt and I was fourteen and had thought droving the most romantic occupation in the world.

Then it was back to Dreyfus to organise the second camp and take delivery of the first mob there. The route was tired already to my eyes, the track rutted and deep in bulldust, the frontage country trampled by the mobs that had gone before. After that we moved across to Neumayer Valley, north-east of Dreyfus, with its homestead on the bank of the Landsborough River. The entire herd at Neumayer Station was being sold off. Ours would be the fifth mob to go: fifteen hundred head of mixed cattle. This was crocodile country for sure, and my first sight of the broad, opaque waterway with its milky-grey colouring made my skin creep. We'd met a fisherman on the way over, a professional come straight from the Landsborough and heading into town with a freezer load of barramundi.

'Want a feed of fish?' he'd asked, and vaulted onto his truck to haul out the biggest one I'd ever seen. It was longer than his arm, a frozen giant with great thumbnail-sized scales.

'I'll cook some for you, too,' I said, but he shook his head.

'Nah, been living on it. But if you've got a bit of corned meat...'

We ate right there in the gidyea where we'd met, the two vehicles parked nose to tail like horses and the plant drowsing in the shade. We'd none of us had barramundi before and found it a wonderful meal.

'Best thing in the Gulf. Well, bar the prawns,' the fisherman said. He told us about his job then, the lonely camps and long hours, the salties in the tidal rivers, the mud, and the problems of getting the boat into inaccessible waters. He and his truck smelt strongly of fish, as though both had been impregnated with the essence of his quarry. And looking at his salt-whitened shirt and the myriad old scars on his hands and forearms, I thought fishing sounded worse than droving.

Our arrival at Neumayer Station coincided with the visit of Padre Brian Walker of the Australian Inland Mission, usually known as the AIM. He came down to our camp below the yards to squat on a swag's end and drink tea with us. We'd never run into him before but he'd heard of us, he said.

'Just talk round the ridges, you know.' He had an attractive smile that lit up his rather sad face. 'Maybe I'll get across to visit you at home one day.'

'I'm a roamin' Catholic,' Dad said. I couldn't tell if he meant it as a warning or a joke.

The padre smiled. 'I won't hold it against you.' He had a slow, easy way of speaking. 'D'you read at all? There's a box of books in my vehicle – just take what you want and put back anything you've finished with. And I've got a film to show tonight up on the verandah. The boss said everyone's welcome to turn up for it.'

'Oh, what's it called?' I asked eagerly. I hadn't been in a cinema since the Saturday matinées of my early childhood.

'*Spring Wedding*. Princess Margaret's the bride – you'll like it,' he said, and both Judith and I did.

I liked the padre too, with his gentle, unassuming manner. I had never met anyone like him before. He dropped in at all the stations to talk and listen, to baptise the occasional baby or marry a couple. He'd once even helped bury a dog, he told me, and I shouted with laughter. 'What, with prayers and the "dust we are and dust we turn into" bit, or however it goes?'

'Prayers never hurt anyone.' He wore an old felt hat and a khaki shirt. Only the crosses on his collar showed that he was a minister. 'And I'm sure they helped in this instance. It was a child's pet – the boy was only ten, and heartbroken, poor little chap.'

'I'm sorry I laughed.' I was contrite, and he smiled, banishing the shadows from his angular face.

'That's all right. You see,' he said unexpectedly, 'I know how hard this country is, and that if you want to last out here you have to be tough. But don't let that seal you off from feeling. We are all of us made to love and grieve. That's what being human is about.'

We saw quite a lot of Padre Brian after that. Whenever he was passing, he'd pull into the camp to share a meal or spend the night, and finally even Dad got round to admitting that he wasn't so bad, as God-botherers went.

They bred greys on Neumayer, and a few red and blue roans which Judith went into raptures over. They were the prettiest horses she'd ever seen, she said. The country itself looked largely grey to me, from the ash-coloured soil to the milky-grey spread of the river. While we waited for the mob to be ready, we camped not far from its bank. Neither of us ventured into it for a bath, preferring to ride up to the station and use the cook's bathroom. The opaque waters, lapping at muddy banks lined with silvery-grey thickets of paperbark, looked too sinister to trust. The plant wouldn't wet their hooves in it – they drank, snorting, from the edge, ears twitching and legs a-tremble for flight.

'There's half of them desert bred, so they can't know about crocs,' I mused, watching them water one day.

'Instinct,' Judith said. 'They know about the feel of things, I guess. And I, personally, feel uneasy anywhere near this river. I saw a catfish on the bank yesterday. Must've been a yard long once, and round as a tea-billy – only something had chomped it clean in half. I'll be glad to head further south, I can tell you.'

When we finally got going, it was with a dog's breakfast of a mob: breeders, dry cows, steers, calves, bullocks – even half-grown cleanskins which, technically, it was illegal to travel. Dad mentioned it to the boss but he said it was the responsibility of the new owner, who had cut a deal with those buying the cattle and didn't want the young stuff branded.

It was late August by the time we got away, the nights warm enough for just a jacket, and daylight coming a little sooner each day. As the bawling mob spilled from the yard, spreading across the tramped white stubble of the paddock, a trio of brolgas, great wings beating effortlessly, flew overhead. Their red caps flashed scarlet in the sun's first rays, and long after they'd passed from sight their bugling voices drifted back. I envied their ease of movement – it was going to be no coaster ride getting the cattle to where they were going. This, for now, was Julia Creek, but the mob, or parts of it, could be sold on the road. Before the war, Dad told us, he'd once done a trip that lasted eight months. Every time he got to where he was going, the cattle were sold again and he'd find himself with yet another six or eight weeks to go.

'But you prob'ly didn't have six or seven thousand head in front of you, gobbling the guts outa the country.' Sian smacked at a persistent fly. 'Half of 'em'll be starving before we deliver.'

'True.' Dad fiddled with his pipe. 'We might have to wander a bit if the route's bad. And that won't be easy in the fenced country.'

We knew what he meant. The little properties further south sent a rider out to see the mobs through their holdings. Under those conditions it was difficult to stray off the route. But cattle had to eat, and it was up to the drover to see they did. And it would be a slow trip; a mixed mob couldn't match the pace of bullocks, which swung along like a regiment of soldiers.

We left the ash-grey soil of the Neumayer Valley for the red of the Talawanta flats, skirting the great grey block of the Tin-Pin

Scrub. The mob travelled at the pace of the youngest calves, the tail straggling behind – like a bunch of gossipy old women, Judith said. They lagged across the stony ridges of Donors Hill and dodged about among the gidyea of Cowan Downs. Their feet grew sore, and they tongued more readily as the days lengthened into September. The route was bad – old, trodden-over stubble all that remained – and the station men vigilant. Of course, there'd been four previous mobs through and each one after their grass, so the men dogged us from boundary to boundary to see that we stayed on the route. We'd never had so many visitors on the job.

By the time we reached Canobie, Dad had added the two dogs to the workforce. Once the cows grew accustomed and stopped trying to attack them, they saved the horses miles a day by driving the straggling tail of the mob. Larry, in particular, could be left to bring along the weaker calves, and would plod behind them, nudging their hocks with his nose to keep them moving.

Between Sedan Dip and the Forty Mile, Harry, the mob's new owner, caught up with us. I took him for a travelling salesman when he first stepped from the vehicle in his pressed white shirt and sheep-killing hat, which was what we called the flat-crowned felts worn by those who worked among the woollies. He had cattle from a previous mob agisted at the Forty Mile and wanted to add to them from the tail of ours. A publican by trade, Harry had grown up on a farm and could sit a horse, but beyond what they were worth, he knew next to nothing about stock. To him they were units to be shifted here or there at a speed that devils with pitchforks couldn't have matched.

Dad grunted agreement to his plan, listened to his hectoring directions to be at the yards tomorrow forenoon, and sent Sian off to point the lead east. When Harry had gone, he said he wouldn't fancy being that bloke's barman – there was something about him really got on your works.

And not only Dad's. Next day we turned up at the rendezvous to discover that Harry had been given twenty-four hours' notice to get every beast he owned, including the five hundred agisted there, off the place. Seated on a drum in the shade of the table, I watched the three of them fighting it out – Dad, the owner and Harry. Dad wasn't saying much; he perched on the yard rails smoking while Bob, the owner, leaned against a post, arms folded and face set, and Harry strode up and down flinging his hands about, his white shirt limp and creased. Dad didn't look very worried, but, I supposed, whatever the outcome, somebody was still going to need a drover.

Time passed. I built the fire up and stood the billy near it, and debated mixing the bread dough. Then Harry left, clashing the gears furiously as he drove off.

Bob walked over to the fire for a drink of tea. He said gruffly, 'Nothing personal, Mac. I'll send a coupla lads along to show you the paddock and help put 'em together.' Then he left too, and Sian came riding in from the mob.

'Well?' He stepped down from his horse, squinting at Dad. 'What's happening?'

'I've agreed to take the agisted stuff on with us.'

'What? Jesus! Are you mad?' Sian exploded. 'There isn't enough grass to feed a goat, and we're barely making six miles a day now! What the hell do we want with another five hundred head? That makes over two thousand – how d'you think you can manage them?'

'I'll manage 'em.' Dad sounded frosty. 'It's only for a week, which I was about to mention when yer jumped the gun. And there's a bonus goes with it. We're getting our pick of a hundred heifers outa the job at a tenner each. I reckon that's worth being inconvenienced for a week.'

'Yeah.' Sian thought it over but his face retained its angry scowl. Eventually he nodded. 'So how're we getting them home?'

'Harry's fetching us a coupla men. You and the lad can walk them back while the rest of us finish the trip.'

'Well, it'd be nice to be asked for a change, instead of told.' Sian went back to his horse.

It took three days to get clear of the Forty Mile, to organise the permits and the new men, muster the agisted stock and draft the heifers out. Sian took a couple of packhorses and a small plant when he left, and seemed glad to go. It certainly made life easier not to have him and Dad constantly bickering over every little thing, I thought, but watching the heifers start off, I wished I was going with them. I was sick of the dust and the dry, burned land and the effort of shoving the weak mob south.

We crossed the channels of the Williams River and dinner-camped one day under scraggly coolibahs at the rock-and-earth wall of a chinaman's dam. We were crossing Dalgonally Station by then – open country, bare as a board, its flatness broken only by a distant fenceline. We had to carry firewood, so the horse-tailer belted dry limbs off the standing timber where it was available and thinned out the fence posts when it wasn't.

I hated the plains. You froze in winter on them and fried in summer, and they offered neither shade nor privacy. I waited until the cattle and horses had moved off and then stripped beside the truck to bathe out of a bucket, but Judith carried her towel with her and stayed behind at the bores to take a quick shower before catching the cattle up again. Most of all I hated the grey monotony of the plains, because there was nothing to fix the eye on but emptiness.

And then one day something different loomed on the horizon, and I found the sheep. I took them for rocks at first, scattered and piled across a sort of hollow where no rocks should be. It was only when I pulled up beside them and caught the scent of old bones and saw the wind rippling dead fleece that I realised the truth. There were dozens, scores, hundreds of them. I turned a slow circle under the wide sky where the little hawks hung, breasts buffeted by the winds, trying to work it out. Somebody – a drover, because this was cattle country – had got caught here in heavy rain. Not recently, maybe two or three years back. And he'd lost a flock, bogged and smothered in the heavy blacksoil that could break a bullock's heart. They'd been in full wool too, and perhaps in poor condition.

I closed my eyes and stood stock-still, with the wind blowing my hair, and saw it all – the rain coming down like Noah's flood; the gripping mud and the panicked sheep milling together, treading one another under, even the strongest wethers struggling to rise against the killing weight of a waterlogged fleece. I saw the exhaustion that set in with the numbing chill of the rain, and later the crows coming for their eyes while they still lived, and shuddered. Padre Brian was right. It was a hard, cruel country. And looking at the bones and the torn white skins standing out like grave markers on the silent plain, I knew I would never leave it. But I still wondered why I stayed.

That same afternoon the station manager came roaring into our camp just as Dad was getting off his horse. A tall, thick-bodied man with a fleshy, high-coloured face, he was hopping mad and went for Dad with a stabbing finger, yelling about thieving Neumayer drovers who could teach Ned Kelly his trade.

When he left off to draw breath, Dad had his say, beard stuck out and hands on his hips. 'I'm not apologising for getting them a feed. That's me job. Take yer complaints to the station. And look at it this way – I'd do the same for your cattle if I had 'em, and what's more you'd expect me to. Who's to say next season the boot won't be on the other foot?'

'I say it!' the manager bellowed. 'You'll never lift a mob of mine while cows calve!' He flung himself into his vehicle, then leaned through the window with a shouted afterthought. 'And don't reckon on using the yards at Gemrock tomorrow. I'll have the police on yer if yer do!'

We hadn't even known about the yards till then. If we weren't handling fat cattle, we sometimes used a station yard to hold the mob overnight. It gave us a break from watching. It was just petty-mindedness, not any concern for the possible damage we might do that caused him to say it, because anyone with eyes could see he was no great shakes as a manager. There were big cleanskins still running with his cows, and fences that hadn't seen a straining fork for years, so the prospect of a loose yard wire or two shouldn't have worried him.

'We'll watch 'em,' Dad said, and looked across at me. 'Go past the yard half a mile or so, and pick a camp. And get the beef-bags down. We'll knock a killer this evening.'

He took the rifle out about an hour before sunset, when the horses' shadows stalked like giants across the plain, and shot a glossy-hided cleanskin within the wing of the yards. It was tender meat but without the bulk of older cattle, so it would not last us long. We had the liver and rib bones grilled for tea and enjoyed the joke as much as the taste of fresh meat.

'I'd like to be there when he finds the carcass,' Judith said, chucking a bone to the dogs who were too full to want it.

'On a pretty fast horse.' I dipped my greasy fingers into the washing-up water. 'Bet he checks up tomorrow to see if we did use his lousy yards.' He couldn't miss the slaughtered heifer when he did, or the unmarked ears that showed it had worn no brand – but he'd never know if it had been a Neumayer Valley beast or one of his.

Matt, who'd taken Sian's place, wiped the fat from his mouth with the back of his hand and belched. He was a hard-faced man in his forties with scanty hair and cheeks bristling with dark stubble. I didn't like him. I could always feel his presence, like a shadow, just behind me. I didn't like the way his eyes followed me about either; the weight of them on my body made my skin crawl. He was coarse in his speech and habits, even rolling himself onto one cheek during a meal to fart. He had never said or done anything I could directly complain of, but he was the first man ever to frighten me.

He said now, 'His sort! Man oughta run the red stag on him. I've seen it done for less'n that. What yer reckon, Mac?'

'Not something I hold with,' Dad said. 'Getting your mob a feed's one thing, but having a yike when you're caught doesn't justify starving anyone's stock – not to my mind.'

With horrified understanding I said, 'Burn him out? Deliberately start a fire?'

Dad nodded. 'That's it. Get your own back on the bosses – just set the red stag running and clear off, and nobody can prove anything. There's men that'll do it, but I won't employ 'em.'

That last bit was a warning to Matt, I thought. Of course there wasn't fuel enough now to warm a quart pot, but with the constant wind I could imagine how the grass-clothed plains would burn. That night, when I dropped wearily into my swag, I dreamed of it, running endlessly from fire that scorched my naked feet and spread horizon-wide. And bounding behind me as I ran a great red stag with Matt's eyes, fire snorting from its nostrils, its hooves and antlers outlined in flame. I was panting and sobbing from the terror of it when Judith woke me for my watch.

SEVEN

We were on dinner-camp, with the mob spread through the scraggly growth of shallow creek channels, when Harry next arrived. The saddle-horses were hipshot in the shade, eyes closed and lower lips hanging. They were losing condition. They flattened their ears now at the touch of the spurs, moving with a heavy unwillingness, weary from the miles they'd covered.

'Stick the billy on,' Dad said as the vehicle pulled up. But that was before Harry explained the reason for his visit. He'd sold the fats out of the mob – two hundred and fifty of the best bullocks and spayers – and we were to walk them into Gilliat to the loading yards and truck them early Thursday.

Dad grunted, poking at his pipe. He sucked on it and spoke round the stem, 'That's Thursday week, right?'

'This week. The twenty-seventh.' Harry tossed the words over his shoulder as he strode around. He lacked the bushman's ability to hunker, and never sat unless a seat was offered to him.

'Jesus!' Dad exploded. 'It's forty-odd miles! Yer think they got bloody wings? On good days we get about eight out of 'em and work for every yard of it, too.'

'Not the whole mob.' Harry waved his arm impatiently. 'I've arranged a paddock for the rest on the next property. There's a buyer coming to look 'em over, so you'll just have the fats. The actual distance is forty-five miles. I measured it. But you've got three days – that's plenty of time.'

Dad shrugged. 'They're your cattle. But it's not how I treat fats, nor yer buyer won't be too happy.'

'They're going down on weight,' Harry snapped.

Dad rose, pulled the billy off the fire and poured its contents over the coals. He tossed it into the box of cooking gear and picked up his whip.

'Stand 'em up, then,' he said to Matt and Judith and the rest. 'We gotta fit a week's work into three days, we better get started.'

We made it in time but only by travelling at night, which upset the routine of watch-keeping and made cooking difficult. The mob, so small and mobile after the vast one we'd been struggling with, was easy to handle but you could see the condition melting off them. Then, on the Thursday morning, the train was late.

We sat round the fire talking desultorily and staring up the metal tracks while the sun rose and glittered on the roof of the Gilliat pub behind us, waiting for the train to come.

Dad limped across to the table and back, tutting with vexation. 'If it doesn't come in the next twenty minutes, we're letting them out for a feed. Might suit Harry to run the guts out of 'em for twenty-four hours, but I'm not –'

'Train's coming,' Judith called. The air throbbed faintly and far up the tracks a dark shape appeared.

'Finally!' Dad said. Then everybody took their pannikins back to the table and made ready to go over to the yards.

They had been held up by a hotbox on one of the wagons, the train drover told me. His job was to ride out on the stock trains and keep an eye on the cattle that travelled back. It didn't involve much – checking the wagons when they stopped, to make sure none of the cattle had gone down, and poking them back onto their feet if they had. His name was Hobbs.

'Bill Hobbs,' he said, shaking my hand. He'd wandered over to the camp while Dad and the rest were loading up, to cadge a drink of tea. I could see why he wasn't in the yards with the others because he moved with a lurching gait, his right foot twisted sideways, as if his leg or ankle had been badly smashed and then poorly set. He'd never move fast enough to make the rails if a bullock were to turn on him. He filled his pannikin again from the billy, gripping the hot metal with calloused hands, asking, 'Got any meat you can spare?'

'Sorry.' I shook my head. 'We're on the last bit of corned stuff ourselves.'

'Ah well, I'd sorta hoped . . . Can't beat a bit o' bush meat, can yer? Where'd the bullocks come from?'

'Up the Gulf. Place called Neumayer Valley – you might've heard of it?'

He shook his head. 'I'm a Channel Country man meself.' He

had grey hair and the pinched-down stare and look of leathery toughness only bushwork produces. 'Poor season out that way, too, this year. What's it like up there at this Neumayer place?'

I told him about it while he listened, turning the enamel pannikin between his hands. About the grey horses they bred and the pretty roans Judith had liked. 'That yer sister, is it? Seen her riding over. Sits a horse well.' About the monster fish and the big salties in the wide grey river, and how, when there was a wind, the dried roly-poly tumbled across the ash-grey flats to set touchy horses bucking when it tangled in their legs.

'You going back there now?' he asked when I stopped talking.

'Oh, no. We've still got a mob – it's paddocked back up the route, right now – to take on. It's just the fats going off today, there's about twelve hundred head left. Mixed stuff – breeders, steers, weaners, you know.'

'Getting late in the year for it. Where're they going?'

'Depends.' I shrugged. 'They're up for sale. Where's home for you now?'

'Charters Towers, since my leg.' His mouth turned down as if in hard-held grief. 'I ride the trains when I can. Gives me a few bob and gets me back out here, away from the towns. Not much of a life there for an old bushie like me.'

'I'm really sorry about the meat,' I said, meaning it.

'Ah, well. Almost as good talking to you, lass. Maybe one day I'll get up there and see those rivers of yours for meself.' He stood up and we shook hands again. 'Sounds like they're loaded, so I'd better go. Thanks for the tea.'

I watched him toil across to the train. He looked older than Dad, maybe sixty-five. I'd met a few like him, busted-up stockmen and drovers no longer fit for station work and condemned to a narrow town existence. They were mostly either single or separated men, because there was little room for wives on stations, and the vagabond life that went with the job would have suited few women. I would never marry a stockman, I thought. It was a high-risk job with little money and few prospects, other than those facing old Bill – the boredom of restrictive town living and, once in a long while, being watchman on a train. Walking the length of it, poking cattle back onto their feet, a task any railman could do. I thought of the wide horizons he used to have and wished I could have given him a decent lump of freshly killed steak – something he'd once have taken for granted but which would now be a luxury, a sort of compensation for what age and injury had taken from him.

～

By the time we returned to our mob in its paddock, it had been sold. The new owner was, coincidentally, another Harry, but as unlike the other as pebbles are to pie. He was an elderly, white-haired wisp of a man in cattleman's clobber of washed-out jeans, cotton shirt, old polished elastic-sided boots, and a shiny new go-to-town felt hat. He agreed without a blink to Dad's terms for continuing the trip, which was a change to contract rates from the flat price per head we were presently being paid, and he volunteered to provide a calf-cart and a man to drive it, saying, 'For you've got calvy cows there, Mac. They'll be dropping any day now.'

Harry owned a property below Kynuna, which was our new

destination. He sketched a mud map of the route that would enable us to bypass Gilliat, shook hands all round and departed.

'Well, even your brother, if he was here, couldn't quarrel with that,' Dad said. 'I like a man that knows his business.'

I sighed. 'How much longer to delivery then?'

'I make it about three weeks, which puts it at the back end of October.'

'And hot as Hades, by then.'

'Well, it's work.' He spoke, as he always did, as if work of itself was all that gave meaning to life. He'd told us often enough of the Depression years before the war, when a man might walk a hundred miles on the mere rumour of a job and arrive to find as many as five hundred other hopefuls there before him. I knew why he felt the way he did but his attitude still irritated me.

'There are other things you can do, you know, besides work. The rest of the world has weekends, public holidays. Seems to me all we ever stop for is Christmas.'

'I've seen the time when half the country'd have swapped all their Christmases for a single week's pay, and that not much better'n fifteen measly bob.' His face was hard and I could hear the tinge of bitterness in his voice, always there when he spoke of the thirties.

'Oh, will you shut up about the Depression!' I leapt to my feet. 'I know things were tough then. I know people went hungry. But that was thirty years ago, for God's sake! Things have changed. The war's over, the Depression's finished. Why can't you forget it? I'm sick to death of hearing about it.'

'You should have tried living it, girl.' His voice was flinty. 'And you'd have some reason to complain. You've got absolutely no idea what the soul-destroying futility of being unable to get work does to a man. You ought to be grateful to have a job and money coming in.'

'Why should I be anything of the sort?' I sounded hot. 'It's not like anyone's giving me the money for nothing! I earn every penny – we all do. And that's okay. All I'm saying is we don't have to fill every day of the year with it.'

'Depends where you want to end up.' He turned away, but the argument ran on in my head and I brooded over it for days. We had all agreed to the belt-tightening exercise that owning our own property would entail, to years of hard work and small wages, and doing without holidays and the little luxuries other people took for granted. Most times it seemed worth it, but now I wondered if we had really worked out the cost. The trouble was there seemed no alternative, beyond a seasonal wages job on a station or moving into town. I thought of Bill Hobbs then. 'Not much of a life,' he'd said, and I knew it was one I didn't want to try.

Harry, as good as his word, produced an old Dodge truck with a crate on the back to carry newborn calves, and an eighteen-year-old lad called Jimmy to drive it. He was a lanky, big-eared boy with brown eyes and floppy dark hair, and from the moment he saw Judith he acted as if he'd been sand-bagged. Dad, on whom most of our admirers kept a pretty sharp eye, might not have existed for him. He unsaddled her horse for her, poured her tea, and leapt around offering her seats as if his own were on fire. Most of the time he seemed too bemused to know what he was doing, particularly if she was anywhere near. And every time she spoke to him, his unfortunate ears turned bright pink.

'He's crazy!' Judith said one dinner-camp as we watched the old Dodge bumping slowly towards us with its load of newborns – the cows had been dropping their calves for a week now. 'He's like a big, good-natured puppy, galloping around behind you begging for a pat.'

' "Gobsmacked" is the only word. It's really quite funny – Pete and Matt rib him all the time. Matt's pretty horrible to him, actually. Dad gives him the odd glare and I swear he doesn't even notice. Walks around like a zombie till you come in and, bang! He's lit up like a Christmas tree. If he was anywhere he could get them, he'd be showering you with chocolates and roses.'

'Thank God he can't!' Then she thought about it and her eyes crinkled as she grinned. 'Well, maybe the chocolates. But it's embarrassing having those great cow-eyes yearning at you all the time. And he's only about fifteen.'

'Nope, same age as you. I asked. It's just love at first sight.'

'Well,' she lifted her shoulders in exasperation, 'I wish I knew how to turn it, or him, off. Without being really awful, I mean.'

She wished it more fervently the next evening when Jimmy came into the camp, his ears flushed with triumph and a very active lamb clamped under his arm. 'It's lost its mother,' he said. 'Thought you'd like it.'

'Gee,' Judith said, 'thanks!' Jimmy mistook her understated sarcasm for pleasure and flushed to his eyebrows, while the lamb struggled furiously to escape. It was no more orphaned than I was, he'd run it down, I thought with an inward giggle, because it was the only handy alternative to chocolates. He couldn't know we'd grown up poddying lambs and thoroughly despised them.

Dad, poker-faced, got into the act as well. 'There y'are, then,' he said. 'Your own lamb to raise.'

When I rode out to relieve her on watch that night, Judith said immediately, 'The minute we're all off camp tomorrow, you get rid of that damned sheep. I am not keeping it! Chuck it back over the fence into the paddock it came from. Orphan, my eye!'

'Its mother probably won't have it back now. Besides, what am I going to tell Jimmy? Who must have a pretty good turn of speed, by the way, to have collared it in the first place.'

'Tell him it ran away. Or you drove the truck over it. And that I'm not too upset because I hate sheep.'

'You can tell him that bit yourself. Maybe you could just think of it as a five-pound block of chocolate,' I said.

'Pretty lively chocolate!' And then we were both laughing in the warm night, remembering the kicking little horror we'd wasted half an hour of our precious sleeping time trying to feed.

Jimmy's devotion lasted to the end. I thought he'd burst into tears when he parted from us, but he just stood there with his heart in his eyes and one hand holding his swag upright next to the old Dodge. I flipped a hand at him, calling, 'See ya, Jimmy,' and swung onto my horse, but Judith gave him a quick, self-conscious peck on the cheek, and as she turned away I saw his free hand go up to touch the spot.

'You've done it now,' I said. 'He'll follow you to the track's end after that. Thought you didn't like him?'

She wriggled her shoulders as if finally free of an obligation. 'He'll find that a chore, he doesn't know where we live. And I don't *dislike* him. I mean, he's a pest but, oh, you know!'

Matt and Pete had been paid off on delivery day, so now it was only us who had to get home. We made long stages, Judith and I driving the weary plant and Dad in the truck. Even with our heads turned for home, it still seemed to take forever. In a patch of scrub on the channels of the William River, north of Julia Creek, we heard, through crackling static that drowned most of the broadcast, Polo Prince win the Melbourne Cup. We rode into an early storm in the Ten Mile paddock on Dreyfus, and Mike the mailman pulled the truck out of Fiery Creek for us when Dad bogged it in the silt of its first run that season. We saw ibis there, stalking, long-billed, on the claypan – the first that summer for they were birds that came with the rain.

After that there were no more storms on the track. The Gregory waters ran silver and green between the jungly growth of their banks, and I watched Prudence, standing shoulder-deep above the ford, trying to snort the current out of her nostrils as she drank. Opal was smarter. She had her head turned downstream, gulping the water as it fled past.

There was only one stage left to Yeldham. Dad went ahead while Judith and I, riding Socks and Pirouette, gathered the horses up and set them jogging homewards over the pebbly river crossing, where, legs tucked high to keep our boots dry, we scooped a final drink with our quart pots. Out through the red country then, to the gullied limestone of Maccadams Creek and the long white miles of Maccadams Plain, where the watery mirages formed narrow lakes along the track. The scrub line marked our boundary and an end to the blacksoil country. The horses' feet crunched in the red sand and the ropy spiders' web glittered in the scrub. A storm had passed across Big Sandy, water lay in the rockholes, warm and leafy-tasting, and birds' tracks were set hard in the mud.

'Two or three days ago,' Judith said. Scarlet-bodied dragonflies flitted above the surface, and there was the faintest tinge of green in the tussocky grass along the bank.

'Look, cattle country.' I pointed at the beginnings of a pad and the dung-dappled camp under a low-spreading bauhinia.

'Somebody must run cows here,' Judith said, and we grinned at each other in the pride of ownership.

We crossed Lemon Flats, plunged back into scrub and came to the turnoff at Little Sandy. There was the old shed and the swamp, dry these many months and beyond, the tightly strained wire of the new horse-paddock fence. Legs whinnied and an answer came from the paddocks. I saw a flash of bay through the trees, then Kelpie came tearing out with Tassle and Joy behind him, tails and heads high. Beyond them was the bore and the trough, with a dozen of the heifers camped comfortably in the shade, and behind it the fly-rig and the vehicles, and Patrick wiry and ragged in a torn shirt coming to drag wide the gate. We were home.

We put down Bendiddy bore that summer. Dad named it after a paddock he used to muster back in the brigalow country. It lay on the far side of that great dividing line that had split his life – the two and a half years he had spent as a soldier in his country's service. 'Before the war' was a phrase we often heard. I visualised it as a place rather than a time because he used it mainly for comparison. Before the war, according to Dad, horses stood taller, feed grew thicker, and the scrub on Kirrimbilly Station (where Bendiddy paddock had been) bred cattle as wild as hawks and as cunning as serpents.

'Yeah, well, maybe we oughta call it something else.' Sian gave him a look from under his hat, but Dad stuck to his guns.

After they'd got our mob of Neumayer Station heifers home, the boys had pegged and cleared a fenceline for the big paddock Dad had spoken of putting up. The Bendiddy bore site was just within the paddock outline several miles east of Trinity. A bit close, perhaps, Dad said, but that was where the indications for water were. I went with him the day he chose it, pacing beside him and watching the forked stick he held begin to dip and bend. The tattoos on his forearms writhed as the pull grew stronger, and his muscles flexed to hold it. Then one side snapped just above the fork and it swung dead in his hands.

'That'll do.' He scored an X in the sand with his boot and went to cut a peg to mark the site. There was a whitewood growing close by, its branches low enough to reach. I pulled one down and broke a Y-shaped fork out of it. I held it as he had, arms cocked, elbows against my ribs, forearms level and thumbs out, and stepped right onto the mark he had made. Nothing happened. I trod backwards, then forwards again, eyes glued to the stick, but it was dead in my hands, as inert as stone.

'Hold it tight,' Dad said behind me. His big right hand closed over my wrist in a grip that squeezed the bone, and I gasped as the green wood rolled in my palm. The end of it pointed straight down with such force that an untrimmed bit, where I'd yanked a branchlet off, pierced my skin. But I couldn't do it unaided. Alone I squeezed the stick until my knuckles shone, and nothing happened.

Dad, belting the peg in, said, 'Squat down and try. I had to crawl round on my knees before I felt my first pull. After that it just got stronger every time I did it, but getting closer seemed to help at first.'

I knelt then, right next to the peg, feeling the heat of the sun on my back and sweat, warm as blood, dripping from my nose and chin. The air screamed with cicada song and the distant, repetitive call of a rainbird. My hands were locked so tightly round the wood my fingernails cut into my flesh, but I ignored the smart because, just momentarily, the stick had moved. I watched it, fascinated, trying to find something different in myself to account for it. It stirred again, a tentative dip such as the weight of a small bird landing on it might induce. Then there came a clang as Dad threw the axe in the back of the 'rover, and I saw he was by the cab, waiting to leave. But he had also noticed the movement.

'You've got it,' he said. 'Seems to run in families. One of my brothers could divine, and a cousin.'

'Do you feel anything special or different when you're doing it?'

'Bit of a tingle in my fingers and that's probably circulation. I've gotta grip it hard. Dunno why. I've heard blokes claim different things – they can feel the power coursing through their bodies, the pull of the water knocks 'em off their feet. Maybe it's true.' He shrugged. 'And maybe they can raise the dead, too.'

I ran a finger over the stick in my hand, then held the ends again, amazed to find that what he said was true; my muscles seemed, of their own accord, to tighten until the wood was grinding into my flesh. I wondered if he was right and it was an inherited gift. Dad had come from a large family on the goldfields of Western Australia but he had run away from home at fifteen and we had only ever known our grandmother and his older sister. I had never thought of my missing uncles and cousins before, but felt suddenly curious about them, wishing I could meet the ones with a talent for divination.

Sian punched the second bore down in a couple of weeks, but not without a huge blow-up with Dad. He was impatient of advice on the job and more than willing to make his own decisions about the hole – a right Dad claimed by virtue of his greater experience. They argued about the actual site the first day while I, grown tired of the exchange, waited in the 'rover. Sian wanted to shift onto a lower level of the flat but Dad refused to hear of it.

'For Chrissake, it's where the water is, boy! There's nothing over there. I've tried it and I know.'

'You mean, you've waved a bit of stick about. What the hell does that mean? There's no scientific basis whatsoever to divining. How can water be here and not there, a hundred yards away? Jesus! The stuff is liquid, it can't *not* spread.'

Dad had his way and the hole went down in the original spot. It was so close to Trinity that most of us were out there every other day to help with the work or to see how it was going. Sian hit a small supply of water at thirty feet and another at fifty-five. The hole was damp, then sloppy, then making water, but in both instances when he let the string of tools out further to deepen the reservoir they punched through into dry earth again.

'Just a pocket o' moisture,' Dad said. 'It happens. The real supply's further down.'

At ninety feet there was sweet water in the hole. Sian drove home to tell us after pumping from it for a couple of hours. It wasn't a huge supply, he said, but it would do.

'Punch 'er down another ten feet,' Dad said. 'It's prob'ly just seeping up from the main stream below. Could double its capacity with another few feet.'

'You don't learn, do you?' Sian put his hands on his hips where his faded shorts were stained with clay. He had a rag sticking out of his back pocket and was burned as brown as wood from working on the rig without a shirt. 'That's how we lost it before. Anyway,' he said with finality, 'I've shifted the rig. The casing's in – all it needs is a block run round it and the job's finished.'

It was a few days later that a man went missing from the road camp about ten miles upriver from the Gregory pub. It was getting on towards Christmas by then and very hot. No further storms had come, though the clouds kept building and blowing away again, and each night the lightning shows flickered for hours along the horizon. I longed for coolness. There was a white glare to the days that hurt the eyes, and you could feel your skin crisping in the heat.

'Jesus!' Dad said when the Gregory manager called him on the wireless with the news. He glanced out through the fly opening at the dancing sky. 'Don't like his chances if he's lost.' But that seemed to be the crux of the matter, because the police, who had come to join the search, were not certain that he was. The missing man, they argued, could have walked out to the main road and caught himself a lift to town. He had a steel plate in his skull and was known to be a bit funny. He'd vanished on other jobs, only to turn up drunk somewhere after half the country had spent days looking for him.

Dad and the boys loaded their saddles and drove in to help search, but were home again, tired and dry, by late afternoon.

'Did you find him?' I stood a second billy by the fire, knowing they'd drink the first one like water.

'The coppers have called off the search,' Sian said. 'I hope the poor bugger's where they reckon he is, in some pub. He's a goner otherwise.'

'The station blokes have got a boat out on the river,' Patrick said. 'Case he fell in and drowned. Charlie reckons he couldn't swim. But there was a croc shooter left Burketown yestiddy morning, and the bloke was gone from the road camp by yestiddy lunch, so he could've got a lift. Might be in Katherine by now, or halfway to Boulia. That's how the coppers are thinking, anyway.'

The following day was even worse, hotter than anything I could remember. Perishing weather, Dad called it. Sweat dried instantly on your skin and birds drooped open-beaked in the bauhinias. At mid-morning a tiny finch blundered into the shade of the fly and fell dead out of the air. The sky grew pink above the scrub, which began to flap and roar in the wind, and anything – not only metal, but even the canvas fly – burned the hand that touched it.

We had all but forgotten the lost man. It was too hot to think or do anything but endure. Judith and I filled a washtub for the birds and just lay on our swags, dully irritable with the heat and flying grit, waiting for the day to end.

When it did, there were dead cuckoo-shrikes floating in the trough and a pelican, ruffled and cross-looking on enormous webbed feet, in the dry bed of Little Sandy.

'Must have got sick o' battling the wind,' Patrick said as we watched it lumber into the evening sky. The air was still now, but cloyingly hot. 'Wonder if that bloke's turned up yet. The coppers oughta have heard by now if he got a lift someplace.'

'Maybe he drowned after all.' I'd choose that over perishing any day, I thought. I wished I were in the river right now, gliding above its pebbly bed, feeling the rush of its cool waters along my bare skin and through my hair.

But I was wrong, and so were the police. The missing man had neither drowned nor left the district. A Lawn Hill stockman, attracted by the flash of light on metal, found his body on our western boundary months later, the plate in his naked skull heliographing messages to the empty sky.

EIGHT

That summer I transplanted the little tree from the swamp. It had been grown in a jam tin originally and when I dug it up I found the root ball compressed within the metal rims. Dad cut the roots free with the tinsnips.

'Give it plenty o' room,' he said. 'Anything that tough's bound to spread.'

So I planted it well back from the marked out area of the shack we were building from bush timber and the iron sheets off the old shed down at the swamp. Our 'homestead' would be little better than a pitched roof and maybe a back wall to start with, but at least it would be more permanent than a fly-rig. You could see daylight through dozens of old nail holes in the iron, and plenty of rust patches, too, but I supposed we could always pull a tarpaulin over it, and, however rough, it would be preferable to sitting out another Wet under the fly.

It was no good being impatient, I thought, pressing the soil down round the tree. We were equipping Trinity bore with a proper stock tank and mill, because previously we had only had a 400-gallon ship's tank connected to the trough, and that hadn't held enough for the horses, let alone the cattle. And we had to have a paddock – somewhere to turn the horses out to spell, and to run the brood mares and bay Ferdy, Judith's thoroughbred stallion. As if that wasn't enough to keep us broke, we'd also be needing equipment for Bendiddy – there was no sense in having a bore you couldn't use. There wouldn't be a penny left over from the previous season's earnings, nor, I knew, from this one, or next year either, probably.

But I could still start the garden. The boys had fenced the area off to keep the horses out of it, and though at present I lacked a hose, there was plenty of channel iron from the old shed at the swamp. I shaped a bit to fit under the tap and planted couch grass roots where the water pooled. I might have to wait for the house, but when we got it, I vowed to myself, there'd be a ready-made garden to place it in. The tree, aided by a timely storm and with its roots free to spread, shot ahead, putting out layers of dark green lacy leaves. It was a matter for joy when, towards the end of summer, it was tall enough to sit under. I used to sprawl back on the thick mat of couch grass and watch the sky through the moving leaves, dreaming of the house we'd build one day, or, more prosaically, wondering what I'd cook for tea, and whether Don, the young stockman from Gregory who was my current boyfriend, would be out that weekend.

Sian was dead keen on a girl that summer. Her name was Lindy and she was a little older than me. She worked in the homestead at Gregory Downs and was very pretty. Judith and I were fascinated by her sheer femininity, and the effect it had on Sian who, for all his plans and hard-headedness over Yeldham, was acting much the same as Jimmy had.

'He's besotted,' I said wonderingly. 'All over pink nails and wavy brown hair.'

The two of them lived in a world of their own all that summer, oblivious to everything and everyone else. It amused and puzzled me. I didn't feel the least bit like that about Don – he was just pleasant company, someone to go into Gregory with at weekends, a companion to swim and laze about with under the trees. If the rather peculiar behaviour of the others was caused by love, then I certainly wasn't in love, nor had I been so with any of my previous boyfriends. And I wondered cynically if it was a state you wished yourself into, rather than something that actually happened, as the books insisted.

Judith was just as uncertain about it. 'I can't believe he can get so, so soppy!' she said. 'Even his voice changes. Have you noticed? He sort of coos at her. And she tells him he's wonderful about twice a minute. How can he swallow that? And he hasn't fought with Dad for weeks. If that's love, there's something to be said for it after all.'

Late one day at the start of March, Red, who was lying by the gate into the garden, stood up and growled. Dad cocked his head. 'Vehicle coming. Now I wonder who that can be?'

It was Brian Walker, the AIM padre, with his wife. It was the first time we had met her, and looking at her rather hard, dissatisfied face, I knew that the tales we'd heard about her had to be true. Brian was universally popular, but it was a different story with his wife.

'So this is Yeldham! It's so good to be here at last,' he said, and you couldn't not believe him. 'We're heading through to Camooweal and wondered if we could camp the night and catch up with you all.' They had their own tent but drank tea with us, sitting on carbide drums under the tin roof of our half-built shack. Mrs Walker fanned herself, squinting at her pannikin as if she thought it might be dirty, but Brian was interested in everything – the new tank and mill, the garden, and the cattle stringing out from the trough.

'It'll make for easier living having a roof. What have you done with the floor?' He scuffed at it with his shoe. 'It's as hard as concrete.'

'Antbed,' Patrick said simply. 'Poor man's concrete. You crush up the termite nests and puddle 'em into a mix with water, then pour it into boxing – just like cement. Dad says all the bush tennis courts are made that way. We could build one of our own,' he said, 'only none of us ever learned to play, and anyway you'd need six dozen dogs to fetch the balls back. Netting costs the earth.'

Brian laughed heartily at the picture this conjured. 'Well, you've got two. That's a start.'

'Larry and Red, chase balls?' Judith looked at him pityingly. 'Working dogs have too much self-respect for that. If you gave them a ball they'd bite it in half.'

'Well, if you haven't got a court you'll still have shade,' Brian said. 'That rain tree'll throw plenty in a couple of years. They grow to a tremendous size.'

'So that's what it is!' I cried. 'I've been wondering for ages.'

Dad grunted grumpily. 'It must be feeling like a fish outa water then. It's the driest Wet season I've known.'

'The rain will come.' Brian sounded very sure, but Dad wasn't convinced.

'Course it will, but the point is, when? Seems to me we had the best of it before. Drovers can shift their plant about when bad seasons come, but you can't tow a property down the stock route.'

Sian jumped up then. 'What are you worrying about? There's still March, that's plenty of time for rain. You got your book box with you, padre?'

Brian nodded and stood up. 'Come and have a look. I've got one for your collection, too, Kerry. Somebody put in Kipling's poems and I've kept it for you.'

I had a carton of books now that he had saved for me out of the ones everyone donated to his portable library. I would write better, he had told me, if I read well, and though at first I found his choice of reading matter dull, I was developing a taste for the poetry and novels he brought me. Afterwards, while his wife was showering and Judith and Patrick were milking the goats, I handed Brian the page from *Hoofs and Horns* containing my first published story. He was the only one I had shown. Even Judith didn't know about it yet, and I was shy of telling Dad.

'That's splendid!' he said heartily. 'Is it fiction or a true story?'

'Oh, it happened, but we sold the horse ages ago. And, d'you know they paid me fifteen shillings for it.'

'Did they? Well, keep writing, and one day I'm sure somebody will be paying a great deal more.'

At breakfast next morning, Mrs Walker put down her pannikin and said, as if it were no more than one could expect, 'There's a goat trying to knock the gate down.'

Judith jumped up. 'Oh, that's just Dotty. Come for her foot.' She went out to let her in, taking down the tiny boot from its nail near the door post and kneeling to lace it on. The kid had been born missing her right foot, and the stump, which lacked a padding of flesh between the leg bone and skin, had remained tender. Judith, who now did all our saddling, had fashioned the boot from harness leather, padding the sole with sponge. It was laced on with soft wire and removed each night at milking time. Dotty came for it every morning, and we had grown so accustomed to the whole thing it no longer seemed strange to us. Brian took her photo as she stood on her hind legs, boot braced against the mudguard of his vehicle.

'Where did the goats come from?' he asked as he put the camera away.

'Thorntonia. They run wild down there. We got a truckload up in December and quietened them down. We keep them for meat, and milk.'

'I don't know what the back country would do without them.' He stood watching the flock string away over Little Sandy. 'They look homey, don't they?'

Mrs Walker was already in the vehicle, face hidden behind sunglasses as she tapped her fingers on the door. She said, 'Come on, Brian,' and he shook hands with us, then got into the vehicle, waving as he left.

Sian, looking after them, muttered, 'Must be a helluva temptation for him.'

'What?'

'Throttling that woman. No one could blame him.'

I was in wholehearted agreement, but it seemed disloyal to say so. Instead I traced the passage of the vehicle down through the paddock by the dust above the scrub. The feed that had grown on the storms was already dry. This time last year the swamp had been full, but it was now so low that it could scarcely water a duck. I was very glad that we didn't have dams to worry about, because it looked like being one of those years when the monsoon didn't make it down from the north.

There were still plenty of dry storms about, though. The heated air seemed charged with electricity, which vented itself in violent displays across the skies. The noise was incredible, but I never considered the actual danger that the storms posed until the day we got back from some errand or other at Gregory and found Cuddles dead by the trough. The lightning had struck her on the wither, scorching a track down her shoulder and foreleg and through the shell of her hoof. The body of her five-month-old filly, Embrace, lay dead but unmarked beside her. They must have been touching each other when it happened, and the charge had taken them both. Staring at the limp bodies on which the stink of charred hide still lingered, I knew I would never again think of thunderstorms as simply noise.

Sian wagged his head. 'How lucky can you get, eh? Imagine if it'd hit the mill!'

But it seemed the worst of ill luck to me. Dad had shot old Wadgeri, one of our original plant horses, only the week before. He'd been so old he could barely lift his feet. And in October bay

Rose had died foaling, Todd and Grace had both been sold; Mort was dead from strangles. Of the original eleven only Kelpie, Clancy and Polly were left.

I knew by heart all Dad's pet phrases about owning stock. They were horses, not people. You owned 'em, you didn't marry 'em. There were plenty more as good just waiting to be caught. But when those you had known for years died, they seemed to take a part of your life with them. Wadgeri had been my first horse. I had jogged him hundreds of miles. We'd double-bunked on him as kids, and packed lambs and calves on his saddle. We'd run brumbies with him, chased sheep about, mustered the Bullshead bullocks on him, and used him as a night-horse in the droving camps. He'd been an honest old toiler and owed us nothing, Dad had said, as he cleaned the rifle and put it away. That was praise, coming from him, but I didn't regard it as much of an epitaph.

March was so dry that the Easter sports were held at the racecourse at the Gregory township. They were planned as a matter of course each year, but mostly only happened when Easter fell in April, for the roads were seldom dry enough to travel in March. We were moving out at the time, heading for Dreyfus where the new manager had given us a couple of months' contract mustering work before the bullocks left in June. Most of the stations were starting early. Horse-breaking and mustering had to be done while the feed was at its best, and now that the weather was cooling off there was no point in waiting longer.

Dad sent for Michael and Jervis, the Aboriginal men we'd employed previously. There were still three days before the sports, so we spent one of them chopping cabbage-tree palms along the

Gregory and carting the tops home to thatch the verandah of the shack. Piled thickly and covered with chicken wire, it made a wonderful dense shade to sit under. Next morning we mustered the plant, and Jervis, swinging onto Judith's piebald pony Confetti, was given a lively few moments before being thrown, saddle and all, into the garden fence. The mare, having got rid of him, stood snorting and shaking and wouldn't let him near her again. She'd never had a man on her back before and plainly didn't like it.

'She's only used to girls.' Judith had run out at the commotion to catch the pony, and now patted her trembling neck. 'She couldn't be quieter, and look at the state he's got her in! Well, he's not riding her again.'

'Jesus!' Dad bellowed, incensed. 'I told him to saddle her. What is this? What's the use of a plant full o' nags nobody else can ride?'

'It's only one horse,' I protested, supporting Judith, but she didn't need it. She didn't often get angry, but she was now.

'I don't care what you told him. She's my personal property. I reared her and I broke her in, and I'm not having any ham-handed blackfella – or white one, for that matter – spoiling her mouth and ruining her back. If she goes in the plant, I'm riding her. Otherwise she stops home.'

Dad opened his mouth, then shut it again – in surprise, I think. Judith was the least combative of us all, but she really cared about her horses. After a minute Dad told Jervis to put his gear on Acrobat, and Judith, having gained her point, buckled the hobbles around Confetti's neck and quietly let her go.

Kevin's droving plant was at Gregory when we got there. We camped beside him on the riverbank, across from the pub, and caught up on the news since our last meeting months before. He was heading out to Calvert Hills where he had a mob waiting. There was only him and the silent horse-tailer we had met a couple of years before. Kevin planned to pick up the rest of his men in Camooweal.

'Saves a few bob on wages,' he said, scratching at his cheek. 'Though I s'pose we'll be calling 'em dollars soon. You hear about old Doug?'

'What about him?' Dad looked up from the billy he was tilting over his boot.

'Poor bugger got his skull stove in. Breaking colts at Lawn Hill. One of 'em kicked and got him behind the ear. Musta been fiddling with its feet, I s'pose – shoeing it, maybe. Anyway, the Flying Doctor took him out yestiddy.'

'Jesus! He gunna make it?'

'They seem to think so. Said he was comfortable this morning, but I reckon that's debatable. He must have a headache a truckload of aspirin couldn't fix.'

Judith came back from watering the horses just then with the news that the hawker's van was open for business. It was pulled up opposite the pub, the side panels (for the whole truck was really one vast cupboard) raised to disclose stacked shelves. There was a small white tent rigged beside it. She and I went straight over. We left the horses and walked, because the new bridge, which had gone in about eighteen months before, now made this possible. There was to be a dance after the sports, and we were both going to get a new dress and shoes for the occasion.

We breasted eagerly up to the counter at the van, but the shelves held mostly western gear: Santa Fe boots, action-backed shirts with embroidered yokes, Levi jeans, and heavy windbreaker jackets. There were belts, felt hats of every size and hue, ordinary cotton workshirts, and piles of heavy woollen socks.

Bitterly disappointed, I looked at the owner, a heavyset man in his fifties who had come to serve us. 'Haven't you got any dresses?'

He opened a door at the back and stuck his head into the van. 'Dulce! Some young ladies for you.' He beamed at us. 'Something for the dance, is it? Don't worry, Miss, we have heaps of every-thing – that's Molony's motto. My wife will fix you up.'

Dulce was petite and friendly. She and her husband came from Camooweal, where they ran a clothing shop, she told us. The dresses were hanging in the tent, which doubled as a changing room, and she took us through them, chattering brightly as she zipped us up and down and tweaked skirts straight. We bought petticoats, step-ins and stockings. Judith got a blue scoop-necked dress and white shoes. My dress was similar in style but with short, caped sleeves and patterned in soft swirls of violet and green. My feet were too big for all but the last pair of shoes, which were black with very pointy toes. The latest fashion, Dulce said, all the rage in town. They felt tight, but I was sure that I could wear them, and in any case there was nothing else.

'They'll be perfect,' Dulce decided. 'The dress will look darker under artificial light, so you don't want light-coloured shoes. Now,' she bunched my plait deftly, pushing my head sideways to show me in the mirror, 'will you wear it up? It gives the effect of height, you know.'

'She needs that like a giraffe needs more neck.' Judith was candid.

She turned to me, trying the effect of a stole, but the colour was wrong for the dress. 'What do you think?'

I shook my head. 'Nah, too dark.'

There were gauzy scarves and wraps and little glittery purses, but we put temptation aside, only succumbing to a set of hair combs each: tortoiseshell with sequinned tops. Then, at Dulce's invitation, we stepped up into the van, to a narrow living space that had been outfitted as a tiny kitchen, and had tea with her. It came in pretty china cups patterned with yellow daisies, with store-bought biscuits on a leaf-shaped plate. There was even a doily on the tray, and a sugar spoon with a saint's head on the handle to go with a fluted bowl. I wondered what it would be like to always live like that, with china and curtains and pretty fabrics. And stealing a look at my hostess I was conscious again, as I was in Lindy's company, of how brown my hands and arms were, and how very large my boots.

By mid-morning next day the racecourse was packed. Everybody in the country seemed to have turned up. Some I recognised as coming from neighbouring stations, others from the pub – closed for the day while a bar was run on the course – and still more I knew as council employees from the road camps. The constable and his wife, who lived opposite the pub, were there, the former in uniform, and a host of lean young stockmen lounging on the rails or hunkering on their heels in the shade. There were solid brown older men like Dad, contrasting with the bright cotton frocks of their wives, kids with their ears bent under the weight of felt hats, and at least eight other girls. The publican's two young teenage daughters were there, as well as Charlie Steen's, the road contractor. Also Sian's girl and a governess from Nardoo, another from further down the river, and two girls from the family who were agisting their sheep on Planet.

There were plenty of riders to contest the events, and competition was keen. Sian was so far ahead in the figure eight he would have won it if Lancer hadn't fallen. The roan could spin like a cat, but this time he made too tight a turn and his feet just kept sliding. Sian, who was very quick, swung his leg clear in time but the fall cost him the race. Patrick won two events, and I came second in musical chairs. After lunch there was foot racing. In the women's sprint, which Judith entered, the policeman's wife tripped over in the straight in front of everyone. Her skirt blew up, and the big man from the hawker's van made a trumpet of his hands to yell, 'She's sportin' Molony's underduds!' Everybody laughed as she was helped up and brushed down. Judith was unplaced, so only Patrick got any ribbons.

The dance was held that night in the hall next to the pub. It had bare iron walls, no ceiling, and a slippery wooden floor. There were backless benches along two sides and an elderly piano with yellowed keys, which was played by the publican's wife. A bow-legged man in a fancy shirt joined her with an accordion and sat patting his foot to the melody they made.

I was nervous and my shoes were very tight, but the look and feel of my dress made up for it. Dad stood up with me first, muttering directions as he steered me round the floor, and in an agony of bumble-footedness I saw with relief that a lot of the young men already dancing were no better than me, sawing their partners' arms up and down as if they had hold of a crosscut. One couple skidded into the end wall with a crash that momentarily drowned the music.

I saw Judith, blue skirt swinging, with Dad, then with a boy from Nardoo. Sian, dapper in a new shirt, was swaying with Lindy, and Patrick, chin on hand in one corner, was watching it all.

Don came to claim me and we trod on each other's toes through waltzes and the gypsy tap. We ate supper, and the little kids went to sleep under the benches. My feet were in agony by then, and my hair sliding out of its clips. Finally the generator faltered, picked up its beat again, then died.

'Run outa fuel,' someone said as the lights went out, and the dance was over.

NINE

The mustering job on Dreyfus was at Scott's Hole, a long lagoon
and a set of yards not far from the bank of Mittaguddi Creek. It
was red country, coolibah flats and pea-bush with a bit of gidyea
back towards Nardoo. Dreyfus shared a boundary with Disraeli,
Morella, Kamilaroi and Nardoo, so each of these properties sent
men to attend muster in order to collect cattle wearing their station's
brand. It made for a big camp – there were the four of us (Patrick
had stayed home to pump for the stock) and Mick, the white man
Dad had put on to break in colts, and Michael and Jervis, the two
black stockmen.

Boydie, a long, lean rider from Disraeli, showed up first. He
towed a packhorse carrying swag, tucker and a folded fly. After
tying the horses he stepped up to the fire, quart pot in hand, to
help himself from the billy, then sunk onto his heels to drink it.

Boydie was an uncommunicative man, never using two words where one would do. Dad invited him to eat with us.

'Righto.' He nodded his thanks, then dumped the packbags by the fire. 'You have this, then.' He had a good stare around, picked a site at a little distance from ours, and rigged his fly.

The Morella Station men, Ben and John, came next from the Myalli out-camp with a battered tent rolled in a hessian bag across their second packhorse. They erected it in the scrub fringing the edge of the waterhole and let their horses go. John was the older of the two, but it was Ben who had most to say.

The tucker-horse had taken a header into one of the creeks they'd crossed, Ben told us, but it didn't matter because their cook had been recovering from a bender when they left, so there'd been no cooked food to bring. He and old Johnno, he said, had just filled the bags with tins, and he supposed a bit of water wouldn't hurt them. In fact, the latter had soaked off all the labels, so that when I came to use them I never knew if I was getting peas or pears.

From Kamilaroi came an experienced station hand called Reg, and Noel, a slight, blond new chum. Reg had a black hat which he was constantly pummelling and belting against his thighs. It seemed extraordinary behaviour, until I realised he was doing it to the hat to keep himself from killing Noel. You could see why from the moment they rode into camp, when the blue-shirted youngster dropped the lead rope of the packhorse so that it dragged through the spiky seeds of the kerosene grass, and then, as the horse pushed into the sedgy ground to drink, was trodden into the mud.

They had a little blue tent, which Reg reckoned wasn't worth the bother of putting up, only Noel insisted – he wasn't getting dressed in the open, in front of girls, he said.

'What yer worryin' about, there's plenty o' scrub to hide in,' Reg told him, but it rained that afternoon anyway. Although it was just a shower, it settled the question of rigging the tent. And still the clouds hung round. It would be too ironic, I thought, if after a dry summer the rain was to set in now, just when the season had started.

A man called Scotty turned up from Nardoo that afternoon, completing the tally of musterers. There were now thirteen of us, and the tents and tarps dotted around gave the place the air of a pioneer settlement. It rained again that night, much heavier falls coming out of a muggy overcast. There seemed to be a million frogs giving tongue, while cattle mustered that day bawled their discontent from the yard. And in the breathless stillness between the rain, when the night pressed down like a smothering hand, I heard the solid whine of mosquitoes swarming outside my net.

Daybreak came in cool and grey with the clouds sitting on the trees. There was no sun, and moisture dripped from the fly's edge and laid a wet sheen over the scrub.

'It's gunna pour.' Sian stared at the lowering sky in disgust. 'God, I hate wet camps.'

'Looks like it could set in.' Dad fluffed up his beard in a way he had when he was undecided. 'I dunno, a camp this size – better call the station and get more tucker sent out. If the river comes down . . .'

He didn't finish the sentence but went across to the bough shelter where Judith was putting the meat away. We hung it each night on hooks cut from fencing wire and bagged it during the day to keep the blowflies off.

'We'd better turn a few killers into the paddock while we've got 'em.' He tipped his head to look at the sky again. 'I dunno what to think, shouldn't be more'n a shower or two this time o' year.'

It was Jack, the new manager of Dreyfus, who brought out the extra tucker. He had a gate-opener with him, a ringer from the Cow camp, who unloaded the cartons of rations for me while Jack went across to the yard where the men were branding. They all came back for smoko, those who'd been working at the ramp stained and spattered with mud. Noel was limping. He'd been flattened by a big calf he wasn't quick enough to dodge, Judith said, adding out of the side of her mouth, 'Nine-day grass ain't much greener.'

When they got up to start back, Jack caught Dad's eye and jerked his head. 'A word in your ear, Mac.'

Dad waited and the gate-opener, catching on, sketched a farewell salute and went over to their vehicle. I stayed where I was and heard the boss say, 'That quiet bloke in the dark shirt they call John – one of your men, is he?'

'Nope,' Dad said, 'stranger. Down from Morella for the muster. Why?'

'He's supposed to be a bit odd. Hears voices, and by all accounts they make some pretty violent suggestions to him. I heard – and it's just talk, Mac – that one place he was on he got hold of an axe. Smashed up the kitchen and chopped a bloke's leg open. Had to call the cops in to get it off him.'

'Jesus, God!' Dad sounded disgusted. 'I've got a hopeless new chum, a personal pronoun,' this was a swipe at Mick, who talked a better job of breaking than he actually performed, 'and now a nutter in the camp as well!'

Jack had an easy, mobile mouth. He looked as if he were going to laugh, then thought better of it. 'Hmmm,' he said. 'He's a good ringer, they reckon – between times, that is. But maybe you should hide the axe?'

Dad kept grumbling but he took his advice. He planted the axe under the truck seat, then, as an afterthought, removed the bolt from the rifle and slipped it into his swag.

'He doesn't look mad to me,' I said. 'If it was Reg, now. He flings that hat of his around like a two-year-old in a tantrum.'

'Well, forewarned . . .' Dad didn't bother finishing his favourite quotation. 'Just watch yourself with him, we dunno what sets him off.' He looked at the sky and stumped away to organise a greater supply of firewood and to get the men to turn half a dozen head of cattle into the horse paddock. If the rain set in, we would need plenty of killers – meat wouldn't last any time in this muggy heat.

They mustered next day but wound up letting the cattle go and splashing back to camp through the wet. The rain came out of the north like an onrushing grey curtain, bending the heads of the trees before it. I ran to get a sheet of iron over the oven-hole where the bread was baking, and to build up the fire and cover it, too. With thirteen to cook for, I couldn't afford to lose the fire because it would take some starting again in this weather. All around, men were snatching saddles and belongings into shelter and checking their swags. Judith's and my stretchers were up against the truck body at one end of the big fly, and we sat gloomily on them watching the rain. This was no passing shower, but a serious fall. It poured down until the ground streamed water and the tautened canvas boomed with its fall.

116

'We won't have to worry about running out of the wet stuff if this continues. Won't even have to cart it.' Judith got up to seize a bucket and stand it under the run-off, and in moments it was splashing over. 'There you are, straight from God. Doesn't come much cleaner than that.'

John, who was helping to carry wood, had darted under our fly when the rain started, and now watched the surface water pouring into the lagoon.

'Have to shift camp if this keeps up.' He scratched his head, squinting into the sheeting rain, and I saw that the distance between the waterline and his fly-rig had almost halved. He seemed eminently rational to me, and far more capable than Reg and Noel.

The latter's tent collapsed that night, its pegs having loosened during the downpour, and at daylight the pair of them crawled out into a grey drizzle to re-erect it. They were to get plenty of practice at the job over the next few days while the rain continued, because every time they put it up it fell down again.

The men killed in light rain that evening and hung the hot beef in a bough shelter at the edge of the camp. It wouldn't keep, I knew. The rain might splash unpleasantly cold on my skin as I skipped between the fire and the shelter of the fly, but the moment it stopped the cloying heat returned, and with the dawn came a million blow-flies. They couldn't get at the meat, which by then had been bagged, but they could and did lay their eggs all over the bags. I scraped them off into the fire, but flies were like mossies – you could never kill enough to make the slightest difference.

It was an uncomfortable week cooped up in the muddy camp, watching the rain fall. Everyone was bored, and in the brief dry spells when the weather held off for an hour or so, the men looked for things to do. On the third day, Scotty, who hadn't that far to go, got his pack-mare up out of the paddock and headed back to Nardoo. Even if the rain had stopped right then, it would still be too wet to muster for several days. Reg and Noel continued to fight their tent, and water now lapped two feet deep over the spot where John and Ben's fly-rig had been. They all played endless card games, gambling for matches, and Boydie, who was a bit of a loner, sat cross-legged for hours dealing patience hands onto his spread saddlecloth. Michael and Jervis seemed to have an infinite capacity for doing nothing. They came out of their fly, which was set a little apart from the rest, to eat, then rolled back into their swags and slept again.

Judith and I read and did crosswords, and in the privacy of the creek-bed where we went to bathe, talked about the men. Noel, too green to know better, had a dozen irritating habits – he never screwed the cap back onto the waterbag after he'd used it, or watched where he put his feet round the fire, and as a result was constantly knocking over billies and sending buckets flying.

'And if he leaves the lid off the sugar tin one more time,' I pressed the top down on my shampoo bottle and set it aside, 'I'll kill him. I had to chuck the whole lot out again yesterday because of the ants.'

'They're just such obvious things,' Judith marvelled. 'You don't have to be a genius to do them right. Still, I'd have Noel over Mick any day.'

I knew what she meant. Faults of character were difficult to hide in stock camps, where each man worked and lived so closely with his neighbour. Mick was lazy, and tried to gloss over the consequences of half-done work with a smarmy sort of charm. He was a whinger too, complaining endlessly about external things like the rain and the mosquitoes, which affected us all equally, but what Judith really disliked was his newest affectation of addressing her as 'darling'.

We had both of us been called 'mate' and 'love' times without number and taken no offence, knowing nothing was meant by it, but Mick's smartalecky 'darling' was different: a sly showing off to the others, a subtle appropriation of more of Judith than she was prepared to give. I had seen her stiffen the first couple of times he said it, then decide to let it pass unchallenged. But it grated on her and by the next day she'd had enough.

Dad, cranky from pain and lack of sleep because the damp made his arthritic hip ache, had just pulled Mick out of a poker game in Boydie's fly with the terse reminder that he was paid to handle colts, not sit on his arse wasting time.

''s too boggy to get 'im outa the yard.' Mick sat unmoving, the cards fanned in front of him.

'Then work 'im in it. Get a packsaddle on him and some sandbags if you can't do anything else. Jesus, man! Yer can't start on a colt then just let him go.'

'Right.' Mick was also good at judging how far he could push things. He dropped his hand and took a step out of the fly, and there was Judith, bent over a bucket of clothes she was washing. He said, 'You gunna tell us where I could maybe find some sandbags, darlin'?'

She spoke very slowly and very clearly, so that even the blackfellas must have heard her in their fly. 'My name is Judith, Mick. Unless you want to call me Miss McGinnis.' She stared at him until he turned away without a word, then went composedly back to her washing.

The horse yard at Scott's Hole was the same sort we used to build in our brumby-running days – rails wired to standing timber in the shape of a rough circle. There were slip-rails at the entrance, held in place by wire loops with plenty of play in them, and because they were lower than the rails, Dad had told Mick always to hang a saddlecloth over them when he was working colts, to block them from jumping out. Mick had done so once or twice, then, in his usual slipshod way, couldn't be bothered.

He was working on a quiet little bay called Dandy. Judith had got him as an injured yearling and had handled him only enough then to treat his injured leg. He had recovered and was now a three-year-old, a cobby little horse, broad as a pit pony and not much taller. Mick thought him a pushover because he was quiet. I had heard him telling Noel, who was easily impressed, that really a man should be ashamed to take the money off old Mac – the colt was that easy he practically broke himself.

He rode him in the yard that same afternoon after the horse had had a perfunctory hour with the pack, not being made to work with it but just let stand there, undisturbed, in order to feel the weight and get used to the gear. Even when his own neck was involved, Mick couldn't get it right. It was true the colt had been lunged and led, and reined about with a minimum of fuss, but ground work was different from having someone on his back. When Mick swung confidently onto him, Dandy bunched up, flicking his ears back and forth and moving clumsily as he adjusted to the weight. Mick tugged his head round, working his legs to urge the horse into movement, and Dandy saw the slip-rails, uncovered, lower than the coolibah barrier around him, and went for them.

He was a funny little horse. He didn't try jumping, as nine out of ten colts would have done, but stuck his head low and shinned under on his knees, dragging his yelling rider off. A kneepad snapped on the saddle, and then he was away, reins swinging, bucking and bolting down the boggy paddock.

Mick's nose bled copiously. His jaw swelled up where he'd cracked it a good one on the rail, and he was mad enough to quit, only there was no point in doing so because the Leichhardt River was in flood and there was no way he could leave.

We had a couple of almost dry days then, and the men, sick of being idle, got the horses up. The black mare that Noel caught after much cursing and chasing (and a good deal of punishment to Reg's hat) pulled away half saddled, and when Noel finally got her back she threw him.

Reg flung his ill-used headgear on the ground and kicked it. 'Yer useless flamin' drongo,' he bellowed. 'Haven't I told yer forty million times to keep hold o' their heads? I seen kids, girl kids,' he yelled, 'could do better. Yer couldn't ride a cart with a pig net over it.'

Noel's face flamed. The whole camp, except for John and Ben who had ridden back to Myalli and wouldn't return until late, were watching. And he was fed up, I supposed, with the constant chiacking and criticism that was his lot. He glared at his mate, yelling rashly, 'I'll ride anything in the damn paddock.'

Boydie, propped like a bent straw against a gum sapling, grinned evilly. ''kay,' he said. 'Try that bay o' mine.'

Fairly caught, Noel couldn't back out, but he looked as if he wanted to. The horse was a smallish yellow-bay mare called Crystal. She had a darker stripe down her spine and a sullen sort of go about her, flattening her ears and stabbing out with her hind foot when Boydie stood her up to be caught. She was short-coupled, without much wither, and would be hard to keep a saddle on.

Dad, who was watching, pulled a long face and I knew Noel didn't stand a chance. I said so, adding, 'They'll wind up getting him hurt.'

He just shrugged. 'Not much I can do. Not my men, or my horse, come to that. Bit o' luck she'll chuck him clean, and if the weather holds we can work tomorrow. That'll sort things out – they're just bored.'

Boydie caught the mare for Noel, and Reg, who despite his earlier strictures was now wholeheartedly backing his mate's attempt, bustled round overseeing the saddling up. Crystal, sidling and snorting, was as jumpy as a cat, reefing away from the approaching saddle, until Reg slapped a shin-hobble on her and got her nearside ear in his fist. He screwed it tight, and Crystal stilled magically while Noel girthed her up. When he'd finished, Reg reached his spare hand across to the pommel to test it. He shook his head and I heard him growl, 'Chrissake, man! Screw it tight. Bitch's got no wither, she'll have that orf in two jumps.'

Finally, Noel cinched in his belt, pulled down his hat, and tugged the mare in a slow circle as Reg stepped away from her head. Then Mick, who'd been passing low-voiced remarks about hopeless wannabe ringers to the two blackfellas, picked up his swag and stepped into the loose ring of spectators, tossing it down just as Noel reached up to swing into the saddle. It was deliberately done. Crystal shot into action carrying Noel, whose hand was locked fast to the monkey-strap, with her. He hit the saddle as she rose under him, and Reg, flogging at his jeans with his hat, roared, 'Git her head up, boy! Keep a-holt of her head!'

It didn't last long. Crystal flashed by in jerky strips of pistoning legs and flying mane. Her ears were flat and she roared like a bull through distended nostrils. Noel's face was a bobbing white blob. There was more and more daylight visible between him and the saddle seat, and then he was gone. Crystal reared as he came thudding down among us, his head smacking with a soft *whump* into Mick's rolled swag. She screamed, more like a stallion than a mare, and one shod front foot smashed down in a strike at Noel's face.

She missed him by no more than an inch. The steel cut through the Berkmeyer canvas, clipping off a tuft of blond hair, which stuck to the swag. Boydie dived, swinging his hat to drive her off, and Noel shot upright so fast you'd have thought he'd sat on a snake.

'Jeesuz!' He stared, gobsmacked, at Dad. 'That bitch tried to kill me.' His hands were shaking. He looked as if he were going to faint.

'Bad horses do that, son.' Dad spoke as if he were talking to a child. He turned his gaze on Mick, and I waited with some interest to hear what he'd say, but Reg, striding up without ceremony, beat him to it. He shoved a work-toughened fist under Mick's nose and thrust a rage-mottled face only inches behind it.

'You!' He was choking with fury. 'Yer try that again, yer bastard, and I'll fu—' He saw Judith and me standing there and adroitly changed the word in mid-pronunciation. 'Flaming well kill yer. Yer hear me?'

'What'd I do, then?' Mick appealed to the circle of faces. 'I never made him ride her, and look at me swag cover – ruined! What about that?'

'Take it up with the mare – she's still saddled,' Boydie said in a hard voice, but Mick wasn't about to tangle with the lean rider, or Crystal. He picked up the damaged swag and sulkily walked off.

'Never a dull moment,' I murmured to Judith. 'You reckon Noel will quit when he gets back to Kamilaroi? If,' I added, glancing up to where the clouds were massing again, 'it ever fines up enough for this muster to start, let alone finish.'

'Not likely. Reg'd flog him silly with his hat. Nope, in a couple of years' time we'll meet him in a camp somewhere – see if we don't. And he'll be just like all the rest, skiting about the horses he's ridden and the rivers he's swum.' She laughed, and Sian going past with his bridle looked suspiciously at us.

'What are you two on about?'

'What d'you think?' I said. 'Men. It's what there's most of round here.'

It rained all night, alternating between steady falls and thundering downpours, when the canvas swayed and creaked under the sheer weight of water. Damp, cold air blew through the fly, and the ruby eye of the fire sank and flared again under its cover of tin. The night roared with water. I couldn't believe the skies could hold so much.

'It's been going on for hours.' Judith's voice came muffled out of the darkness.

'I know. We must have had four inches, at least.'

'The Kamilaroi tent'll be down again. Betcha.'

'Yep. They might even have turned into frogs come daylight. Noel'll be a tadpole. And Mick,' I giggled with sudden inspiration, 'a toad.'

'What'll happen,' she said with sleepy portentousness, 'is that Mittaguddi'll flood.'

She was right. Daylight came with a rushing sound I took for wind, only the trees dripped stilly in the calm air. The rain had stopped with a finality that suggested, and later proved to be the case, that we'd had our whack. We all, save Dad, looked about for the source of the noise. He was already stumping towards the creek, his towel in his hand. Then a ripple ran over the sodden flat, a surging tide of brown water all heading our way.

'The creek's coming!' I yelled and ran for the shovel.

Judith stopped to help and so did John, the man who was supposed to be mad. The rest of them took off like kids, whooping and splashing through the spreading flood while we three battled furiously to save the fire. The water was ankle-deep through the camp when we finished, and rising, but we had built a dike about the precious flames. The burning logs were safe and dry behind ramparts of mud and firewood. And as we leant on our shovels, grinning in shared camaraderie, the clouds to the east peeled apart and let through the first sunlight we'd seen in a week.

TEN

The rain had been widespread across the Gulf Country. When the river had run down and the roads were dry again, the boss drove out with more rations, and a letter from Patrick. It was full of his doings from home, and we read it avidly. He had measured fourteen inches, he wrote, and fixed a bad leak in the roof. Everything was fine. Big Sandy was running, but he'd been round the fences and the stock looked prym.

Prym? I wondered what he meant. Judith took the scrawled page out of my hand and studied it.

'He means prime – you know he can't spell. Says he'll write again next month and how do you make curry?'

I wrote out the recipe and posted it, along with reminders about keeping the water up to the garden once the ground had dried out again. I knew that he was driving into Gregory Downs each week, more for the sake of seeing another human being than for the ostensible purpose of collecting the mail. I wondered how he was managing alone. He only had Larry for company and the care of the other animals to fill up his days. And it now seemed very likely, the way things had gone with the weather, that we wouldn't be home for weeks. He'd be grown up when we got back, I thought, not in years, but in experience and responsibility.

In April we moved on to Cassidy's Yard, a coolibah camp on the opposite side of the river from Scott's Hole. Mick left, the men attending muster collected the cattle belonging to their various properties and departed, and I retrieved the axe from its hiding place under the seat. I bogged the truck crossing the river, not in the sandy bed, but in the soft red soil of the cutting where the track climbed the far bank. The boss came along while I was stuck there, and after a lot of (to me) incomprehensible hand signals that served only to bury the back wheels deeper, he hooked his new Toyota onto the tow-chain and pulled me out.

'Where did you learn to drive?' he asked while we were getting the chain off.

'My father taught me.' I met his eye, guessing his thoughts. 'Okay, it was a lousy idea. Dad couldn't teach a duck to swim. He's too impatient, or he just hasn't got the knack of imparting knowledge. He thinks if you bellow louder, the idea sinks in quicker.'

'Ah.' He nodded and lifted the bonnet. 'Well, your radiator's boiling. I think your fanbelt must have gone. You'd better see if there's a spare I can put on for you.'

The steers we were shifting to Cassidy got to the river just as he finished the job. They crossed downstream from the road, and standing by the truck I watched them pouring through the timber down the far bank to splash into the water, heads and tails high. Dad was on the lead on Simon, who plunged recklessly through showering spray to keep abreast of the mob. Jervis was behind him, while Judith and Sian worked the far bank. The first of the cattle were almost across, swimming strongly, while the tail of the mob was still entering the river, when something startled them, perhaps a bird or a surfacing croc, but it fizzed panic through them like a shorting wire.

Cattle went everywhere – the lead into the river thickets, some upstream, some down, and more into a milling pile-up treading one another under on the far side. There was quicksand in the Leichhardt bad enough to trap and drown stock; the boss hadn't been on Dreyfus long, but long enough to know that. There was nothing he could do on foot though, so he tugged his hat tight as if he were about to go somewhere and said, 'Oh, shit!'

We waited, watching the action, which was mostly a lot of crashing and yelling in the channels, and a brief glimpse of Simon's forequarters rising above the burr in a magnificent leap over a fallen tree. Sitting on his heels in the shade thrown by the truck, Jack said, 'It's a bit unusual, a family stock camp. What d'you all do when the season's over?'

'Just keep right on working. No, seriously,' I bit off a grass stem and slid down onto my heels by the front wheel, 'we bought a property up near the Gregory. It was unimproved land, but we've got a couple of bores down on it now and a few cattle. When we finish the droving, we go home and muster, or do a bit of fencing, clear a road. There's always plenty to do.'

'I see. Build it up while you're contracting. And I expect when you've got cattle old enough to sell I'll have to find myself another droving team?'

'Something like that. I daresay you'll be trucking the bullocks out by then, anyway. It will take years – the property, I mean – but you've got to be doing something with your life, haven't you?'

'Hmmm, and there's worse things than the land. And when old Mac retires, Sian'll be there with the experience to take over.'

'Yep.' But it would most likely be Patrick, I thought. Sian would never stay. He couldn't work with Dad because they both always wanted things done their way. They were equally to blame, both convinced they were right and neither willing to listen to the other. 'Your brother always wants to be a bloody chief instead of an Indian,' Dad frequently growled, and I wondered how he could expect Sian to be running a camp and making his own decisions one day and then taking directions over every little job the next. Patrick would probably be the same, but at least he was younger, which meant that Dad would be that much older and, I hoped, more willing to listen when Patrick got round to challenging his every decision.

Across the river Michael and Jervis had joined Sian in getting the rest of the steers back in hand and shoved across to join the lead. Finally there were just half a dozen struggling in the shallows, spreading glinting ripples in the golden light. Sian pulled off his boots and shirt and dumped them on Trinket's hanging reins to hold her there on the bank, but Michael, having left the plant to help, was more reluctant. He made a great production of tying Rachel's reins and his words carried clearly to us.

'Might be croc, eh? Might be smellin' his dinner 'ere?'

'No fear, mate.' Sian skied his hat up the bank. 'Only little fellas. I'll take his head, you get his tail, eh?'

It took a long time to haul all six out. Both Michael and Jervis went in fully dressed, boots and all. The black men were very modest in the camp, always removing themselves half a mile or so upriver, or wherever, to bathe – even in the hottest weather I had never seen them shirtless. They shared the camp life but were apart from it, having their own fire to sleep about at night and their own shade on the dinner-camp. Their meals were served to them; they ate apart from the white stockmen in the camp, who had to rustle their own grub, and their wages were lower. Because they were under the Aboriginal and Torres Strait Islander Protection Act, they couldn't legally enter a pub or buy liquor, and because they were protected people their employers were responsible for transporting them to and from the job and making provision for their accommodation and meals en route.

Even the grown men were referred to as boys, a habit of speech that had grown out of the Aboriginals' childlike dependence upon the white man, imposed by the State. There were more of them working in the droving camps than on the stations, to which the white stockmen tended to gravitate. This was partly because the Aboriginals could not choose their jobs but were assigned them by the mission superintendents responsible for finding them employment, and partly because it was difficult to find good white ringers who wanted to go droving. It was a mug's game, as Mick, our erstwhile breaker, had not been the first to tell us.

Cassidy's was our last camp on the contracting job. After the steers had made it safely down to their paddock that day, we spent a week mustering the river country and then, as the bullocks weren't ready yet, left the plant in the Ten Mile paddock and went home. Patrick was tinkering with the pump-jack when we drove up, changing the rods over from the mill to the diesel. He waved a spanner at us but went on tightening the bolts, then checked the belt and started the engine before walking across. I remembered a time when he would have run, bursting to hear our news and impart his own, but six weeks on his own had changed that. It was ironic, I thought, watching my youngest brother, that Dad had done it again – given to Patrick the same responsibility and authority that had forced Sian into early maturity, and conflict with him.

We had a week at home, time enough to become accustomed to the changes wrought in our absence – new kids in the goat yard, a healthy growth of vines in the netted area beside the tank where I had scattered the pumpkin seeds. We mustered the horses from the big paddock and gelded the colts, and on Wednesday Patrick and I went into Gregory Downs in the truck to meet the mail plane. We took the truck because Sian was doing a wheel alignment on the landrover.

'When'll you be back?' Dad asked as we were leaving.

'After lunch I suppose.' I slammed the door, settling into the passenger seat. 'If the plane's on time.'

It turned out, however, to be a great deal later than that because while I was waiting for Wilma, the manager's wife, to sort the mail, Patrick wandered off to the sheds. Half an hour later he was back to announce that we weren't going home yet. The Gregory men had just finished pulling down the station windmill. They'd been about to tow it away for scrap when Patrick turned up, so he'd asked them to wait while he saw the manager. 'He gave it to me,' Patrick said simply.

It was an old mill but still serviceable, and as the station was putting a diesel motor on the pump in the river they no longer needed it. So we would be taking it back with us. 'Soon as we get it loaded,' Patrick said.

'How?' I stared at him. 'It'll never fit. The wheel . . .' I thought of the vanes and tailpiece, the great height of the tower. 'You'd need a semitrailer!'

'Don't be dense. Not in one piece. Of course not! They've already got the head off. And the tower's just bolted together, like a meccano set. It won't even hang over the tailboard if we load it in two sections. All we've got to do is unbolt it in the middle and get a sling round it. Easy.'

It wasn't difficult, just slow. The tower, even in pieces, was weighty and cumbersome, and the wheel took up the full width of the truck. The platform had to be dismantled too, and some of the nuts were frozen in position. The mechanic helped us load up, swinging a cable over a sturdy tree limb and using another vehicle to lift and lower the heavy slings of steel. We finally got away about four but the drive home took hours. The load shifted on the blacksoil sections, and twice we had to stop and tie it down again. The sun was setting when we finally drove in through the horse-paddock gate to see the carbide light burning brightly in the shadowy hut, and our own mill outlined against the darkening sky.

Dad was furious. 'Where the hell have you been? After lunch, you said – what time of day d'you call this?'

I was astonished. I dropped the letters on the table and tossed my hat aside, staring. 'We got held up. That's all.'

'And you couldn't have sent a message? You're hours overdue and it never occurred to you to let me know why?'

'For Pete's sake, Dad! We went to Gregory, not Outer Mongolia.'

Patrick just shrugged. 'What's the big deal? I've been driving to Gregory for weeks. We've been pulling down and loading a mill for Bendiddy. It's on the truck, if you're interested. How did I know how long it was gunna take? And I couldn't see any point in coming back till it was done, even if it meant midnight. What's wrong with that?'

'You're getting too big for your boots,' Dad snapped. 'The whole damn lot of you are.' And behind him I saw Judith cast up her eyes in exasperation at the familiar refrain.

We had a third bore site picked out for the drill rig, north of the road where the scrub gave way to open plain, not far from the Gregory Downs boundary. Before the rig could get out there, we had to have a road through the scrub, and we'd been working on it when the telegram of notice came through on the wireless. I took it on the twelve o'clock traffic list and gave it to Dad when he came home that evening. We had sent hundreds like it, but this was the first we had ever received and he read it aloud.

'"Entering your run Thursday twenty-ninth twelve hundred Lawn Hill bullocks regards Fin." Well,' he looked round at us, 'behoves us to do the right thing by our first drover. Couple of you better see him through. He could prob'ly use a hand in the scrub.'

In the end it was Patrick and I who rode out to meet the mob at Stony Creek a little before mid-morning next day. I had my brown mare, Lady Meg, and Patrick caught Widgie, a flashy little mare, also brown, with four white socks on legs capable of a spanking walk. The morning was fresh and clear, with a little breeze teasing the tops of the turpentine, now dusted gold with blossom. We heard the black stockmen hoying at the bullocks as we picked our way down the ridge into the creek, where myrtle and ebony grew. There were still little pockets of water under the bank and we let our mounts drink. Meg was blowing like a grampus, her shoulders creamed with a sudsy lather because it was her first ride of the season.

Fin, a stocky figure on a raking bay, waved his whip in greeting. He was about Dad's age, I guessed, with a family we had never met and a small property outside Camooweal. He was doing exactly what we planned to do and went droving to support his family on the station. He had come from Anthill camp that morning and had to get the cattle through to the boundary to find a clearing large enough for a night-camp. The mob was travelling well, its centre holding to the road, while on either sides the bulk of the bullocks slid in and out of view through the scrub, which stood shoulder-high to a rider.

'We'll make Greenhide Plain for dinner-camp.' Fin popped his pocket watch back in its pouch. 'Tell Mac I appreciate the hand. When do you start lifting the Dreyfus bullocks?'

'Second of June. We're heading back end of the week. The plant's already down there, and the men. Dad loaned 'em to the station till we get back. Who've you got this time?'

'Oh, coupla Camooweal lads. The horse-tailer's a bit green, couldn't find his own backside in the dark.' He screwed up his eyes, weaving his head about to watch a beast on the wing of the mob. 'That roan bullock's trouble. Been try'na sneak off all morning.' He jumped the bay over the tumbled rocks of the road verge and took after it, body swinging easily to the horse's movements, his checked shirt ballooning in the wind.

Greenhide Plain was at the bottom of our horse paddock, where the two fences made a corner – a patch of open, grassy ground scooped out of the solid wall of scrub. The council was talking about pushing up a dam there to water travelling stock, Fin said, but he doubted it would be done in his time.

'Why not?' Patrick refilled his quart pot from the billy, glancing out of habit across the mob camped in the angle of the fence. The cook, a middle-aged white man, addressed as Poisoner, was asleep, the horse-tailer, an angular youngster with reddened peeling skin, gloomy and silent. From the far side of the vehicle came an occasional murmur from the blackfellas, and the jingle and snort of the saddle-horses tied in the shade.

'Stands to reason,' Fin argued. 'Station's buying a roadtrain.'

'What, Lawn Hill?' I was astonished.

'So they reckon. And not too many other cattle come this way. Few hundred from Bowthorn, the odd mob down from the Territory. Time they get round to making a water, there'll be nothin' left to need it. Trucks'll be doing it all.'

'That's what the old man says,' Patrick said. 'A good thing, too. This lot, f'r instance, you'd have 'em at the boundary in half an hour instead of needing the rest of the day for it.'

It took us till sundown to reach the fence. Patrick turned back at the gate, with the dusk already pooling under the scrub as the sun vanished, but Fin insisted we stay for a feed. A night wind had got up on the plain, carrying the smell of cattle and smoke from a smouldering fire.

Poisoner was using a sheet of tin for a windbreak, and the flames eddied and sulked as a result, gusting smoke into your face if you went too close. Bushes were better, they let a fire breathe. We tied our horses, took plates from the stack set out on the side board of the truck, and helped ourselves to raggy, overcooked corned meat and underdone spuds. The bread had a soggy centre and a crust so black you could only peel it off, and the tea seemed to have been stewing for weeks. I tipped mine out when the cook's back was turned. They didn't call him Poisoner for nothing, I decided.

It was strange to be watching the familiar routine as an outsider, with everything, from the outline of the truck to the shape of the tea billy, slightly different. Even the horsebells were off-key, their tones unlike ours; the animals were walking, too, the clanging too regular for feeding horses. I thought the horse-tailer hadn't done as he was told and taken them down for a drink at Sandy Creek, and now they were looking for one. They'd be spread to hell and gone come daylight. Only the sky was the same, when you gazed up away from the red beam of the smoky fire – that and the black mass of the mob hunkered down like some monstrous beast on the open plain. I wondered if Fin liked droving, or if, for him also, it was just the means to an end it had become for us. It was the dream of most old drovers I had met to quit the road and have a little place to hang their hats, and a paddock for the plant, because few could envisage life without the horses who had shared it so far.

I yawned, thinking of Fin's wife and wondering how she managed in his absence. Any bushwoman could kill a snake or mend a fence, but what did she do if the bore broke down, or the lighting plant wouldn't start? Paying extra wages was a luxury most little properties couldn't afford, so with the husband away there was very often only the wife and kids home. She must have been lonely over the years, particularly when the children were off at school. I yawned again, thinking of the miles still between us and our beds.

'Come on, Patrick.' I stood up. Around me the men were already kicking their swags open and pulling off their boots. 'Thanks for the feed, Poisoner. Safe trip, Fin. See you down the route.'

'Righto. Thanks for the hand. I'll give you a watch on my way back.' He toed his swag open and dropped his hat on the nap. Flipping the reins up onto Meg's neck, I heard him grunt as he sat down, then we were moving away into the monochromatic night, with the rising moon a pale glow at our backs. It was only three nights past the full, but it would be half gone by the time we took delivery at Dreyfus. I thought of the dusty, trodden route, of the chapped hands and split lips that came with cold weather, and the wearying length of the watches, and sighed, wondering how many more years it would take.

It would be nice to ride home every night. To grow a vegie garden and a few flowers perhaps, and to have a stove – and a kitchen to keep it in. I was sick of water buckets and sooty cooking pots and having nowhere to keep my growing collection of books. To keep them properly, on a shelf, instead of humping them around in cardboard cartons, with saddles and swags being dumped on them, and always the danger of getting them wet.

The track unrolled steadily before us, parts of it already with our own history, despite the shortness of our tenancy – the soft shoulder where the mailman had been bogged, the bend where we had the blowout that had nearly rolled the 'rover, the spot where Tumbler had thrown Judith . . . The horses knew they were headed home. They had settled into a long stride, their hooves crunching the sand of the track, their ears pointing sharply ahead. I could see the sheen of Meg's eyeballs and the pallid blur of Widgie's facemark whenever Meg's faster walk put her ahead. We trotted for a couple of miles standing in the irons and listening to the hypnotic beat of hooves interspersed with the creaking of saddles and the chime of bit rings. Once Widgie blasted a snort, shying sideways and crashing into my leg, breaking Meg's even stride. Something small fled under her nose and she flung her head up, snorting in turn.

'What was it?' I pulled her back to a walk as Patrick cursed Widgie, gone giggle-headed with fright.

'Dunno. Cat, kangaroo rat, maybe. Walk, yer faggot!'

A dingo howled from out of the scrub on our right, shockingly close in the dark, and I felt the hair brush up on my neck. Another answered from further away, the sobbing wail spiralling up to hang just under the stars like bones for the wind to blow through. The horses pricked their ears, pacing on, and then the track curved and dipped and their hooves struck loud on the layered stone of Sandy Creek. Water glinted upstream under the far bank, and we rode across the crunch and suck of damp sand to let them drink, ears tuned to the night sounds of crickets and leaf rustle in the myrtle thicket above the bank. Something scuttled in the sand as Meg blew gustily and lifted her head. Droplets plinked from her muzzle, the sound lost as she whinnied at the tread of a fast-walking horse on the track.

'Old fella musta sent out a search party,' Patrick said. He whistled, 'Over here!' But all that came back was a whinny. We heard a curlew call, then a scramble of hooves over rocks, a snort, then the beat of trotting feet going away.

'Hoy! Who is it?' I yelled. The words hung and died unanswered. We smelled dust and heard the urgent hoof strokes change to a canter, and that was all.

'Strange.' Patrick, head up, was sitting like stone. He had reined Widgie about as if prepared to go after the rider, because there was no doubt that the horse had been ridden.

'There's no point.' I put Meg at the bank. 'He's only got to duck into the scrub and you'd never find him. Wonder who it was.'

'Or what he's up to,' Patrick said.

We were never to find out, but that didn't stop us speculating on it for the rest of the ride home.

ELEVEN

Next day, our last one at home, was spent packing up and servicing the vehicles. Dad kept thinking of things to remind Patrick about, like checking that the mill was greased, and making dead sure that when he topped up the cooling tank for the diesel he didn't leave the hose hanging there.

'Because it'll siphon back, and if the level's too low, the motor'll seize up.'

Sian would have fired up at the unnecessary advice but it was water off a duck's back to Patrick, who was very even-tempered. 'I know what I'm doing,' he said, which didn't please Dad at all.

'You think you do! You all seem to think you know everything. You're so bloody complacent it scares a man.' He had a way of including all of us in the sins of the offender.

I tried to say something but was drowned out by Dad developing his argument and Patrick maintaining that he had never once left the hose in the tank.

'Will you all shut up!' I almost had to yell to get their attention, and wondered why men wanted sons if all they did was fight. 'God! It's like living in the middle of a battlefield. I've been trying to tell you there's a vehicle coming – it looks like Padre Brian.'

It was. He had his wife with him again and they pulled up out front just as the goats, their shadows long beside them, were stringing into the yard. They would have been along earlier, Brian said, only he had done a tyre and lost the muffler off his exhaust on the trip down from Burketown. He'd been lucky, though, he added, because the mailman travelling behind him had shepherded him into Planet Downs where the mechanic had sleeved his tyre. It could still do duty as a spare, but the whole business, combined with the dreadful state of the road, had put them behind their intended schedule.

'Well, you're here now,' I said, pleased. 'And lucky for us, because we're heading off again tomorrow.'

'Whereabouts this time?'

'Dreyfus, same as always. Years may come and years may go, but the good old DPC, which is the Dreyfus Pastoral Company, in case you didn't know, keep right on breeding bullocks for us to drove. Thoughtful of them, isn't it?'

'Very,' he agreed with a smile. 'Your garden's really come on since I was here last. You've got good green thumbs. Like my wife – she can grow anything, you know.'

I was astonished to hear it. Mrs Walker was so unapproachable it had never occurred to me that we might actually share an interest. I said, 'Oh well, I got the mulberry cuttings from Gregory. And the lemon tree has flowered this year, but look there, see?' I pointed triumphantly. 'There's fruit on the cumquat.'

They pitched their tent beside the tank and it was only later, sitting round the table with us, eating curry in the flare of the carbide light, that Brian broke the news he had come to tell us. It was his last visit. He had been posted to a new patrol area centered on Katherine in the Northern Territory.

'Where, at least, we'll have a base,' Mrs Walker observed acidly, 'and conditions might be a bit less primitive.'

We didn't know if she meant less primitive than Yeldham (she'd just had a cold-water shower in our tin-and-canvas bathroom, so perhaps she did) or the Gulf in general. Even Brian didn't seem to know, so the remark fell, as so many of hers did, into silence.

I was dumb with dismay. I had come to treasure Brian's visits. Now I would have nobody to talk to about books or the stars or anything else beyond the range of stock camp interests. Brian must have realised what it would mean to me because just before we all turned in, he excused himself to get something from his vehicle. It was another book, E.M. Forster's *A Passage to India*.

'I didn't bring the book box this time – most of our stuff is packed up for the move – but I thought you'd like this. You'll find an address on the flyleaf.'

I thought he meant an address I could return it to, so I didn't bother looking just then but folded the book in my arms.

'I'll miss your visits. Will they send someone to replace you?'

'Oh, yes. Padre Frank is coming up from Charleville. He'll visit you all – I'm sure he reads too. And if he hasn't got one already, tell him about the swap box. Then it'll be just the same.'

'Yes,' I said miserably, but I knew it wouldn't.

Next morning when we rose we strapped our swags for travel, but breakfast, in deference to our visitors, was later than normal. We had the wireless on listening to the flow of station-to-station chatter, when the Burketown police cut in, calling Gregory Downs. They wanted to know the whereabouts of Padre Walker, the sergeant said. The matron's husband had shot himself and they needed the padre back in town.

'What, dead?' Gregory's manager sounded as stunned as we all felt.

'As last week's mutton,' the policeman confirmed.

Dad got up from the table then, and thumbed the mike. 'Burketown. This is Yeldham. He's here with us and he heard that.' Dad looked across at Brian, who nodded vigorously. 'He'll start back soon as he breaks camp.' He switched off the wireless and sat down again into a silence, broken by Mrs Walker, who hadn't let the news stop her eating breakfast.

'Silly old fool,' she said crossly. 'Why couldn't he have done it yesterday while we were there?'

'My dear . . .' Brian looked as if he didn't believe he'd heard right, 'a man is dead!'

'And because of it we've got to drive back over that ghastly road.'

'Well,' Patrick saw nothing incongruous in the idea he now mooted, 'maybe you'll find your muffler on the way. You could get it welded up at Joyner's joint, y'know, Padre.'

I didn't know whether to cheer or kick him, and was rather afraid I was going to laugh.

After they had gone, we threw the swags on the truck, sat the saddles astride them, and snugged the lot down with ropes. Larry was staying with Patrick, who'd been threatened with death if either goats or lack of water killed off the garden. Red was coming with us. Dad slapped the side board and he sprang onto the load, panting, showing the red slash of his tongue.

Sian and Judith had gone ahead in the landrover. Sitting in the passenger seat of the Bedford waiting for Dad, I picked up my new book. It fell open to the address that Brian had mentioned – not, as I had thought, a place to forward the book to, but a secondary correspondence school in Brisbane. He had spoken of it to me before, when I had told him of my desire to write. I could enroll with the school and further my education at my own pace, he said. It was a marvellous institution and entirely free, costing nothing but postage and the price of textbooks. I remembered the day we had talked about it, and read what he had written underneath: 'I hope you do it, someday. I know you can. Best wishes. Brian Walker. AIM Patrol.' And reading his neat script, I promised myself that one day, when we had finished droving, I would.

～

Dreyfus was much as we had left it, busy as a dog with a burr in its ear, as all the stations now were. They had suffered a fire in the men's quarters which had burnt out the front wall of one room and weakened the steps (the building was on stilts for coolness) to the point where a newly hired stockman, arriving drunk on the mail truck, had gone through the top one and broken his leg.

'Which makes nonsense of that stuff about drunks not being able to hurt themselves,' Judith said. She and Sian were just leaving for the boundary camp, having checked for mail and picked up spuds and onions at the station store. I went up to the big house to talk to Jack's wife Nola, and found her in the garden attacking the bougainvillea arch with a pruning saw. I helped her until she called a coffee break, waiting while she went indoors to make it.

Nola was a small, intense woman in her thirties, with a great passion for growing things, as the garden testified. I had never seen it look better. She had removed a lot of the easy-care shrubbery and dug out some of the lawn area to plant rose bushes and create colourful flowerbeds. It looked a picture in the pale winter sunshine, and as we sat drinking our coffee on the wrought-iron bench I told her so.

'It is nice,' she said. 'And it'll look even better when I get that arch under control – there're three colours in it, you see, but there's so much old wood there it hardly blooms. By the way, did you want something? I mean, I never asked before, and then we were getting so much done, I forgot.'

'No, I'm just filling in time. Dad and Jack are down the horse yards, they've got colts in to geld. And Dad,' I said with remembered indignation, 'got all Victorian about me going over for a look at the horses. As if Judith and I haven't been helping brand colts for years! But no, it would embarrass the men, he said. Huh! I'd be astonished if you could.'

'Men are funny sometimes.' Nola put her mug aside, and then, as if the topics were related, she said, 'Think you'll ever get married, Kerry?'

'It's possible, I suppose.' I looked at her, a little taken aback by the 'ever'. She seemed to put an emphasis on it – I was sure I hadn't imagined it. 'I'm only twenty, it's a bit young to be tied down. What d'you call that creeper on the shed, the one with the pink flowers?'

'It's pretty, isn't it?' She rose, picking up the saw again. 'It comes in white, too, but that pink one's maiden's blush.'

I felt myself redden behind my tan. I had wanted to change the subject but had picked a dilly of a plant to ask about.

Later, driving down to the boundary camp where the blackfellas should by then have had the horses mustered and waiting, I went over the exchange again, puzzling about that 'ever'. It almost sounded as if I, or at least my single status, had been exhaustively discussed. It was an unsettling feeling to suspect that you had been watched and gossiped about and put under the microscope of public interest. Even though I was one of only six unmarried girls in the district, it had never occurred to me that other, older women might be interested spectators of my private life. Except that nothing was private, I thought hotly. And now I came to think of it, there weren't six in the sisterhood at all, but five. Kevin had married the other one, a girl called Barb who now rode and watched beside him, early last summer.

The season went by as others before it had, with skies permanently pinkened by dust, not only from the cattle this year, but from work on the new main road. Its construction had been pushing ahead for months, the scars of its creation visible for miles. The ground had been cleared first, and everything, from scrub and anthills to giant old coolibah trees, bulldozed aside. Culverts and floodways were built, the raw earth formed and rolled and graded, storm drains cut and the edges cleared. A permanent fog of red dust hovered above it like a banner, and the movement of men and machinery never seemed to stop. Some day it would be gravelled and then sealed, but some day they were going to build a bridge across the Leichhardt River, too, or so it was said. At present it was easier to battle the truck along the old stock-route track, except where the two converged, and then, if the section was already graded, you had the pleasure of driving on the new road.

I was doing so the day Steve, a white stockman we had that year, spurred across from the feeding mob to drop off his jacket. He was riding Star, a gentle old brown mare with a silken mouth, and instead of waiting for me to pull up he came cantering in at an angle to the slowing vehicle and tried to lob the jacket through the moving window of the cab. The wind caught the garment and Star, shying away from its flaring shape, slammed into the shoulder-high butt of a big coolibah which the bulldozers had uprooted. It was black-heart coolibah, the name practically synonymous with iron, and a root, broken by the 'dozer into a splintered dagger, ripped into her chest, which instantly fountained blood.

By the time Steve had jumped off and I had got myself out of the truck, the powdery road dust was drenched with blood, his boots and jeans splattered, and the air thick with the stomach-turning smell of it. I grabbed at the hole in Star's chest, getting a hot sticky spray up my arm, and tried to hold it together.

The mare's neck was sweaty, I could feel her flesh moving against me, and my fingers kept slipping. I couldn't stand there forever watching her life leak away but my brain seemed stalled in neutral.

Steve said, 'Jeez, old Mac's not gunna be best pleased,' and, as if the words had provided the spur, I could think again. A scrap of memory surfaced – an Irish voice, one of the flying doctors giving the Sunday morning talk: '... because first aid is just applying commonsense. If you can't stop the bleeding any other way, shove a towel in the wound.'

'Quick! Give me something to plug it with.' My voice sounded screechy with haste, like a nail on slate. 'The cloth off the bread bowl. Hurry!'

The bread cloth was soft calico, the size of a tea towel. Wadded tight and forced deep into the wound, it cut the flow as if a tap had been turned. Only seepage remained. I watched the makeshift cotton plug slowly redden and cautiously took my hand away.

Steve had pulled the saddle off by then and dumped it clear of the blood. He was fumbling with his hat, one eye on Star who looked as glassy-eyed as a colt on a choking rope. At length he produced a curved saddling needle, something many ringers carried in their hatbands. 'If we had a bit of string or something,' he made sewing motions in the air, 'we could stitch her up.'

The words jogged a memory of one of Dad's yarns about a dog of his, almost gutted by the ripping toe of a big roo. He had rolled the canine's head in a cornbag to stop it biting, then sewn it up with horsehair plucked from his mount's tail.

'Cut a bit of her tail hair,' I said. 'I'll get the pliers.'

I gave her a drink when we had finished, and before I pulled the bridle off and let her go I refilled the bucket, wedging it against the fallen tree where it couldn't be knocked over. I could return tomorrow to fill it again, and perhaps by the day after that she would be strong enough to get into the river herself.

She looked pretty wonky right then, gaunt and tucked up in the flanks, as if she had lost flesh as well as blood. And washing the stains off my hands, I remembered the fluttering panic I had known feeling it spurt through my fingers. It was the engine oil of the body, and when it was splashed around in such quantities something, its slick viscosity or the urgency of its colour, galvanised you into action the way a shrieking alarm would.

Star survived the accident. We glimpsed her on the return trip standing alone under a tree, the blackened bloodstains striping her chest and forelegs. She probably wouldn't work again if she recovered, and certainly not that year, but might still breed a foal. I could no longer tally the number of horses we had lost through injury, poison and disease; they were as vulnerable as humans and a good deal harder to help. Now, with Star's survival no longer an issue, another problem loomed, because Gypsy, the pony mare, had vanished. She had failed to turn up with the others one morning, and despite Michael's best efforts (and he was a good horse-tailer) couldn't afterwards be found.

'She might have got into a patch of quicksand and drowned, I suppose,' Judith said doubtfully when our two camps met up and she heard the news, but I couldn't see it – the horses were always taken to water.

'More likely that somebody was going through and pinched her.' I thought about that. 'He'd have a sour little pony on his hands if he did – the whole plant's tired, especially the night-horses, after that last mob.'

'Well, only one more to go,' Judith said. 'Then they can all have a spell.' Characteristically, her thoughts returned to the pony. 'I do wonder what's happened to her though, and where she is.'

⌒

Michael and I found Gypsy halfway through the final trip. The brown pony had been missing for almost a week when we stumbled on her trapped in a breakaway at the edge of the Leichhardt River. When the muffled whinny sounded, we stared bemusedly at each other across the firewood we were loading, then gazed blankly about. The call had seemed both near and far off, but no horse was visible, only the trampled feed and patchy scrub of the paddock, with the dusty pads leading out and anthills bulking like red gravestones in the middle distance.

'Come from the ribber, I reckon,' Michael said. He flung back his head, imitating the call, and was answered with shocking suddenness from almost beneath our feet.

'The breakaway!' I rushed the dozen yards to the edge of the steep erosion gully and there she was, six feet down, jammed between banks of red earth beneath a crisscrossed lace of dead tree roots. She had lipped up all she could reach of the leaves and windblown grass, and chewed the bark from the slender stem of a box sucker that had found a footing in the walls of her prison. She was as herring-gutted as a racing dog; the flesh had melted from her frame, and her eyes were sunken and dull.

'Poor thing, she's perishing.' I grabbed the bucket and when Gypsy smelt the water she whinnied and tried to rear, hitting her knees, which immediately bled. They were scabbed with old wounds from earlier struggles. The gully was gouged behind her. She'd struggled twice her own length along it since falling in, ending up against a sheer earth wall she couldn't possibly climb.

It took ages to free her. Michael scrambled down to hold the bucket under her head, then dug away at the imprisoning earth with the shovel while I scooped lucerne chaff into a nosebag for her. She looked almost too weak to stand, but I knew we'd never get her out unless she helped.

We chopped out the roots, then kicked and broke down as much of the lip of the breakaway as we could. While Michael widened the channel behind the pony, I threw gear off the load. Dad had told a story once about a farm horse that had fallen into an underground concrete storage tank. The local farmers had come to him for help in extricating it and this he'd done by dumping a truckload of baled hay into the tank. They'd built a series of platforms, one atop the other, to lead the horse up, which was exactly what I needed to do for Gypsy.

I had no hay, of course, but there were the feedbags, the swags, and the folded tarpaulin we carried but seldom rigged. Michael had inserted his large bulk under the pony's neck, forcing her back as he shovelled, and into the space thus gained I lowered a full bag of feed, then the swags with the tarpaulin doubled over the top. It looked too steep and the pony would still have to jump the last couple of feet to get out. Studying her emaciated frame, I didn't think she could, so I filled my cast-iron bread oven with dirt and packed it under the last swag to lessen the height of the jump.

'What d'you reckon, Michael – think she can get up that?'

'Might be. Only more better we chuck some dirt on, eh? Stop 'er slipping.'

It was sound advice. If she lost her footing and fell, she'd never get up. And a couple of inches of padding over the tarp would prevent hoof damage – the first thing you learned about expensive canvas was not to walk on it.

When all was ready, I replaced Gypsy's nosebag with a halter. She pushed forward, mad for the feed, and made her first stumbling step up the ramp we'd built. Michael got his arm round her barrel because she was trembling with weakness, and supported her weight. At the top she heaved frantically with her forelegs but the effort was too great, and as she slid backwards we both rushed behind her to prop her up. I put the nosebag back on while she had a breather, then, standing one on each side, we gripped hands, our heads separated only by her bony rump.

'Ready?' I braced myself to push, looking across at Michael, who nodded, and I smelled the musky sweat of his exertions as his grip tightened. 'Hup, girl!' I cried, and as we heaved together, hauling her hindquarters forward, Michael suddenly bent his head and bit her, snapping his teeth shut like a dog.

The pony leapt convulsively. She made a sound between a snort and a whinny, and her forequarters were over the bank.

I yelled, 'Now!' and we surged forward, carrying her back end between us, and she was out. I tripped, falling into the bank as the weight went, but Michael let out a 'Yackai!' and clacked his teeth like castanets. I goggled at him, and at the wet shape of the bite on Gypsy's hide. It was beyond belief but it had certainly done the trick, and the pony was fine. As soon as she'd got her balance, she'd dropped her head to the nearest grass, trying to snatch it up through the folds of the hessian nosebag.

'I reckon she be too much sorry she went down there.' Michael began hauling at the folded tarp, loosing a cloud of red earth over us both. The chaff would be full of dirt, too, and I'd have to scrub the camp oven, but it was a small enough price for averting the sort of death Gypsy had been facing.

On dinner-camp that day there was general rejoicing over the pony's recovery. She was too weak to travel far, so I'd left word with the Kamilaroi manager as I was going past that afternoon, and Michael dropped her off in the stony horse paddock where the young ringer had been killed a couple of years before. She wouldn't pick up much condition on dry feed this late in the year, I knew, but the spell should strengthen her enough to let her walk home when the trip was over.

Once the mob was trucked at Kajabbi Dad took Michael and Jervis back to Dreyfus, where he put them on a plane to the mission. Then he continued back to Yeldham, leaving Sian, Judith and me to follow with the plant.

We picked up Gypsy on the trough a week later when we came back through with the plant, finding her thin and cranky, her ears going back at the first horse to jostle her in the mob. She was in season, too, and that night while we were hobbling up she got into a kicking match with Trinket. The rest of the horses scattered about them, leaving the two mares squealing as they hammered at each other, until Judith appeared swinging her bridle.

'Hey. Hey! Cut it out, will ya?' She clouted Trinket, who bucked away, shaking her head, stubby ears still flat.

I was standing next to Gypsy, carrying hobbles for her, and had just reached to touch her shoulder and grab her neck-strap when she attacked. She came at me like a thunderbolt, teeth bared and forelock flying. There was no time to dodge or swing the hobbles in defence. Her jaws closed on the side of my neck with a jolt that put my teeth through my tongue. I fell backwards, banging my elbow on a stone, and as the pony tore past, her near hind foot stabbed out, catching the side of my thigh.

Judith came running. 'You okay?'

'Yes, no, of course I'm not!' I cried furiously. I lifted the hand off my smarting neck and clasped my elbow instead, rocking forward in pain. 'Is she a wolf or something? The rotten little bitch tried to tear my throat out. And she kicked me. Next time I find her in a breakaway, I'll shovel it in on top of her.'

Judith looked me over critically. 'You sound all right. Your neck's red, sort of grazed really. Where'd the blood come from?'

My shirt was spattered, I saw, and my hair had come loose and was full of dirt. 'I bit my tongue. Give me a hand up.' I struggled to my feet with her help, and back in camp she tipped some Condy's crystals into a bowl so I could wash my neck. We had grown up with an almost religious belief in its efficacious qualities as an antiseptic. Handing it to me she said, 'It mightn't kill germs but –'

'Yeah, I know,' I finished our old childhood quotation, 'it sure turns 'em purple. You can get back to the horses. I'm okay. And clout that little slut for me!'

'She's just weak and cranky,' Judith said.

'Yeah? Well, I'd hate to cross her when she's feeling strong.'

That night Sian, who had driven into Dreyfus to pick up some meat, said out of the blue as we ate our evening meal, 'I haven't told the old fella yet, but I'm thinking of leaving.' He watched us for a moment, waiting, and Judith finally said, 'For good, you mean?'

'That depends, but not initially, no.'

It came as unwelcome news to me but was no surprise. 'What will you do?'

'Well, first off, it wouldn't be immediately. I'd stay till the mustering was done and that other bore we've talked about was put down. But I'm planning on drilling. Riversleigh want a couple of holes, I know, and I've been talking to Jack about it here too. Do it on a contract, half the money coming home for the hire of the rig, the rest for me. It'd keep me going through summer, and after that . . .' He sat staring at the fire, then roused himself to say briskly, 'Well, we'll see. But I can't work with the old man any longer. Just thought I'd tell you.'

He chucked the ends of a burnt stick into the flames, which flared up, illuminating his face. His eyes and hair were the same colour as mine, and our ears had identical lobes, but we weren't much alike inside. I wondered if he was serious about Lindy, and if that had something to do with his decision, but decided not to ask. We had all of us always been careful of each other's privacy, not from any particular delicacy of mind, but so that we, in turn, would be spared prying questions. The fewer physical barriers you lived with, it seemed to me, the greater the need for personal space. You could be more private in a crowd than you ever could in an unpopulated landscape, where even the arrival of a letter, if not its contents, must necessarily be public knowledge. If I wanted to know how Sian felt about Lindy, I would have to wait for him to tell me. I thought about what his absence would mean in terms of the work at home, but offered no opinion on his decision, and neither did Judith.

Next day we mustered the remaining horses out of the Ten Mile and started for home. It was good to be leaving the bare river route, with its dust and dirty camps, behind us. The road was so familiar now that the plant could have walked it alone, from the old wagon crossing on the Leichhardt to the grey banks of Top Water and the wide, Mitchell-grass miles of Maccadams Plain.

At Gregory, an empty space gaped beside the pub where the hall had stood. It had collapsed, as if hit by a giant's fist, into a pile of lumber and iron.

'Willy-wind,' the publican said.

'And it knocked a building down?' It seemed incredible.

'Yep. Shonky work – the roof beams were tied together with fencing wire. Contractor's long gone, o' course.'

Some of the iron was still sitting on top of the piano, and the edges of the exposed floorboards were already lifting in the sun. What was left of the benches was still there, although a broken one had been pulled out onto the woodheap, and the pub was using it for firewood. I remembered the fun of the dance we had attended after Easter sports, and hoped that the council would rebuild. Without the hall, the township had shrunk by a third.

༄

It was good to be back. Larry came rushing to meet us, whiskery jaws barking a welcome as I reined Mary-Ellen in by the horse yard and stared about me. The lawn had spread amazingly – the tin shed now sat in a patch of vivid green, which was darkened by the shade of the rain tree. There were finches bathing in the broken camp oven under the tap, and red flower spikes on the cannas I had planted by the gate. The wild plum at the stock tank was starred with blossom, its scent heavy in the still air. I sniffed it in, and half a dozen cattle stringing in on the pad over Little Sandy paused to stare as I pulled my saddle off and swung it over the rail. I was glad to be back. No more basin baths or sleeping on the ground, for a few months anyway.

We bought a stove and a washing machine that summer and branded our first calves. The stove was a double-oven Crown with a ten-foot chimney length and curved steel legs, big enough to handle shearers' meals. I had chosen it from the Queensland Pastoral Supply catalogue and had it railed up from Brisbane to Cloncurry. The mailman brought it out to Gregory, and Dad and Patrick drove in to pick it up. They had already boxed in a section of the shed floor and laid a concrete slab to receive it. While it cured, a slow process requiring frequent wettings, they returned to the fencing the job had interrupted. They were building a stallion paddock for Ferdy and the brood mares, which meant the existing big paddock would be available for Judith's use. She could start seriously looking for a sire and mares for her pony stud.

Sian had left by the time the stove arrived. He had taken the drill rig up to Riversleigh and was working there. Dad had accepted his decision calmly enough, although I think it had come as a shock to him. He had gone still when Sian broached the matter with him, looking down for a long moment at his plate and the meat he was cutting into as if he were wondering how it had got there, then he shrugged, spearing the piece onto his fork.

'If it's what you want, I can't stop yer.' And while the dishes were being washed they had worked out the details of the hire of the boring plant. Sian had already quoted for the hole at ten bob a foot.

''s not enough,' Dad objected immediately. Judith gave an exasperated sigh, but for once Sian refrained from arguing.

He left straight after completing the third bore on Yeldham, which he named Trubbidy, after a character in a book he was reading. It was a deeper bore than the others, but the water, though in plentiful supply and suitable for stock, tasted vile.

'Think he'll come back?' Judith asked as we were watching the rig head out towards the Lawn Hill road. Sian had his swag stacked on his tin trunk next to his tuckerbox, and an old shirt tied on the end of the sinker-bar which, longer than the rig, hung out the back.

'Not permanently. But I s'pose as long as he returns for the droving season, we can manage. I wouldn't mind getting a job, too, just over summer, you know,' I said, surprising myself. 'Make a change, earn a bit of extra money.'

She looked startled. 'You'll be wanting to leave next.'

'No. Mind you, if we lived in town we'd all have left by now – well, maybe not Patrick. But a temporary job might be fun.'

Gregory's fallen-down hall still hadn't been rebuilt by the time the Country Women's Association Christmas party came around, but a working bee had cleared away the mess so that a dance could be held on the floor. The corrugated iron and the broken piano had been removed, and all the lumber stacked around three sides

158

of the floor, partly to hold the lifting boards down, but also to stop people dancing straight over the edge, because the floor was a good two feet off the ground.

Geoff, the local constable, had drawn the Santa suit for the party, and suffered in it, because it was a sweltering day in late November with a purple glaze to the building stormclouds. The poinciana trees in the pub garden wore skirts of vivid crimson, and the heat struck upwards from the baking ground. There was a cricket match in the morning, followed by lunch spread out on tables under the shade of the river paperbarks. All the women took something along for it – my contribution was a cold leg of mutton and a watermelon from the garden. After the meal, Santa made his appearance with a chaff-bag full of presents, but his first utterance proved unfortunate.

'Ho, ho, ho, young fella, who d'you think I am?' he asked the nearest kid, a sharp-eyed station boy with ears bent double under the weight of his felt hat.

'You're the copper pretendin' to be someone else,' the boy said. 'An' your beard's not real. What's in the bag?'

The rain started while we were swimming, a quick patter of big drops dimpling the water and stinging bare skin. It was over before the dust was fairly laid, but thunder continued to rumble and you could see the storms advancing in a black line across the plain. They never actually reached Gregory, but those whose homeward journey lay across the blacksoil country immediately packed and left. Nobody wanted to end the day bogged.

Only a dozen of us remained for the dance, and all the musicians had gone. A line of coloured bulbs strung around the floor made enough light to see your feet, and the publican's youngest daughter borrowed her mother's gramophone and roped in her kid brother to change the records. It wasn't very successful though, until somebody hit on the idea of rolling a petrol drum across next to the dancefloor and standing the gramophone on it. That stopped our stamping feet causing the needle to jump out of its track.

The records were an eclectic collection, ranging from 'All I Want For Christmas' to 'Marie Elena'. We fitted our steps to the beat as best we could, doing barn dances and the gypsy tap for the faster ones, and colliding happily around the floor in a jazz waltz, which only Stan, a slim, part-Chinese stockman, could do properly. He was partnering Sian's girl Lindy, who didn't seem to be missing my brother much, I thought, and he'd just swung her back to the stacked lumber we were using as seats when she screamed.

It was a nerve-drilling sound that made my heart jump and brought the hair up on my neck. Somebody yelled, 'Snake!' and there it was, a huge brown, sinuous and deadly, coiled on the timber ready to strike.

Stan seized Lindy, yanking her away. The skirt of her dress flared out and the snake struck it as she scrabbled backwards, screaming again. The Augustas head stockman threw a short baulk of timber he had snatched up, but the brown rippled from sight untouched. Somebody else levered at the stacked wood, yelling, 'Get a light!' The publican's son was dodging around the men, and the needle had jammed on the record, but nobody noticed.

The mindless iteration of the song was shredding my nerves, which felt prickly and raw from the fright I'd had. I ran down the steps from the dancefloor and clicked the machine off, my eyes darting at pooled shadows and every one of them a snake. Without the music, I could hear the thud of the pub generator, which had previously faded into the background, and the cries of dart players in the bar. Dad had gone there earlier with Patrick while Judith and I attended the dance, but it was over now. We all wanted to be somewhere away from the shadows in clear bright light.

Stan took Lindy, who was jumpy and shaking and still hiccuping sobs, over to the pub verandah, and Judith and I, starting at every hump and hole underfoot, crossed to the landrover where we found Patrick asleep. I shook him awake and sent him in to get Dad. The night smelt of rain, and upriver distant lightning flashed like far-off messages.

Everybody was leaving; car doors slammed and headlights cut tunnels in the dark. The yellow glow at the police-station window went out as we backed up, then there were only the pub lights and the string of coloured bulbs above the ruined hall, which we'd all forgotten to turn off. Judith, crushed beside me on the front seat, shivered suddenly and a rush of goosebumps ran up my arm.

'Snakes!' she said. It had been a dramatic ending to the dance.

TWELVE

In early December the job I had been thinking about turned up, and I went as relieving cook to Lawn Hill Station, thirty-two miles west of Yeldham, filling in for Mrs Russell while she and her weedy husband took a holiday.

Dad drove me over with my tin trunk and the secondhand typewriter I had recently bought out of my droving wages. Lawn Hill was a big place and kept permanent staff on the books right through the Wet. Apart from Harry de Bois, the manager, there was a bookkeeper, a mechanic, a windmill expert and his offsider, a carpenter, a cowboy/gardener, a camp cook, a head stockman, a boundary rider and a ringer. And those were just the white workers. They also had two Aboriginal women helping in the kitchen and house, and four black boys for odd jobs, like bringing killers in.

The Russells lived in one of the cottages on the Hill, but Mrs Russell showed me to the cook's room which adjoined the kitchen. It was a plain box of a room which still seemed the height of luxury to me, with a wardrobe, chest of drawers, wall mirror and a comfortable bed. It had a screened verandah attached, and there was a tin-walled shower with a plain concrete floor under the tank stand in the garden, for my personal use. Mrs Russell showed it to me, observing with satisfaction, 'Of course it's only cold water, my girl, but that won't harm you.'

Her attitude towards me was ambivalent. On the one hand, she hated the idea of my being in her kitchen (she had worked at the Hill for five years); on the other, I was less of a threat to her future on the station than another couple might be. Her husband was a hopeless alcoholic, and she herself past sixty – she feared losing the cottage as much as the job. She was also entrusting to me her cat, and a flabby great lump of a cattle-dog called Boof. He was so fat he snorted as he walked, and spent most of his days lying expectantly in front of the kerosene fridge. He ate literally anything.

Big Sally, the housegirl, demonstrated that. She flipped him bits of cheese, stale cake, raw potato and sliced beetroot, and he snapped them up as if he were starved. 'Missus always gave him the scraps,' she said.

'Well, from now on we'll give them to the chooks,' I told her firmly. 'That fella's been eating in the same paddock you have.'

She screamed with laughter at the truth of this because she was just as fat as Boof. Her plump cheeks shone like polished ebony and she rolled when she walked. Her tasks included the dishes, the vegetable preparation, the floors, and cleaning the enormous washing tub in which I let the bread dough rise. They ate a lot of bread on Lawn Hill. I baked four loaves a day, five days a week, and was in constant anxiety when unexpected visitors arrived in case I ran out.

As with most company-owned places, there were three tables to serve: one for the blacks, one for the men, and the third in the big house where the boss, the bookkeeper and I ate. Had I been married, I would have eaten in the kitchen with the men. Everybody who worked on or visited the station had his place, and most didn't need telling where it was. Owners, managers and the padre would go to the big house; vets, head stockmen and drovers to the kitchen. The Aboriginals had a separate table under an outside shelter.

It was hard work but very well paid. A cook on male rates and with overtime earned as much as a head stockman. I started at four-thirty in the morning and finished at eight each night, my last task that of laying out the chopping board, knives and frying pans for the breakfast steak. Sundays were different. Only the cook worked, but breakfast was an hour later. There were neither morning nor afternoon teas, and, in the absence of Sally, the men did the midday dishes. I don't know if that had been their practice with Mrs Russell, but Cass and Normie, Johnny and Don, and whoever else was present for the meal, did them for me.

There was a kerosene fridge in the kitchen, another in the big house, and out in the shed a wooden-walled coldroom where the meat hung. The power came on each morning at four when Cass started the diesel motor, and again in the evening, but as the kitchen had no electrical appliances it served only to light the place and run the coldroom. I beat the cakes with a wooden spoon, ground meat for rissoles with a hand mincer, and made toast by propping it on a fork at the open door of the firebox. The kitchen, despite its size, was always hot, and meal preparations endless. The stockpot lived on the stove, for there was soup in the evening as well as main course and sweets. And then there was the baking – a dozen men could eat their way through a lot of cake and bread.

Mrs Russell's husband had done the cowboy's job – chopping wood, feeding the chooks and the pig, bringing the meat to the kitchen each morning – tasks now performed by Sally's husband, Bill Ryan. I only saw the boss at meals, which were taken at the long table in the bush-built dining room that looked out over the valley to the purple wall of the Constance Range. The roof supports were tall posts, the rafters adzed bush timber, so nothing fitted properly and chinks between the louvres let in the rain. The boss was a widower; in consequence the big house was a womanless establishment, kept clean by Rita, the other housegirl, but wiped surfaces and stacked papers were all she ever achieved. I put flowers on the table sometimes and pulled the sofa and chairs around to soften the angles of the room, but next day they were always pushed back to their original positions.

I had little time off, but plenty of company because the men were constantly dropping in, starting with old Joe at daybreak. Being the oldest inhabitant, under Mrs Russell's regime he had established the right to his own pot of tea before breakfast. He was the station oracle, full of advice about the meals and the men and the stove, all of which I pointedly ignored. I hadn't taken the job just to pass from listening to Dad to listening to Joe. I missed having Judith to talk to but, that apart, I was enjoying being out on my own.

The most regular visitor of all was the mechanic, Cass. He was Polish, with an unpronounceable surname, and had taken the job at the station after the mining venture he was involved in had failed. He was thickset and muscular, a blond man with blue eyes and very broad cheekbones. His English was poor and I was often hard put to understand him, but Sally had no such problems.

'He looking for girl, that one,' she said one day, watching Cass whistle his way out the door after one of his brief visits.

'Is he really?' I was startled. Cass was old, at least forty, and I had thought he was just lonely, as most of the men were. Her words put a different complexion on his visits, and I resolved either to be busy or out of the kitchen the next few times he dropped in for a chat. I liked him, for his weathered face and ready humour, but no more than any of the others, and dreaded being put in the position of having to tell him so.

Christmas came and went in forty-degree heat, with the storm-clouds clustered purple as grapes above the valley, and a rainbird's maddeningly repetitive call sounding from the creek. The men, self-conscious in good shirts and slicked-down hair, trooped into the big house's dining room for Christmas dinner, where only Cass looked truly at ease. We had the works, on Mrs Russell's say so.

I had boiled the ham a week before but experienced a last-minute panic over the gravy, which was to accompany both the roast beef and the poultry, when the flour didn't brown in the pan. It was half an inch deep (I needed a lot of gravy), but trying to make it darker with Worcestershire sauce only resulted in disgusting white lumps which wouldn't cook out. I sent Sally, who was helping me prepare and load the dining-room trolley, for a sieve and dumped the gravy through it, stirring in a good dollop of tomato sauce to disguise the taste of raw flour. I'd roasted onions, potatoes and pumpkins – the only fresh vegetables there were – and the rest came out of tins. Mrs Russell hadn't trusted me with the pudding, making it before she left, so I had only to boil it for an hour and cook the brandy sauce. I did this using lemon essence in place of brandy; even Christmas wasn't excuse enough to bring spirits onto the station. Beer was served with the meal, and luscious red wedges of watermelon which I heaped onto a large platter and set between the nuts and crisps.

Johnny, Normie and Cass pulled crackers and donned their party hats, but even these valiant efforts could not lift the constraint from the table. They were like schoolboys summoned to dine with the head, I thought, and catching Cass's hurt glance (because my policy of avoidance had worked) and the boss's bored one, I wished I were back home with Judith and the rest. I felt suddenly displaced, like the men, who only wanted this festive ritual to end so that they could escape to their own, more congenial environment.

The new year of 1966 came in with showers and violent thunderstorms that seemed to shake the very ridge the station complex was perched on. The boss went off on annual leave, then Normie decided to take a holiday as well, and two of the black boys returned to the mission.

There were fewer visitors – only the mail truck on Saturday mornings, with its load of freight and often hungry passengers to feed. And then one day, as I stood at the door beating the length of bore casing that served as a dinner-bell, I saw a dustcloud above the stockyards and horses moving within it. Two men were toiling up the steep pad towards the kitchen, a tall old blackfella with grizzled curls under his hat, and a lame white man.

I said, 'Bless my soul entirely,' by way of greeting.

Dad just answered with a question. 'Any tea in the pot, girl?'

After a meal he sat out on my verandah, which caught what breeze there was, smoking and passing on the news from home. Watching him tease and rub the tobacco flakes in his palm, I thought it was these little details I had missed – the smell of pipe smoke, the squint of his eyes where the lines of crow's feet wrinkled his skin, the blarney of his voice. He could talk anybody into anything, could Dad. Had I been paying attention I would have seen he was doing it now.

He and the old blackfella, whose name was Long Charlie, were headed up through Lawn Hill to take a look at the country north of the station boundary. Charlie knew the area well, and Dad was allowing himself a week's poking about to see what was there.

'But why?'

'Just a bit of a holiday. Well, you're all doing your own thing – the boy's away drilling, you're here – I thought I might as well enjoy meself, too.'

'I wouldn't call cooking for fifteen a holiday, exactly. Have you finished the stallion paddock yet?'

'We have. And Patrick's got himself a new horse, an entire. He's calling him Decimal Currency to remember '66 by. That bay mare o' yours'll be in foal to him by now. He's just what we want – Ferdy's a touch fine-boned, I've always said so. Bit o' strength in a working horse's legs never hurt.'

'But hang on, that means you've got Ferdy in the new paddock and Patrick's horse in the big paddock. What about Judith's pony stallion? Where's he going?'

'She's gotta buy him yet. And before she can do that she's gotta find him. Anyway, bit of a pony, she could run him anywhere. Buy feed and stable him, come to that. When are you finishing up here?'

'The end of February, that's when the Russells get back.' I fanned myself, looking out where the garden trees hung limp above their black patches of shade. 'You picked some weather for riding.'

'We'll just be poking about,' Dad said. 'Early starts, long dinner-camps, and pretty short days. We'll do okay. You can trust a blackfella to know the short cuts an' the best camps.'

'And you're not saying what this is all about?'

'Told you,' he said blandly. 'Bit of a holiday.'

He left in mid-afternoon, with a disparaging look at Boof, melting under a bench in the kitchen. 'Useless-looking sooner.' There was no worse insult, its meaning hidden in the abbreviation of 'sooner eat than work'. But despite the aptness of the description I found myself defending the dog.

'It's not his fault. Some people have got no business owning animals.'

Long Charlie was waiting patiently in the shade of the tank. Standing at the door, I watched them both crab down the steep path to the yards, then head out across the paddock under the threatening sky. I was glad that Dad had Charlie with him; it was a dangerous time of year to be wandering around alone. When the curve of the hill hid them from sight, I went for a shower, stopping en route to give poor old Boof a pat, an action that surprised him nearly as much as it did me.

The evening brought a violent electrical storm that seemed to rattle the building on its foundations. Little rain fell, but the thunder roared and cracked amid the rocks of the hill, splitting the sky with blue-white flashes that seared your sight. The first detonation brought Boof howling through the mesh of the screen door of the verandah to hide under my bed. He lay there whimpering, shaking the bedframe with his trembling, until the storm passed. I was torn between pity and annoyance, because the instant the wind and spitting rain stopped, the mossies swarmed in through the torn screen.

Don, the carpenter, fixed it next day, but our night together seemed to have polarised Boof's loyalty. Now when he lay under the bench, his eyes followed me about the kitchen, and whenever I left the room he rose and accompanied me.

Dad returned at the end of the week, apparently satisfied with his journey. It was pretty country up there, he told me, and there was an impressive amount of water.

'There's holes along the Nicholson River you could float the *Queen Mary* in. And springs everywhere. Just little ferny hollows, y'know, at the foot of cliffs, with moss and tiny wildflowers, and the water bubbling up clear as crystal.' He had always had a gift for describing things. 'And talk about fish, the holes are just teemin' with 'em.'

'So you had a good time?' I filled his mug again from the teapot, mopping at my sweaty face.

'I did. Old Charlie took me into a couple o' the big gorges — you'd have to see 'em for yourself. One thing's certain, a man'd never go short of a drink mustering that country.'

'What will you do now, then?' I still had no inkling of his plan.

He scratched his beard. 'Camp the night here. I want a word with the head stockman anyway, and old Joe, then I'll head off in the morning. Weather's due to break any day and I'd sooner be home when it does. You're okay here, are you?'

'Of course I am. They're a good bunch of men, and I've learned to put up with having plumbing and electricity. Even old Boof's starting to act like a dog. So yeah, it's not too bad.'

Mrs Russell returned just before the end of February. Her husband got off the plane sick and hung-over. She brought treats with her – fruit for the big house, and five pounds of sausages for the men's breakfast. She looked jealously about the kitchen, switching over the dippers on the wall pegs beside the stove and straightening the mat. The cat came purring to her, but Boof, though he stood to be fussed over, continued to follow me.

Next morning, while the dew still glistened on the roofs, Joe backed up the landrover to the verandah and loaded my trunk and typewriter, while I took a final look round and pulled on the hat Big Sally had made for me out of cabbage-palm leaves. I had already collected my last cheque and said my goodbyes to the boss and the men and the housegirls. Now there was only the Russells and Boof, lined up under the dinner-bell, to see me off.

'You right then?' Joe was waiting.

'I think so.' I pulled the door open and there was a whine behind me, a scrabble of paws, and Boof went flying past me onto the seat. He wouldn't be called out. I had to grab his collar and haul him every inch of the way to Mrs Russell's feet. She had a face on her like thunder, and I knew she would never forgive me for alienating his affection. Her husband hung onto him while I jumped back in, and the last thing I heard as I left was Boof's heartbroken howling.

I had spent three months cooped up on the Hill, too busy to notice the seasonal changes, but now my eyes were everywhere in an effort to take it all in. The country was lovely dressed in its summer green. There were long stretches of water across and beside the track, glittering in the early sunlight, and the little plains between the hills were rippling seas of grass. Archie Creek had run big – there was a tide-line of flood-wrack high up the bank, and the hole above the road crossing was full and starred with pink waterlilies. As we crossed the snappy gum ridges into Yeldham, a bush turkey ran before us up the track, its feet squirting silver spray out of the waterlogged wheel ruts.

When we arrived, Joe wouldn't stop for a cuppa. 'Don't like the look of that sky,' he said. Dad gave him a packet of mail to post, and I flipped a wave, then turned back to stare again at the garden.

'Everything's grown so much.' I could hardly believe the change. The lawn had filled the yard, and the trees were feet taller. 'But where's the cumquat?'

'The white ants got it.' Judith kicked at the stump. 'There was a willy-wind came through one day and snapped it off. It was all hollowed out inside – a wonder it could still stand up, really. Hey, what d'you think? I've got a job. I'm going down to Dreyfus on Wednesday to do their saddles. It'll take weeks because there're about twenty of them. Jack says I could be there until we start droving even. It means I can go ahead and buy my ponies.'

'Have you found them yet?'

'I think so.' She had a page of newsprint torn from *Country Life*. 'There's a place here – Pea-Tree Creek, see? They've got a six-year-old horse and three mares, two of them creamies, one with a six-month foal. The stallion was grand champion in the ag. show two years back. They sound perfect.'

'But that's,' I peered at the fine print, 'Biloela, for God's sake! How are you gunna get them up from there? It's halfway across Queensland.'

'Ah,' she grinned. 'That's why I'm going to Dreyfus. They'll be backloading for Mike. You know he does freight trips when he can get them, between running the mail? Well, he's taking a load from Cloncurry down to Toowoomba pretty soon, he said, so he can bring them back. Shouldn't cost more than the saddling job's worth.' Her head went up as a strident whinny sounded down the paddock. 'That's Decimal Currency, Patrick's new horse. Come and see him.'

He was a chestnut, big-barrelled, with a star and a couple of white feet. His legs were clean but a bit straight in the pastern, I thought, and Judith agreed.

'The idea is to geld him after a couple of seasons. There's no real blood there. Dad has just got this thing about Ferdy breeding 'em too light-boned. Lot of rubbish, I think.'

'Yes, he said something about it to me. The fence looks good. Did Bill 'old gloom-and-doom' Foster come across again to tell you it wouldn't hold stock?' It was a well-worn joke. We were the first ones in the district to put up suspension fencing using high-tensile wire and spreaders between the posts. The strains were a quarter of a mile long, as opposed to the short panels and frequent strainer posts of conventional fencing. It was quicker and cheaper to stand, but the Gregory Downs manager had been outraged by its sloppy appearance. 'Your eye just has to become accustomed,' Dad had told him. 'It looks okay then.'

'Where's Sian now?' I asked Judith.

'At Riversleigh.'

'What, still drilling?'

She shook her head. 'He got a bore eventually, after two dry holes. No, head stockman. He's gunna run the camp there. He'll come back for the droving, he said, but he's keeping his job until then.'

'And this business with Dad traipsing round up the border country, what's that all about? Dad doesn't go riding for fun like some weekend cowboy.'

'Search me. He just said he was going and went. I didn't think about it.' She had been too immersed in her own plans, I thought, to do so. But it was odd, all the same.

About a week after Judith had gone off to her job on Dreyfus, Dad announced that he was heading into town. I should make up a list, he said, and he'd pick up the stores for the droving season. And there was a fella in there called Branson, a pub owner, he wanted to see. He could be interested in doing a deal with us.

'What sort of deal?' Patrick sounded as mystified as I felt. It was a name we had never heard before.

'Depends what he wants. He owns that bit o' country I was looking at the other side o' Lawn Hill. Runs a few scrubbers up there. He's not even a bushie, let alone a cattleman, so he could be interested in selling.'

'But we don't want it. I mean . . .' Patrick looked round and I felt my heart sink. 'We've just got this place paid off. What would we want with two? We'd never be able to work 'em.'

'God, stone the crows! I dunno what's wrong with young people today. Where's your sense of adventure, son? What have we got here we can't just as easy sell if something better offers?'

It was out in the open now and dismay filled me. 'What about my garden? The trees will be fruiting next summer.'

'You can always grow some more.' He was impatient. 'Jesus! You could be middle-aged, you're all so cautious. No one turns down opportunity for a patch o' lawn. Any road,' he ended suddenly, 'nothing's settled. All I'm gunna do is talk to the man.'

It mightn't be settled yet, but I knew it wasn't going to go away, either. Dad had talked us into many things over the years – into horses we hadn't wanted to buy (but they'd turned out well), into mobs we hadn't wanted to take (but we got them there), and bank loans I was certain we'd never be able to repay (but we had). He had obviously been thinking about this latest scheme for some time, and he had maintained, right from the start, that Yeldham was too small.

'The first one of you that marries, where'll we be? There's not a living here for two families.'

Useless to say that nobody was getting married yet.

'The time to plan for the future is before it gets here,' he said.

We were going to sell, I knew it in my bones. We'd talk about it, everybody having their say. We'd go up there and look the country over for ourselves, and discuss the price and work out if we could meet it. And in the end Dad's enthusiasm would kindle a like response, even in me. Because it was true, you could grow another garden, and besides, we were all of us accustomed to the challenge of change.

'What's it called then?' I asked, the echo of a question put many times, and in many places, before.

'Bowthorn,' Dad said.

THIRTEEN

In the end we borrowed old Joe from Lawn Hill to caretake at Yeldham for a couple of weeks, while the three of us – Dad, Patrick and I – went up to Bowthorn for a look. We took about twenty horses because we'd need packs to get about. The only track in went as far as the Station Hole on Accident Creek, where the yards and shed were. It stopped there because the station was on a dead-end road.

My ears pricked up. 'What shed?'

'Looks like it was meant for shearers' quarters,' Dad said, off-hand. 'It's about sixty feet long with a concrete floor, verandahs front and back, and a sort of kitchen alcove one end with a stove and sink and table.'

'So how big is the property again?'

'Five hundred square miles. It's range country,' he said. 'Don't go expecting Mitchell grass. It's a battler's block, same as Yeldham, but Branson'll guarantee three hundred head, and from what I've seen we'll muster more. The cattle are wild, which is why Branson's men never tried to get 'em, but I haven't seen the scrubber yet that could beat me. And there's more cleanskins than a man could wave his hat at.'

'Are there really?' I watched the country going past. We had crossed Lawn Hill Creek and the land was rising into spinifex-clad hills cut by sharp gullies where snappy gum grew, scraggy and twisted like poor relations. We passed from that to swampy flats and wide, scalded claypans, and after that, though not all in the same day because we could travel no faster than the horses, there was timber again, box and carbean, and the rolling blacksoil plains behind Mt Oscar.

It looked to be good bullock country. Behind it the Constance Range bulked in shades of ochre and mauve, like something painted on the pale sky. The Mitchell grass was thick but almost white already, and only a trace of water remained in the coolibah swamps further on.

'Light season.' Patrick, squatting over the dinner fire, waved his hand to disperse the smoke. 'Seems to be getting dryer the further we go.'

'Means you can see what you're getting,' Dad said.

I knew what he meant. It took a bad year to show up a good waterhole. If you could still get a drink there when others were dry, it was a hole that would last.

Next day Dad and I got the new Toyota, which had replaced the old landrover, bogged in a tight creek only a few miles short of the boundary. Patrick caught us up just as we finished digging ourselves out, and the horses wandered on while he got himself a drink.

'Whoever made this road must've gone looking for soft country.' He capped the waterbag again. 'Hey, did you see the buff carcass back at the swamp? Big old bull with a great set of horns. I'm gunna call it Buffalo Swamp.' It was the first natural feature to be named by us, even though it wasn't within the lease.

A bit further on we came to a fence across the road.

'The boundary,' Dad said. 'It's an old check fence. Runs from the range there to the creek. The horse paddock's just up the track a bit.' The front wheel crashed into another hole, rattling our teeth. 'Jesus! We could do with a council grader on this goat pad.' He was starting to sound like Patrick, as if we had already bought the place.

'Nobody delivers the mail, do they?' I said.

'Nope. We'd have to fetch it ourselves from the mission – it's only fifty miles away. Here we are.'

The creek-bed was wide and shallow, full of tumbled black rocks that we lurched across in first gear. I could see the water stretching away upstream; it was low for so early in the season. Further along, where the deeper water lay, was the silvery grey of paperbark foliage. A jabiru was fishing among the rocks at the creek's edge and beyond it a little croc floated, legs hanging, only his snout and eye knobs breaking the surface.

The paddock, which wasn't much more than a square mile, seemed full of horses. There were actually only seventeen, but they had been there all summer and the short grass was chewed over and dotted with old black dung, and the pads leading into the watering lane were dusty from use. The shed stood on the creek-bank, a solid, cyclone-proofed building with some groceries and half a dozen packs and riding saddles stored inside.

'There's no water laid on,' Dad said. 'No bathroom, no dunny. Still, it's more than we started with at Yeldham, by a long way. The yards are rubbish, too.'

He was right about that. The contractor had built them from ti-tree, which rotted after a couple of years in the ground. There were no gates, only skinny slip-rails with the bark still on them. I climbed onto one when I heard the bells coming, and it snapped under my weight.

'Fat lot of good they'll be with a yarding of wild cattle.' I banged dirt off myself with my hat, and nodded at a hip-roofed structure next to the yards, a patchwork of rusting iron weighted with stones under which a shabby truck was parked. 'What's in there?'

'Junk mainly. Wants a firestick chucking in it. Except for the vehicle, and Patrick can check that over. Let's get the horses hobbled outa the paddock, then run the rest of 'em up and get a look at 'em in the yard.'

Next morning we took a drive down to Old Bowthorn, a deep lily hole hidden behind a rocky hillock half a mile off the side of the road. It had been the original station site back in the forties, but it wasn't the rubbish dump we went to see, or the concrete slab which was all that remained of the old hut, but the yard. We left the vehicle and walked, scrambling through the gully to the back of the hill where huge sandstone boulders, some of them ten feet high, were scattered about like toy blocks. The yard butted onto the rocks. In places the rails were even sunk into them, creating a solid holding yard with an entrance between two boulders. Long Charlie had showed it to him, Dad told us, and there were a couple more like it on the place.

'Poddy-dodgers' yards. It's been open slather up here for years for the moonlight riders.'

We went across to Elizabeth Creek next, on an incredibly skimpy track that wound through and over the range. It was so bad Dad hadn't bothered including it in his description of the place, and it took three hours to do the thirteen miles to the bluff above Elizabeth Creek. When Dad pulled up there, I stared out over a vista of gorge and valley and plateau-topped ranges spreading to the horizon – and down, with horror, at the wheeltracks tipping over the edge of the bluff.

'We're not driving down there.'

'It's not as bad as it looks.' He shoved the four-wheel-drive lever forward and I gripped the door with both hands, turning my eyes from the drop.

The track had been bulldozed out of the side of the hill, with a straight fall into the creek far below. I could see water glimmering through gum and myrtle scrub, and on the other side, where the hill rose ever higher above us, the brilliant yellow blaze of flowering kapok trees. Rain had gullied out the middle of part of the track. Dad stood on the brake while Patrick and I rolled rocks into it to allow us to get past, and we continued on down to the bottom.

It was certainly pretty country. We walked up the gorge, inspected another hidden yard, this one buried in turpentine scrub, and

found some of the springs Dad had mentioned, overhung by flowering shrubs and with mosses and delicate ferns filling the interstices
in the rock around them, just as he had described.

It was dark by the time we got back to the horse paddock. The
shed looked derelict in the headlights and I suddenly wished we
had brought Red or Larry with us. A dog made the loneliest camp
homely.

Patrick and I put the horses together, and by the time we returned
Dad had a light going in the shed and was stirring a corn-beef
curry on the stove top. After we'd eaten, we sat on in the pool of
yellow thrown by the carbide light, going through what paperwork
there was, which wasn't much: the boundary descriptions, a
certificate of brand registrations, and receipts for horses bought.

'These are farcical,' I said. 'Listen to this: "One kicking colt, paid
five pound." Or this: "Black filly, blind eye, bought off Willie B.
Paid for same." Who was running this show?'

'Nobody.' Dad flicked through the papers. 'I doubt if Branson
ever came out o' town above once or twice. He'd put blokes on to
do a bit o' mustering or build a yard, but he knew nothing, so of
course they put it over him. The solid-built stuff like this shed here,
and the original cattle – they were his father's doing.'

'And you reckon the numbers are here – six hundred head?'

'Stake my life on it.'

'Fifteen and a half thousand quid is a lot of money to borrow.'
I could see the moon rising behind a pair of giant carbeans growing
beyond the fence that surrounded the shed. Their trunks glimmered
palely against the soft darkness.

'It's thirty-one thousand dollars in new money.' Patrick looked up from the brands he was copying down. His mathematical skills had always been better than his writing ones. 'And that's what? Another ten years' droving? If the roadtrains haven't taken it all by then.'

'Oh, we'd quit the road if we bought,' Dad said. 'Well, maybe do a bit this year – we couldn't walk out on Jack until he'd found someone else, but we'd have to be here to work the place full-time.'

I looked at him. 'So, if we buy, where does the money come from? Until Yeldham is sold, I mean – and that might take years, for all we know.'

'From the cattle here, of course. That's why Bowthorn is a better proposition than Yeldham. We've got another four years there before we can sell anything, unless we start on the steers and that's not good business. But up here we could sell this year, and as long as we kept the branding figures up we'd have bullocks to turn off every year after. I'm not saying it'd be easy, just that it'd put us four years ahead of where we are now, and that's well worth considering.'

Next morning we were packed up and riding by daylight, heading west up the Accident Creek. It was pleasant in the mild April weather to be jogging behind packhorses again through new country. We were riding up a broad valley bisected by the now dry creek-bed. I could see the southern range behind the creek timber, its rocky slopes almost too rough to climb. There was an abundance of wattle and silver-leaf box, and the sturdy trunks and narrow foliage of forest ti-tree. We crossed brumby pads just before the sand country gave way to a gravel ridge thick with turpentine bushes, and then a narrower, deeper pad indented with the twin half-moon crescents of cattle tracks. Dad grunted with satisfaction.

That night we camped under the shady tree that gave its name to Shady Hole. It was huge, the largest girthed tree I had ever seen. Dad didn't know its name, but Charlie had told him the blackfellas called it boat tree, because in the old days they'd used them to make dug-out canoes.

'This one must have been growing when Cook barged into the Barrier Reef,' I said. 'The waterhole here's better than the station one. What if that goes dry?'

'We'd put down a bore,' Dad said. 'I'll try it with the stick when we get back.'

Next day we blocked up a couple of small mobs of cattle and found the tracks of more. Also brumbies, bush turkeys, and dozens of sturdy little rock wallabies that bounded up the rocky outcrops like they were paved roads. There were dingoes, too – a big yellow dog with a sleek coat trotted across in front of us and Dad cracked his whip at him, but instead of bolting he stopped to stare.

'Never been shot at,' Patrick said. 'The place is crawling with them – did you hear them last night?'

'Nothing a bit o' strychnine won't fix.' Dad gave the dog a baleful look and shied a stick, which missed by a mile.

We went north to the river, dodging the rougher range country where we could because the horses were unshod, and checking out the creeks and swamps still holding water along the way. By the number of fresh cattle-camps we came across and the evidence of well-used pads, Dad was satisfied that the cattle were there. We saw few actual cattle, but then scrubbers didn't hang around waiting to be looked at.

We camped in spinifex one night at a short distance from the Eight Mile Creek, and soon after moonrise the brumbies got among the horses. The harsh squeal of the stallions, of thudding hooves and the clangour of galloping bells carried clearly to us. Patrick went out with the rifle, and lying in my swag I heard the blasting snort as the first brumby scented him, then the sound of galloping hooves. Patrick fired twice, the shots splintering the night apart, but in the morning, although a stallion lay dead in his blood, the chestnut mare Lucy was missing.

We found her, Dad and I, five miles back towards the range, her front feet bloodied from galloping in hobbles. She had been chasing the wild ones and was still at it, lunging forward with tail half cocked, when we caught her up.

'Bitch of a thing's in season.' Dad sounded cranky. 'How'd we miss that? She shoulda been left in the paddock.'

I fashioned a headstall from the neck-straps and led her back, maintaining a good pace because the morning was well advanced. Dad, riding behind to toe Lucy along, said suddenly, 'Left, girl! Left! Way you're going, you'll miss the camp.'

I turned obediently, putting Fandango into the gully that we'd been riding alongside. He lunged out of it and straight into the path of the first scrub bull I'd ever seen – a huge red and white beast just standing there scratching at his hide with one great horn in a cloud of buffalo flies. It was like coming up against a tank. I had just an instant to take in his massive horns, his matted poll and piggy eyes before he dropped his head, lifting the great hump of muscle on his neck, and came at me like a thrown spear.

Fandango let out a snort and made a leap that was half a rear,

185

then bolted. For a few dreadful seconds I thought he wasn't going to make it, but he was a fast horse and the bull had nothing but weight and malevolence, which was no match for speed. He pulled up, shaking his heavy head, drooling strings of lather, while I reined Fandango in a wide circle, the blood still pounding in my ears. Dad was catching Lucy, who'd taken off again when I dropped her lead.

'Hell's bells! What got into him?' I wondered aloud, my heart thumping as I took the mare in tow again.

'We just got too close, is all. A bull like that is king o' the scrub.' Dad's eyes gleamed. 'Frightened o' nothing and worth damn near as much as a bullock at the meatworks.'

There were cattle on the creek when we rode into camp, mostly cleanskins. They scattered at our approach, and afterwards, packed up and riding north again, we cut the pads they had come in on. There were more on the red sand flats at the river, feeding out around the bronco yard there. They broke, galloping for the timber, but we blocked them up and held them for a while, all except the bull, another big cleanskin that barrelled his way past me, horns spread like curved spears above his wicked eyes.

There was a grave behind the yard. It had no marker, and half the posts and rails had rotted away. We sat on our horses looking at it. I wondered who could possibly have died here so far from anywhere.

'We'd have to fix that,' Dad said. 'Be gone for good pretty soon. Come on then, there's a place along a bit where we can camp. And then I'll show yer what a proper waterhole looks like.

It was several miles upstream. We crossed sandy channels where water lay in flat sheets iridescent as satin in the sun, or pooled under the spreading boughs of paperbark. Our mounts' hooves crunched across damp sand and gravel banks as we dodged through dense channel growth of eucalypt suckers, deadly nightshade and girth-high grasses. And finally we rode out onto a beach of white sand and saw the water spread before us, far up the reaches of the gorge until it was lost in distance, the surface, choppy with wavelets pushed up by the wind, glittering under the wide blue sky.

'Holy mackerel!' Patrick said. 'Beats Sandy Creek by a yard and a bit, doesn't it?'

Awed by the sheer size of it, I had to agree.

FOURTEEN

Judith was home when we got back. She had had her hair cut short and was wearing a new shirt, blue with an embroidered collar. Padre Frank, Brian Walker's replacement, had brought her home from Dreyfus two days before.

'I like your hair. And the shirt. Did the hawker's van come while you were down there?'

'No, I went into Cloncurry. Annie Simpson – you know her, the mechanic's wife at Dreyfus – was going in, so I went with her. The road's great now, crowned nearly all the way.'

'Where'd you get the shirt? It's pretty.'

'Oh, Clarkie's. I got some other stuff, too, a brunchcoat and shortie 'jamas and a new lipstick. I'll show you. Then I got my hair done. We stayed in a pub.' She pulled a face. 'It was a bit rough but I shared a room with Annie, so it was okay.'

'Which one?' I had only been into Cloncurry a couple of times, and it had seemed to be full of pubs.

'Oh, Prince of something – Kent or Wales. I forget. What's all this about buying a new property?'

'How did you know about –? Oh, Joe, I suppose.'

'Nope. I heard it down at Dreyfus.' She felt at the edges of her new short hair. 'I haven't got used to it yet. We were having lunch one day at Dreyfus and one of the Webber boys dropped in. He told us. He said, "Mac McGinnis has just bought Bowthorn."'

'Well, he hasn't. God, if you sneezed round here they'd have you dead from pneumonia before you got your hankie out. But we are thinking about it. I wasn't too keen at first, but it could be a good move. Dad reckons there're enough cattle to live off, so there'd be no more droving. No more bores to equip either because there's water everywhere. And there's a big shed with a concrete floor and proper doors. It's got a kitchen one end with a table and sink and stuff, and the other end is already partitioned off. We could have it as a bedroom. There's a fence around it – round the shed, I mean – but the water's not laid on. Oh, I forgot, it's on a creek – Accident Creek. It doesn't look the best waterhole in the world, but they put the shed there so I suppose it must be okay. I think it might be a good idea now I've seen it. It's a long way out, though.'

'Any horses go with the deal?'

I flapped a hand. 'There're s'posed to be thirty-seven, according to what Branson told Dad, but there're actually seventeen. I'm not surprised – they were all in a paddock no bigger than this one, with nobody to check on 'em all summer. Hey, what's happening with the ponies? Because that's something, there're no paddocks up there you could use.'

Judith shrugged. 'Doesn't make any difference cos it all fell through. Mike didn't get the freight after all. I rang up Bruce – the fella selling the horses – while I was in town.' She saw my surprise, because neither of us had ever used a telephone, and grinned. 'Well, Annie helped. She got the number and rang it, and I just talked. I felt such a fool. Couldn't stop saying, "Over," like it was the wireless. Anyway, Bruce had another buyer and didn't want to wait, so I had to tell him I couldn't take them now.'

'Well, maybe you'll find some more, somewhere closer,' I said. 'Though that's another thing, it's just crawling with brumbies up there. I dunno what we'd do with the horses, there's not even a spell paddock.'

'What about Sian – does he know about it yet?'

I grimaced. 'Why not? I daresay the gossip makes it to Riversleigh, too. Dad's going to see him, of course. I mean, if we sell Yeldham he's due his share, but even if he wants to come in on the new place he probably wouldn't stay. He'd still be working with Dad.' I stretched, looking sideways at the old shack with its verandah of rain-spotted pandanus thatch. 'Looks an awful dump, doesn't it, when you've been away for a while? I reckon it'd be worth buying Bowthorn just for a better roof.'

'What about the garden?'

'Well, Dad is right, I suppose. You can always grow more stuff. If we buy, I'd make another.'

It wasn't until August of 1966 that we actually signed the paperwork for the property. It took four months to organise the bank loan, find a buyer for Yeldham, and sell off two-thirds of our cattle to get a deposit together. In between all this, we did the usual mobs from Dreyfus into the railhead. Dad told Jack it would be our last year, and when we pulled out it was with all our horses, even old Star, who had spent the previous twelve months in the Ten Mile.

We left the goats behind at Yeldham for the new people, a family called Perry, but took the chooks, the dogs, and Judith's tortoiseshell cat. It was amazing how much we had accumulated during our three-year tenure: tools and engines, the arc welder, chairs, stretcher-beds and two kerosene fridges. There was the washing machine, the stove, a set of tubs, even a mango in a pot, and various garden cuttings, all to be fitted onto the two vehicles somehow with the saddlery and ordinary camp gear. And, perched incongruously atop the Toyota, the tall rectangle of the corrugated-iron toilet, its door latched shut and wooden seat in place.

It was Dad's idea. 'You can't live anywhere without a dunny. We'll take the building up, then we've only gotta dig a hole, and Bob's your uncle.'

'And what about the buyers, the new people here?' Patrick asked.

'They can build one for 'emselves, same as we did,' Dad said, adding, as if he were giving away free samples, 'they'll still have the hole.'

The horses and the eighty-odd heifers that we had kept back from the sale went up last of all. We had a hundred and twenty horses, counting the foals, and our first task was going to be finding somewhere safe to keep them all. We tailed the heifers out on the creek for a week to settle them down, turning them up towards the big Shady Hole when we let them go because it had become

191

obvious that the water at the station wasn't going to last the season out. You could trust an ignorant townie, I thought resignedly, to pick the worst hole on the place to build on. Dad was itching to go mustering, but it looked like we'd have to punch a bore down first.

Sian, his head stockman's job now finished, had come home again. He took the truck down to Riversleigh to bring the boring plant back, and while he was away Judith, Patrick and Dad took the stallion and brood mares across to the Elizabeth Creek country, where between the steep-sided ranges were some valleys that could be closed off with less than a mile of fencing. Water was no problem there, with springs at the foot of the range and even a couple of artesian bores, drilled and then abandoned by the mining camps a decade before, which still bubbled water into swamps of quag and bullrushes. The rest of the horses had been turned into Horse Gorge, a natural paddock deep in the range country south of the homestead, which was what we had fallen into the habit of calling the shed.

The first bore site was divined just twenty paces from the back verandah, the next one a quarter of a mile distant at the mouth of the watering lane, and the third, in desperation, across the creek. Sian had been against that.

'Jesus, man! How are you gunna get the water to the house? It'll be nothing but a headache.' His arm shot out, pointing over the shrinking hole. 'Look at the height o' the floodbanks. This is a big creek when she runs.'

'What the hell is the use of worrying about getting it where you want it?' Dad roared. 'I'd just settle for getting the bloody stuff!'

The drilling had already been going on for weeks, but none of the holes had got much beyond thirty feet. In the second one Dad had resorted to explosives, tamping the shot with hundreds of gallons of our precious water, but the blast didn't even dint the impervious layer of stone that had stopped the first hole and would also stop the third.

'Jesus!' Dad was fuming. 'It's harder than bloody diamonds.'

We had lain prone behind logs awaiting the explosion, not knowing what to expect as we counted off the seconds, and at the last moment Red had ambled across to the foot of the rig and hung his head over the hole.

'Come behind, yer great drongo!' Patrick bellowed. He started to get up just as there came a loud *whump* from deep in the earth. The derrick swayed fractionally and Red snarled, snapping at a spray of silver droplets that suddenly shot past his face.

Later, investigating the results with a mirror, we could see that the blast had travelled sideways, carving a cavern out of the hole.

The third site fared no better. By the time the bit was clanging on the same layer of stone that had defeated us before, the foot valve of the pump that Sian had rigged in the creek was barely covered by water. The boys dug a soak, and Dad brazed two-inch pipes into four of the ubiquitous 44-gallon drums to join them together, then raised them on a stand to provide a tank to pump into.

It was the beginning of a long battle with the water supply, but one which, in the end, I was grimly determined to win. The water was there under the rock. I could feel it with the stick, but we were going to need a rotary drill, not an outdated mud-puncher, to get at it, and that took money.

I could think of nothing else but rain. While the others were away on the run mustering, pulling the rickety yards together with lengths of cable, getting the feel of the place, I watched the sky and waited for rain. My mango seedling was still in its pot, along with half a dozen little poincianas I had grown from seeds collected on my first trip to Doomadgee Mission, which, fifty miles to the east, was our nearest neighbour. I could have had cuttings too – bougainvillea, hibiscus, crepe myrtle, even bananas – but there was no point at present. Looking at the dusty wasteland about the shed, with its clumps of dead grass and drifts of old bauhinia leaves piled in corners of the netting fence, I knew I didn't have enough water to grow a cactus.

The Wet was late that year. It was bound to be, of course. I knew well that the miracle of the timely storm happened more often in movie scripts than in reality. There were odd storms, it was true, through November and December, but they had a half-hearted feel to them. There was no verve in the build-up, just a limp muttering which did nothing to break the searing heat or hint at an end to the dumb endurance that simply getting through the day required. Sometimes, as Christmas approached, a shower would fall, and then for half a day there'd be a muddy pool on the flat where plovers clinked, or perhaps a sinkhole in a creek half full of black, leaf-stained water. But never enough to fill or run the Accident, where the deep drifts of sand were as dry as fifty-year-old bones. The soak still made a foot or two of water an hour, but there was endless trouble with the pump.

'The lift's too great.' Patrick had studied the problem, and on his say-so we moved pump and engine, mounted together on a heavy metal frame, down into the cutting. Next day, twenty minutes after starting it up, I checked it and found the whole affair vibrating inexorably towards the soak. I drove a peg into the earth to hold it, and wished I had faith enough to make praying for rain a reasonable option.

On Christmas day, with the paperbark heavy with blossom, the smell of it thick as smoke in the air, we carted water, because the soak had finally given up. We took half a dozen forty-fours down to Old Bowthorn and formed a chain, passing the buckets from the rock where Dad was dipping them to Sian on the bed of the truck, who hoisted them up and emptied them into the drums.

'Some Christmas chore.' I wiped my sleeve over my face to get rid of the sweat. 'I bet they're sitting under my tree at Yeldham with all the sprays going, and the tank overflowing too, very likely.'

'Shouldn't be surprised,' Judith said. 'It's what I'd be doing if I was there.'

'The rain'll come,' Dad said. And early in the new year it did. Only Judith and I were home. Dad and the boys were camped out, still mustering despite the heat. Many of the open-range places continued their stockwork into summer because the early storms brought the cattle together on the new feed, making them easier to find. It had rained on the Elizabeth country, and at the river even the Eight Mile Creek was full. Now, at last, it was our turn.

The storm massed for hours in the west, inky piles of cloud that sent the sun early to bed. We stood on the back verandah snuffing the scent of it as it came, then yelling to make ourselves heard above the hammering on the tin roof. Water poured from its unguttered edges as from a fire hose.

'Drums,' Judith mouthed, splashing out into the downpour to manoeuvre an empty forty-four under the torrent.

'But the creek will fill,' I yelled.

She shook her head. 'Dirty water – take a week to settle.'

We filled all the drums, then paddled down the path to the creek-bank to watch the creek come down. The rain had lightened off to a drizzle, and the layers of dead leaves felt spongy underfoot and smelt of rot. Water ran in trickles and shooting torrents down every pad and gutter into the creek, but the sand swallowed it all like a sponge, and I wondered in dismay if, after all, the storm would do no more than revitalise the soak.

There was a hollow in the sand directly opposite where we crouched, its surface littered with debris – curled bark and sticks, and a scattering of dead ti-tree leaves. The litter suddenly moved, and I nudged Judith. 'Look, the sand must be filling up, it's breaking through the low spots.'

What actually appeared wasn't water but a tiny crocodile, ten or twelve inches long. It clawed its way out of the sand and sticks under our bemused eyes, and was followed immediately by two more. Then a sort of hissing filled the air. I turned my gaze upstream and saw the water coming, curling like a wave around the island that bisected the channel at that point, a dirty red torrent with a crest of soiled foam. It spread when it hit the wider section of creek-bed, swamping the hollows and shooting over the sand at better than walking pace. I saw the baby crocs lift with it and float until only their tiny eye-knobs were visible, and marvelled at their imprinted knowledge. Tons of sand were displaced when creeks ran this way; had they not dug themselves out before the water arrived, they might never have done so. The vibration of its passage must have triggered their emergence, I thought.

Then Judith leapt to her feet as though she'd been stung. 'The pump! We forgot the flaming pump.'

It was as well she'd remembered, because by the time I had backed the old International truck, which had come with the place, into position against the fence and hooked a chain around the back axle, then joined a cable onto the frame that both pump and engine were bolted to, the water had already covered the lower end of it.

I let in the clutch and the wheels gripped, then spun, and I saw Judith in the mirror waving her arms. 'Hold it! You're pulling it into the bank,' she said when I climbed out and ran back. 'The slope's too steep and it digs in. It'll tip over and smash next.'

'Better than getting it drowned.'

'Don't panic.' Judith was always calm in a crisis. 'It needs something to lift it. Like . . .' her eyes roamed around seeking inspiration while I stood fidgeting. 'A forty-four. That'll do. Have to empty it though, or we'll never hold it down the bank.'

It worked just as she had said it would. When I let the clutch in this time, the engine frame rode up behind the drum, its front end lifting to the pull. Once it was out of the cutting, Judith kicked the drum free and I pressed my foot down, and then she was running and yelling again, arms going madly.

I slammed the brake pedal down and stuck my head through the window. 'What?'

'You crazy woman! You're taking the fence with you! The hook must've caught in the netting.'

I stared appalled at the drunken posts and scrunched wire,

dragging behind like a chained dog fallen from the load. The tight, stretched look of it was so similar that I put my hands over my mouth and started to laugh.

Judith looked at me as if I'd gone mad. 'You've ruined it!'

'Yeah, I know.' With a final spurt of laughter I backed up and freed the offending hook. 'We'll have to fix that before the men get back and see it.' She knew what I meant. We prided ourselves on our ability to handle things, so mortifyingly silly mistakes like this were best rectified and forgotten.

Next morning the sky was clear, the creek, a brown tide topped with dirty foam, sliding effortlessly between its banks. Our water worries were over. And as if to celebrate, everything shone – the periwinkle sky, the carbean leaves twisting in the light air, even the white stalks of old grass. I dug a hole for the mango tree and planted it out, then we went walking, up the track and across the swamp, where the silver-leaf box now stood ankle-deep, through water glittering like glass in the sunlight. It was alive with the chirrup of frogs and aswarm with their jelly-like eggs, and the corpses of crickets and drowned ants. There were red-waisted dragonflies drying new wings, and iridescent beetles, bright as jewels against the drab trunks of trees. It was hard to believe that yesterday the whole paddock had been as sere as a desert. This was why the blackfellas went walkabout after rain, I thought; not just for the harvest of new food a deluge brought, but for the marvel of renewal and the bright, evanescent beauty that lay hidden behind the harsh face of the land.

The men came home that afternoon, all three of them in the Toyota, now a uniform red from mud. There was mud even on the cab roof, and great gobbets of clay hanging off the underside of the tray. All you could see through the arc the windscreen wipers had cleared was Patrick's head behind the wheel.

'Did you get the rain?' I called. Then, seeing no camp gear on the back, just their swags and two shovels, the handles smeared with clay, I added, 'What's up?'

'Accident,' Dad said. 'Open the gate, will you? Sian's been hurt.'

FIFTEEN

It was his right leg that was injured. He had been throwing a big mick, which got up when it shouldn't have and took to him, and now he could put no weight on the knee, which collapsed under him when he tried to stand. The flying doctor, when we got him on the wireless, was quite definite in his diagnosis: the cartilage in Sian's knee was torn and needed immediate surgery. What, he enquired, was the state of the Bowthorn airstrip?

'Non-existent,' Dad said. 'We'll have to get him to another one by road.'

Doomadgee was the closest, but I thought of the miles of ti-tree swamp, and the second, much deeper crossing of the Accident separating us – and that was without taking the Nicholson River into consideration – and I knew there was no chance of getting a vehicle through. We would have to try for Highland Plains, sixty miles south-west across the ranges. There was an airstrip there and George Doherty, the owner, listening in to the medical call, had volunteered help from his end.

'We'll have to give it till morning to let the creek run down a bit, and I'll need you along, champ,' Dad said. He'd called Patrick that when he was a kid, but he rarely did so now. It showed how rattled he was by what had occurred. We had been lucky over the years – Dad had been injured, but the rest of us had suffered only minor hurts. Until now.

I packed food for the journey, which should take no more than a couple of days, there and back, but I packed for a week anyway, thinking it better to be safe than starving. The others loaded the jacks and lifting blocks, and the shovels and cables and axe, and fuelled the vehicle up. Then there was nothing to do but wait and hope that the rain we had been so glad to see only twenty-four hours before held off for the next couple of days. Sian was sleeping by then, his knee strapped, and the painkillers the doctor prescribed from the medicine chest inside him. The chest contained everything likely to be needed in an emergency, from scalpels to kidney dishes, along with a wide range of prescription drugs, of which morphine was the most important.

They left next morning, Judith and I accompanying them to the creek crossing. Patrick covered the engine and we two stood watching on the bank, hardly breathing as the Toyota nosed into the creek and surged across with a bow wave breaking over the bullbar. The horn gave a watery toot as they breasted the far bank, then it was gone into the great emptiness stretching around us. Normally, I never noticed it, but now I could feel our isolation in the immensity of scrub and sky and range. I had a sudden mental picture of Bowthorn's position on the map, and, dotted like mileposts along the track leading out, all manner of dire emergencies from snake-bite to heart attack just waiting to happen. Of course, they almost certainly wouldn't, but looking around me at the vaguely menacing emptiness, I wished the old comfortable familiarity with my surroundings would return to draw the cloak of usage over this unsettling strangeness.

It rained again that evening, and during the night, when the clouds had cleared and a half-moon was standing above the carbeans, we both woke to a great clamour on the roof, followed by a breathy beating of wings.

'What was that?' Judith sounded as startled as I felt.

We went out onto the verandah with the carbide light and found a wild duck dead on the damp ground, its legs bloodied and all but sheared from its body.

'Must have been the moonlight on the roof. Fooled it into thinking it was water. Poor thing, it's hit the edge of the iron.' I turned it over, admiring the perfect fit of its feathers, the pale appropriateness of its webbed feet.

'More rain coming.' Judith was looking at the moon. 'It's standing on edge, see, to tip it out. Wonder if they've got there yet.'

'God, I hope so.'

But they hadn't. It ended up taking them five days, and half of that time was spent digging themselves out of bogs while the storms and showers continued. We had still to learn that there was nothing as treacherous as the range country once rain fell, unless it was the ashy deserts where the ti-tree grew. The earth quaked like sponge beneath your feet, and from every bank and hollow water bubbled and leaked; soil turned to ooze when weight was applied to it, and vehicles, horses and men sank into it like stones in soup.

By the time Dad and Patrick arrived home on borrowed horses, having left the vehicle at Highland Plains, Sian's operation was over and he had started on the several weeks of physiotherapy necessary to reverse the muscle wastage in his leg. The creek had run down by then until it purled between the black stones of the crossing, and only light showers continued to fall. It was going to be another poor season. The swamps dried rapidly, the grasses seeded, and minuscule wildflowers appeared, tiny specks of colour in the grass. My mango tree now stood waist-high, the other cuttings were flourishing, and, at the foot of the clothesline, behind the newly finished bathroom that had been built in stages throughout the summer, Judith and I had started a lawn.

In March, when the roads were dry again, Sian returned, with only a small scar to show for his injury. He had caught a ride out to Highland Plains and driven the long way round, through Camooweal. Unusually for him, he couldn't remember the state of the creeks or the road, but the latter can't have been bad because there was very little mud on the vehicle. He insisted on washing it anyway, and as there was no one else home we both went down to the crossing, rolled up our jeans and began scooping water over it.

He was very cheerful, full of talk about the hospital and not the least interested in my news. When I had twice asked him the same question and been answered with a burst of melody, I slapped my cloth onto the bonnet in exasperation.

'What's the matter with you? You're not even listening.'

'Nothing.' His face was alive and there was a little-boy charm in his smile. 'I've met this girl – she was a nurse on the ward. I'm gunna tell the old fella tonight, so you can hear it now – I've put my name down for a job at the mines. I'll be leaving as soon as I hear from them that I've got it.'

'You mean it's serious this time? What's her name?'

'Oh, it's the real thing,' he assured me. 'We haven't made any long-term plans yet, it's too soon for that, but I think we'll be getting married. Her name's Leoni.'

'That's pretty. Is she – would she make a bushie?'

'Live out here? Without power or proper plumbing? No.' He was firm. 'I wouldn't ask her to. That's why I'm going into the mines.' He took up the song where he had left off, while I stood with the water pushing at my calves, thinking that there was just the four of us again to handle things. It would have to be enough.

Sian left a week later, Dad driving down to Mt Isa with him to bring the vehicle back. We branded the colts while he was away, and Judith and Patrick caught a few of the three-year-olds, even though we hadn't yet got round to rebuilding the catching pens in the old yard. Patrick had sunk a bloodwood post against one of the outer panels instead – it meant you at least had something to whip the head-rope about and know it was going to stay there. Earlier on, Chorus Girl, a mad, patchy-coloured roan and white filly, had flung herself at the rails and the whole panel had keeled over before her as the posts snapped off. We'd be better off without a yard, Patrick said furiously, the heap of rubbish we had would only teach colts bad habits.

It was soon after this that the chooks started to disappear. Remembering the baby crocs we had seen come out of the sand, I suspected their adult relatives – the hens were always scratching around in the long grass down by the creek. I put out more water so they had no need to drink down there, but the very next day the speckled broody was missing, her clutch of eggs gone cold in the nest.

'Snakes,' Dad said.

I stared at him. 'A full-grown hen? What sort of snake could swallow anything that big?'

He pulled the pipe from his lips. 'Don't be daft, girl. There's some up here can swallow wallabies.'

My knees felt suddenly weak and my skin crawled. He wasn't joking. I looked at the open doors and unscreened windows. 'Well, I just hope none of them come into the house!' And, having said it, of course one did.

It was Coochy, the tortoiseshell cat, who woke us, yowling like a banshee in the kitchen in the small hours of the morning. She'd had kittens in the enclosed space beside the fuel tank under the fridge, and when I finally got a light working and Dad, pushing the noisy cat aside, gingerly ripped the hinged flap open, the area behind it seemed entirely filled with snake.

'Cherr-ist!' He took a step back, grabbing up the .303.

'Don't hit the kero tank!' I shrieked, but the snake was already moving, its coils unrolling over the metal framework as its head slid swiftly into the shadow of the iron wall. Dad fired and the snake whipped its tail around, as if trying to knot off the broken bit. It heaved and writhed, smearing the walls and floor with blood, and Coochy yowled again and struck at its moving head.

I pushed her off with the broom. Her kittens were dead, their tiny bodies crushed by the strength of those muscular coils. She rushed between them crying, her fur on end, then suddenly seized one by the nape and sprang out, growling in her throat.

'It's alive,' Judith marvelled. 'It got pushed under the tank where the snake couldn't reach it. God! I'd never sleep again if that had happened to me.'

'Me, either.' I shuddered, then Patrick sneaked up behind me and dropped his whip across my ankle. The light leapt as I jumped and screamed. My heart froze, and there were snakes in every shadow until I caught his grin. Rage replaced fright then, and I swung the broom and caught him a crack across the shins that made him yell and hobble huffily back to bed.

In daylight the python measured a bit over nine feet. I incinerated its body along with the dead kittens, and for a while there were no more casualties among the poultry.

∾

In April the horses were mustered and the packs readied once more for the new season's work. Dad and Patrick and Judith went out, leaving me behind, and one morning in May, while I was digging weeds from the cabbage bed, a yellow landrover drove up to the gates and I met Giuseppe Morani. Visitors were an infrequent occurrence at Bowthorn. Stock inspectors came by, and the occasional crocodile hunter plying his lonely trade along the northern rivers, but we had no close neighbours and the distance was too great and the road too bad for casual callers.

I had seen the yellow landrovers years before, down near Kajabbi, and knew they belonged to the Bureau of Mineral Resources. It was the practice of the Canberra-based bureau to field large camps of surveyors, geologists and geophysicists, who established a base camp then worked out from it, investigating and recording the mineral potential of the country. Giuseppe's camp was thirty miles down the road at Spectacle dam, on Lawn Hill.

There were two men in the vehicle when I walked over carrying the digging fork. They got out, and I brushed the dirt off my hand and stuck it forward as they introduced themselves.

'Frank Paxton,' the tall, grey-headed one said. He had knobby knuckles and a stoop, and looked about fifty.

'Giuseppe Morani. How do you do.' He was dark – dark eyes, dark brows, dark hair, olive skin – very good-looking.

My ear hadn't caught it. I said 'Giu— I'm sorry. What was it?'

He laughed. 'Call me Seppe, everyone does.'

'It's Italian, isn't it?' I swung the gate open. 'Come in. But you were born here?' He had a pleasant accentless voice, with no sense of foreignness. And a truly engaging smile.

'True blue, despite my wog name.'

I was still holding the fork. I bent to stick it into a garden bed, then wiped my hands on my jeans, suddenly conscious of grubby nails and hair falling over my face. 'Well, come inside, both of you, and I'll make some tea.'

There were nine men, counting the cook and the mechanic, in the Spectacle camp, and over the six months of their stay we would meet them all, but Seppe came most frequently. He was a geologist and called in whenever his work brought him in our direction. He invited us down to the camp, with its screened mess tent and gas fridges, for barbecues, and he frequently drove over to spend Sundays with us. Sometimes the family were home, sometimes not. We would swim and fish, and once I tried taking him riding, but he was ill at ease with animals, even old Larry, so often we just sat on the verandah and talked. I had never met anyone like him. He lit up my world like a thousand suns, and everything I touched and saw and read had meaning, because in a week, or a day, or an hour, Seppe would be there to share it with.

I lived in a blaze of happiness week after week, and Judith, watching me dreamily wash a dish at the sink after he had driven off one evening, said, 'What on earth do you find to talk so much about?'

'Oh, I don't know, ourselves, books, food, the world. He lives in Melbourne but he's been overseas to lots of places. Makes you realise what dull lives we've had. He was telling me about his family today – one of his brothers is a priest. His parents run a delicatessen –'

She was blunt with me. 'You're in love with him, aren't you? Oh, for heaven's sake, give me that dish!' She almost snatched it from me, and I swished my empty hands through the suds and smiled at her.

'I think I might be.'

'Only think? Can't you tell?'

'Oh,' I said, suddenly more certain than I had ever been, 'when it happens you can tell. Believe me.'

'I thought so. You even look different, sort of lit up. Dad's noticed, too. It's partly why he's taken such a scunner to him. Pity his name's not John Smith.'

'Yes.' I sighed unhappily, my mood broken. There were no grounds for Dad's dislike beyond that of Seppe's name. Dad had fought in North Africa against the Germans, but his racial prejudice was reserved for the Japanese and the Italians. He hated the former because he had lost a brother in the prison camps, and he despised the Italians. The Japs, he had often said, were treacherous bastards, the Eyeties simply useless ones.

'Dad,' I had flared once, furious at hearing Seppe referred to as 'that damned dago', 'he is not. He's as Australian as you or me.' But it made no difference. We had had a bitter row about it and had scarcely spoken to each other since. I would not forgive him for the things he had said about Seppe, retorting that it wasn't his parents' nationality Dad didn't like, but the fact that Seppe was different. 'If he wore riding boots and talked about cows,' I yelled, 'you wouldn't care if his name was Hiroshima!'

His eyes went flinty behind his glasses. 'I'm trying to stop you making a mistake.'

'No you're not.' I felt bitter. 'You just want your own way.'

I was glad when all three of them left again next day, heading for Connolly's camp on the river, where they would begin picking up bullocks for sale. Then, late the next afternoon, just as I was pulling the saddle off Dubloon at the yards, I heard the strange bell. It was light and sweet-toned, coming from across the creek. Puzzled, I stood listening, then the grey put his ears up and whinnied, and half a dozen horses, followed by a rider, trotted out of the timber and followed the fence around to the yard. There was a pack on the leading creamy, which also wore the bell. The rest had a workmanlike look about them – tails pulled short, hobbles round their necks, and when they pulled up in the angle of the yard wing, nickering across at Dubloon, a glance at their tracks was enough to show they were shod.

The rider was a lean old bushman, grizzled and half deaf, and he hadn't expected to find anyone living on, much less working, the country he had come to regard as his own mustering preserves. He offered his hand and his name, which I immediately recognised as that of the poddy-dodger they called The Batman – for his habit of living in caves rather than camps. He was jolted by my presence, but he pulled the pack off the creamy and said in his soft, deaf-man's voice that he'd come to attend muster. He had the handle of a branding iron sticking out of one corner of a packbag, and coils of greenhide ropes buckled under his swag straps.

I wasn't very helpful. 'The family's over on the river country somewhere – you'll have to find them.' The creamy arched his neck over the rails, whiffling at my grey, and I stared. 'Good Lord! That's not a stallion, is it? You take him out into our working mares, Basil, and my father will have a fit.'

'Oh, he's no bother,' he said. 'Old Sultan won't look at strange mares.'

It was such an absurd claim that I could find no answer to it.

Basil came over to the house for a meal but slept at the yards and was gone by daylight. He would find the stock camp all right, I thought. He might have some funny ideas, as our conversation over dinner had evinced, but I would have bet money on his bush-craft. Basil and a few similar old rogues had been finding their way about this country for years, dabbing their brands on purloined stock and making a good living at others' expense.

When Seppe arrived on Sunday, I told him about the comical surprise Basil had shown on seeing me, and the line he had fed me about his stallion. Seppe showed no appreciation for the humour of the situation — I realised, too late, that he couldn't be expected to understand about the horse — but only concern for me.

'I don't know what Mac's thinking of, leaving you here on your own with men like that likely to ride in. Anything could have happened to you.'

I gave a hoot of mirth, I couldn't help it. 'Seppe! I grew up with men like that. I've spent my life among them.'

'What, thieves?'

'Don't be silly. Bushmen. Actually, he was rather sweet — very polite. They are, you know, those old fellas. He told me about breeding eels.' I laughed across at him. 'You put a horsehair into a bottle of water — he'd seen it himself, he said — and it turns into an eel.'

'Typical.' Seppe's voice had an impatient edge to it. 'That's what I hate about the sticks, the ignorance you meet with.'

'Hey! Come on. It's not a hanging crime to have funny ideas. Basil's a long way from ignorant, he's just had no education. He was probably out working at twelve.'

Seppe looked quizzically at me. 'Why is it that all you people up here are so slow to condemn faults? I've noticed it before.'

'Are we? I guess it's called tolerance.' I jumped up, hurt by his lack of understanding but determined not to quarrel — it was bad enough to be permanently at odds with Dad. 'I have to feed the animals, d'you want to come?'

'No.' He picked up his hat. 'My tolerance doesn't extend to being mobbed and trampled. It's time I was getting back, anyway. I'll see you next week.'

He waved as he drove off. I raised my hand in reply, then stood there with the calf feed at my feet and the memory of his impatient tone echoing in my head.

SIXTEEN

It just showed that there was always something left to learn about animals, because when Patrick next rode home, he said Basil had spoken no more than the truth about his stallion, Sultan.

'Queer sort of a horse. Never went near our plant.' He scratched his cheek where the down had turned to stubble now that he was eighteen. 'Had any visitors?'

'Only the BMR boys. Bob, the mechanic, came with Seppe on Wednesday – they'd cracked something on the trailer and wanted to weld it. I told them to go ahead. What about Basil? Has he gone? Did you pick up any of his cattle?'

Patrick snorted. 'One. Runty little steer. We're sending it off with our mob. I don't reckon he'll be back next year, especially as we put a match to three of his yards. We found a cave up the river, too, that's been one of his regular camps. All set up with a horse yard and fly-rig. There was a packsaddle in the cave with his brand burnt into the treeboards, a coupla ropes, and a bit o' tinned tucker. We kept the food and made a bushfire of the rest. That was before he turned up, of course. I think he'll have got the message.'

'And the bullocks? How's the muster going?'

'That's what I came in for. Dad wants the buyer out to look at 'em next week – we'll be in with them by then, so he can see them here – and the trucks are to be booked for the thirtieth. You can tell them you'll confirm it and give them the truck numbers on Thursday. They'll load at the Lawn Hill yards.'

I scribbled the telegrams out as he talked, remembering that day at Lily Hole, years ago now, when we had first spoken of a dream – selling our own cattle instead of droving others.

'How do they look – a good mob?'

'No more than fair, now,' he said. 'But that's from being in hand for weeks. They were very good. We'll just have to get a holding paddock up so we can muster into it in future, instead of dragging them around with us.'

'The creek's dropping pretty fast.' Now I had the garden in, water preoccupied my thoughts.

'Yeah. Well, it is August. The river's dropped a bit, too. You can see the sandbar at Connolly's. What about a feed?'

'Kettle's on. I'll just catch the next traffic list with the telegrams. Everything else okay out there?'

He was making himself a sandwich, too hungry to wait for the tea. 'A coupla the horses are crook – well, three. I noticed this morning that Wombol's not so hot either. We dunno what's wrong with 'em, but Judith's talking about some sort of poison – we've

214

come across a few dead brumbies, too.'

My hand, reaching for the wireless knob, stopped. 'That doesn't sound too good. Which ones are sick?'

'Oh, Beau. And Huckleberry, and Wombol. It's hard to tell, really, if it's the same thing or not, because they've all got different symptoms. I mean, Beau's poor and rough-coated and he drags his feet. Judith's still riding Huckleberry, but she said when you gallop him his back end wanders around like a crippled spider. He's lost a bit of condition, but then he never carries much, and when he's hot he sounds broken-winded. Wombol's got a gutsache. He was down, kicking at his belly when I left.'

'That might be colic.' The kettle was whistling and I lifted it off. 'He could recover – well, so might the others.'

'Yes,' Patrick said, 'but the brumbies didn't.'

I saddled Dubloon and rode out to meet them the day they brought the sale cattle home, but one look at Judith's gloomy face destroyed my pleasure in the ride and bustle of activity about me. It had been quiet at home without them.

'Keep away from the bulls,' she said, and I saw that they had half a dozen big scrubbers in the mob, massive beasts with horns to match, like the one that had chased Fandango and me last year on the Eight Mile. 'We've got them pretty civilised. They'll turn if you yell, but they still charge if you get too close.'

'The buyer's coming,' I said. 'And the trucks are lined up. What's the Friday face for?'

She looked behind, where Dad was poking along with the horses. I could hear the bells and see Simon's head bobbing through the wattle, but that was all. 'It's this sickness, or whatever. Creamy's got it now. He was blundering about on the dinner-camp, falling over logs and into bushes. Just couldn't seem to stop moving. We had to tie him up to keep him out of the cattle. Yet he was as right as rain yesterday.'

'What about the other three?'

She sighed, flipping a stick at a lagging bullock. 'The same, more or less. Beau's just wasting away. He's dragged the toes of his hind feet square – it's like he can't lift them. Wombol's as hollow as a drum. Huck seems all right until he gets hot. I've quit riding him, it's too dangerous when he can't control his legs.'

It was my turn to sigh, then I remembered my news. 'I've heard from Sian. Seppe was at the mission meeting the plane; he picked up our mail and brought it across on Sunday. They're officially engaged now. The wedding's in Brisbane in January. I forget the date but it'll be on the invitation. That should arrive in the next mail.'

Sian himself was working underground in the mines at Mt Isa, going to nightschool and off-siding for a builder on the weekends. He had, he wrote, put his name down for one of the mine flats at Star Gully because there was an acute housing shortage in Mt Isa. The flats were only for married couples, so they'd move in straight after the honeymoon and live there until their own house, which he planned to build himself, was ready.

'What's he know about building a house?' Patrick said that night when he had finished reading the letter.

'You know Sian.' I shrugged. 'By the time he's finished working for the builder – everything.'

~

Seppe and Frank Paxton came by the day the cattle left for Lawn Hill. We had shot poor Creamy by then, unable to bear the sight, or sound, of the agony he was in. Seppe, helping himself to a drink from the fridge, recoiled from the labelled plastic packs that filled the narrow freezer compartment.

'Liver,' he read out, 'kidney, long gut – what *is* this?'

'Organ samples. Dad post-mortemed the horse we shot. We're going to ask our stockie to get them analysed, see if we can find out what's killing them. We think it's something they're eating because the brumbies are dying, too.'

'That's bad luck,' he said, but I could see he was thinking of something else. 'Look, I talked Frank into bringing me along today because I wanted to tell you I'm flying out tomorrow. I've got a job interview in Sydney. I'll be gone about a week.'

'Are you pulling out of the BMR, then?'

He laughed shortly. 'I'd do that this arvo, if I could. I never knew there were so many flies in Australia till I came up here. Still, there's only a bit under six weeks to go by the terms of my contract, so I'll see it out. This job came up about a month ago and I applied then. It's with Rio Tinto, the company I worked for when I was in Peru. I'm pretty confident I'll get it on experience alone, with South Africa and Peru under my belt, not to mention Western Australia.'

'Of course you will. Where would they send you though – not overseas again?'

He grinned, hat at a rakish angle, the light from the door falling across the brown column of his throat where the gold chain glittered. 'Nowhere, it's a managerial job. That means an office in Sydney and the beaches, my girl, and the harbour, and surfing. Ever been surfing?' He laughed buoyantly. 'No, of course you haven't. You'll love it after being stuck out here. Don't look so gloomy – I'll be back a week tomorrow and belting over that frightful road of yours with the news.'

'I know it's bad. You don't really like the bush much, do you, Seppe?'

'The understatement of the month, dear girl. Give me civilisation any day.'

He kissed me and went out, and soon I heard the throaty bellow of their vehicle – they must have lost the muffler again – as it drove away.

Dad and the rest got back before Seppe, having seen the cattle safely off. The main roads were still not wonderful, but it was now possible to get a big truck over them. The Normanton to Cloncurry bitumen, we had heard, was nearing completion, but there was still years of work ahead before they could think of sealing the Leichhardt road. The stockie, dropping in on his return trip from Westmoreland, had taken Creamy's organ samples off to town, sealed in an ice-filled esky. The tests would take time, he warned, and, in answer to my question, he wasn't aware of any neighbouring properties having problems with horses.

'Not that it means anything,' Judith said. 'The Lawn Hill horses live on the blacksoil country, so the vegetation's totally different. Corinda isn't being worked, so it doesn't have any horses to get sick. And nobody at the mission would have a clue about their nags' condition. I'll bet they don't even have a horse book.' There had been no change in the sick horses, which had been left behind in the house paddock, and no further illness in the plant.

'They don't seem to be getting worse,' I said.

'No.' Her lips compressed. 'But they aren't getting better either, are they?'

They had stopped on their way home to pull and roll a load of secondhand wire out of the old fence at the Seventeen Mile where the road divided, one heading south to Lawn Hill, the other winding off east to the mission. All three of them were out reloading it to cart it back to build a spell-horse paddock, which was to run from the creek to the old check-fence, the day Seppe returned.

He had got the job. He gave me the boxer's victory signal as he got out of the landrover, a grin lighting up his face.

'You are incredibly good-looking, you know that?' I said as he hugged me. 'Especially when you're pleased. You got it, then? Congratulations.'

'Well, you might *look* a bit happier about it,' he said humorously. 'Are you? Really?'

'That's my famous poker face.' I put my hand on the warm, hard flesh of his arm. 'I'm happy if it's what you want, Seppe. Shall I make a cuppa?'

'No, I shouldn't stop. Shouldn't be here at all, really. We're in a bit of a rush with these last few sites, and my taking leave hasn't helped. But I just had to give you the news and bring you this. You said you liked chocolate.'

'I do. Thank you.' I slid my fingers under the ribbon and slit the glossy paper with my thumbnail, but there was no point delaying. 'You see, Seppe, it's just – I mean, I don't know how to tell you this, but –' It came out in a rush, not at all as I had planned, 'I can't live anywhere but the bush.'

I looked unhappily at him and, as his mouth opened, hurried on. 'I know. You think the city scares me, because it's strange, and – and crowded and big. But it's not that I couldn't learn to cope with that, it's that I couldn't leave this. I don't expect you to understand – city people don't ever seem to. All they see is the surface things, like the flies and the bad roads and not being able to get newspapers.' I paused to draw breath, then rushed on again before my courage failed me. 'I met an old man once, a Channel Country bushman who got smashed up and couldn't work any more. He had to move into town, just a country town, not even a very big one. He was train-droving when I met him and, you know, I could have cried for him. He was pining like an old scrubber that had been fenced off its range and couldn't get back. I would be like him. It's not a reasonable way to be, not to people like you. I know it, but it's how I am.' I felt the smart of tears and said desperately, 'I love you, Seppe. But it wouldn't work. I can't – it would be like putting myself in prison.'

'You don't mean it.' He grabbed my shoulders and stared, then let his hands drop. 'Christ!' he said in baffled incomprehension, 'you do. I thought –' He walked past me and banged his fist down on the bonnet, then turned back. 'I rang my mother and sister from Sydney. I bought a ring. I mean, how can you tell me this now?'

'Because I didn't know before. I was just happy having you here. I never thought about living anywhere else. I suppose I assumed you'd always be doing this sort of work, that you'd be in the bush.

You didn't ever tell me that you hated it. I had to work that out myself.'

'For God's sake! Is it a crime to want to have clean and comfortable living conditions? Look,' he glanced at his watch, 'I have to get going. I'm supposed to be taking gear out to the boys. But we've got to talk this out. I'll come back this evening.'

'Not tonight. The family's home. Sunday.'

'This can't wait that long. I –'

'Sunday.' His mouth set mulishly, and I said sadly, 'It's no use coming sooner, Seppe, because I won't change my mind. I can't.'

He got into the vehicle then, slamming the door hard, and I stood there watching, holding my box of melting chocolates as he drove away. He hadn't offered to give up the Sydney job.

I thought of Sian moving into town for the sake of his marriage, but he had never felt about the bush the way I did. Dad had not been able to stand the city life, and in that respect I was like him. I thought I knew now why the old blackfellas had died when they were taken from their country. Leaving it was like having a fish hook pulling at your heart.

The others returned in the early afternoon, having unloaded the wire along the proposed line. They had enough now, Dad reckoned, counting the few coils on the old wire dump near the yards, to put up a two-wire fence, which should do to hold horses.

'Whose were the tracks on the road?' he asked.

'Seppe's,' I said, then took up my hat and went out into the garden to avoid any further questions.

༄

Seppe came twice more before the BMR camp pulled out in late September, to argue and plead with me to change my mind. He looked as wretched and unhappy as I felt, and in the end we parted, I in misery and he in anger. Frank and the rest of Seppe's colleagues wanted to put on a farewell barbecue for us all, but Dad and Patrick and Judith, having stood half the new fence while the plant had a week off on the fresh feed over the creek, had gone mustering again, and I had no desire to socialise.

I lay late in bed the morning they broke camp and headed back on their long return trip to Canberra. The casual workers – the cook and camp-hands – would be paid off in Cloncurry, but the rest, including Seppe, would drive the string of yellow vehicles south. He would be half a continent away from me. And one day – in a year's time, or three, or five, or when I was forty – he would be no more than a name. Just someone called Giuseppe who had grown up in a flat above a delicatessen in one of Melbourne's inner suburbs. Someone I had met on a May morning and said a last goodbye to the following September. I lay there until the sun appeared to flood the carbean limbs with rosy light, thinking of the convoy of vehicles bumping along the track through the silver-leaf box, turning left where the road forked, vanishing behind the storm of dust their going produced. Lying there with eyes closed, hugging my pillow and feeling him go.

SEVENTEEN

Late in October there was a government-stamped envelope in the mail – the Department of Primary Industries report on the analysis that had been done on Creamy's organs. The horse had been poisoned, it said, by ingesting the *Crotalaria retusa* plant, a weedy bush that flourished on sand flats and creek-banks and bore the common name of rattlepod. There was no treatment available and no antidote to the poison, from which horses did sometimes recover, though with impaired motor ability in their hindquarters. The squared-off hooves we had observed in Beau and Wombol were, it appeared, the classic marks of the condition.

Judith said, 'But it grows everywhere, that stuff. In Horse Gorge and over on the river. The new spell paddock's full of it.'

I recognised it, too, from the black and white sketch enclosed with the letter. It was a pretty little bush of prolific habit, with bright yellow flowers and the characteristic seedpod from which it took its name. We looked at one another in dismay, but there wasn't much we could actually do. 'Landowners,' the letter had ended, 'are encouraged to control the growth of this woody weed, or pasture their stock in paddocks clear of the pest.'

'Simple!' Patrick was sardonic. 'I s'pose the bloke who wrote that thinks he's talking to someone on a ten-acre farm.'

'It sounds like it,' Judith said. 'It's a great place to start a pony stud, isn't it? I guess I should be thankful Mike never got that loading, or they'd probably be dying, too.'

'Well, maybe we'll just have to keep 'em away from the sand flats, hobble 'em back in the ridges, shift our camps about,' Dad said. 'Now we know what it is, we can watch for it when we go back out.'

This happened on the last day of the month, with the packbags being filled and paired up and the horses run in to continue the muster. The cattle were so wild that they melted back into the scrub and ranges whenever they were disturbed. But because they were territorial, all but the bullocks, which tended to range further, soon returned. So the only way to get them was in a series of quick raids back over the same country.

They left on a clear, still morning, with dry sticks and last year's leaves crunching under the horses' hooves, and smoke from a distant bushfire smeared like cloud along the northern horizon. I had been down at the pump fixing a broken belt (we were back on the soak), and came up the bank in time to see Dad cantering Pigeon towards the garden fence. The horse was flouting his tail and making little sideways steps, the ear on his blind side swivelling back to his mates trotting away up the road behind him. Seeing me, Dad called gruffly, 'Would you fetch us a tin o' tobacco from the store? Mine's empty.'

Though the cause of our original quarrel was gone, we had neither of us lost the constraint it had put upon us and spoke self-consciously to each other, like strangers.

I found the Log Cabin on the store shelves and took it out and handed it to him. Red, who ought to have been accustomed by now to staying behind, was whining in the bauhinia shade at the chain's end. Dad was sixty-one that year, lame and stooped and slow. He was thicker through the waist than he had been and the brown was long gone from his hair, but he still sat light in the saddle, with the best hands on a horse I had ever seen. He rode off at an easy canter, his bad leg sticking out, and I stood watching grey Pigeon meld with the silvery scrub foliage, until Red suddenly put back his head and howled. The sound pimpled my skin, as if a ghost had touched me, and I snatched up a stick and hurled it in his direction.

'Shut up! will yer? You sound like the hounds of Hell.' He flattened his ears and whined. He would have to stay on the chain until tomorrow, or he'd simply make off after the plant.

The days drifted by with their quota of chores and wireless chatter for company, and more than a week had passed when I woke suddenly in the dark of a moonless night to the flat, urgent thud of hooves coming up the road along the creek. I had been dreaming, some muddled tale of colts and mustering, but sleep had vanished and this sound was real. My heart jerked in fright, for a rider in haste, at night, could bring only bad news. I was out of bed fumbling for the lamp when the dogs' noisy challenge sounded, then Patrick was at the gate on a heaving horse, face tight and strained in the flickering light.

'The old fella's had a fall,' he said. 'He's in a pretty bad way. We've gotta get a vehicle and the wireless back to him quick smart.'

It was still an hour or two to daylight, the morning star had just begun to rise behind the carbeans. Patrick pulled his saddle off and dumped it where he stood, letting the sweat-sodden mare go. It was Widgie, I saw. She just stood there until he pushed her neck, then she wandered off and lay down. He had been coming all night, he said, finding his way by dead reckoning across the series of ranges that ran between the Accident valley and the river. He'd got pushed too far east by a rugged spur that he couldn't cross, and hit the track about eight miles down the road, this side of the Mimosa waterhole.

'You still haven't told me what happened.' There was no time to light the stove for tea. We were bolting breakfast standing, knowing we'd need it later, but I could hardly swallow for the weight of fear on my chest. It was twelve hours since the accident had occurred.

'We were yarding up at Batmans Hole and a beast broke back. Dad went after it – he was riding Silver, and I dunno, she plaited her feet round an anthill and somersaulted. Landed right on top of him on her back. And the horn o' that Yankee saddle he uses got him fair in the guts.'

'Oh, God!' My knees felt weak and my hands were clammy. I snatched up the wireless, which I'd wrapped in a blanket, and the coil of spare aerial. 'We want a mattress and the medical chest. Come on, let's get moving.'

It was a nightmare trip to the mission. Dad was south of the river, geographically closer to Bowthorn than Doomadgee, but Doomadgee had a hospital and an airstrip. We'd still have to carry him out across the river because there was no way to get a vehicle over it. So we'd need to drive east to the mission, crossing the river en route, get a stretcher from the hospital and men to help us, before heading west up the Corinda track until we were opposite the point where Dad lay, then walk the rest of the way. I was working it all out while Patrick drove, first on headlights, then, as dawn came, into the glare of the rising sun. He had insisted on driving, on the grounds we'd get there sooner, but he kept blinking off at the wheel. He had been in the saddle for twenty-four hours and was dead on his feet.

Alan Hockey, the mission superintendent, was accustomed to emergencies. He organised an extra vehicle, a stretcher, a nurse called Isabelle, and two other men: Rob was the nurse's husband, the other was called Nev. Alan bustled them into the mission vehicle, then piled in himself before I could convince his wife that I didn't want the tea she was insisting on making me. Leaving the cup untouched on the table, I ran out and woke Patrick, who had fallen asleep over the wheel, and we sped on our way.

We drove west, crashing over potholes and slewing round sandy corners with the dust pluming behind us, catching vague glimpses of the following vehicle. It was new country to me but I was too anxious to take it in. When Patrick finally swung off the road and began a bumpy progress across the timbered flat, I clung to the shock-bar on the dashboard, searching ahead for the river timber.

It was mid-morning by the time we had negotiated the steep

banks and heavy sand-drifts of the riverbed, and noon by the shadows when we finally reached the place where Dad lay.

Judith sprang up on sight of us, her face pale and wild. 'At last! Did you bring an injection? He's in awful pain.'

Isabelle had morphine in her satchel. One of the men pulled down the blanket that Judith had rigged over sticks to keep the sun off Dad, and Isabelle gave him the injection while I looked fearfully at him. His eyes were closed and his face, where it wasn't grey, was mottled with purple bruising. The flesh seemed to have shrunk, emphasising the bony contours of his nose and eye sockets. His glasses had broken in the fall and the splintered plastic had cut his cheek.

'I thought he was going to die in the night,' Judith said. Her voice trembled. She looked as if a touch would collapse her. There were dark shadows under her eyes, and her hair was matted with sweat. She lifted an arm to sleeve it from her face, for there was a bite to the midday sun. 'That poor beggar of a mare's been up since dark last night, too. She needs a drink.'

Peronel, tied at a little distance, was shifting about, pawing at the ground. Dad's saddle was dumped on the flat beside a long skid mark and a patch of crushed grass where Silver had fallen. We were close to a rocky outcrop, a tumbled mass of huge boulders, and there was an emu-apple tree, its leaves green as new grass against the red sandstone. I stared round at it, with the burn of heat across my back and great banks of thunderheads building to the west. And I wondered if he would die here before we could mend our quarrel.

'How long since you ate something?' I asked Judith. She just shook her head. 'Well, you should go back to camp – water the mare, get yourself a feed. Maybe you could get a fresh horse and bring some tea back? It'll be a couple of hours at least before we reach the river, it has to be a good four miles.'

My estimate was hopelessly optimistic. It was nearly sundown before me made it. We had all taken turns with the stretcher because it was killing work in the heat, with the heavy sand dragging at our boots. We had to rest every hundred yards, for Dad weighed fourteen stone or more and the mission men were not used to physical labour.

Judith rode back, at some stage, with the tea, and an hour later we saw another white man and two blackfellas straggling through the scrub on our tracks. The flying doctor was on his way, they told us. The plane would be at the mission in another couple of hours, and with one accord, because their arrival coincided with a rest stop, we all stared westward where the clouds were massed into a lowering storm that could stop any plane.

It was just on dark when we reached the far bank of the river. Wind howled through the bending gums, and somewhere up ahead a thunderbolt shattered the night, but no rain fell. Dad seemed to be unconscious most of the time. He groaned now and then, and he had twice, in a thread of a voice, asked for water, but the nurse would only give him ice from the small esky she carried.

'In case of internal rupture,' she said. Isabelle had a pleasant face and rich chestnut hair braided about her head. She couldn't have been kinder. During the rest stops, she squatted beside Dad, fanning him and laying wet cloths on his skin. He was badly dehydrated, she said. They would have to get him on a drip the moment we got back.

The lightning strike had started a fire across the river. I could smell the smoke as we loaded the stretcher into the closed back of the mission vehicle. Rob was to drive and Isabelle sat beside him, twisted in the seat to look back at her patient. I climbed in beside Dad and as we drove with excruciating slowness out to the road, I could see the hungry flare of fire crackling its way through the dry grass.

The plane had beaten the storm and the doctor was waiting. Dad was received into the long, bungalow-type hospital, and all of us – Alan the superintendent, and Peter, Rob, Nev, the two black men and Patrick and me – sat on the verandah, weary unto death, eating chunks of cold watermelon, which satisfied both thirst and hunger. None of us could get enough to drink. Judith had stayed at the camp to pack up and take the horses back home, and Isabelle was inside with the doctor.

I saw him later. Dr O'Leary was a fleshy Irishman with a high colour and fading red hair. He was a rough-spoken, unmannerly man, but everyone he ever treated had implicit faith in his medical skill. 'Well,' he said staring hard at me as if I were one of his patients, 'the news is fair – fair to middlin'. I was prepared to operate if the spleen was ruptured, but I'm satisfied it's not. We'll stabilise him overnight and get him down to the Isa in the morning.'

'Then he's going to be all right?'

'He's a very sick man,' he said, almost surly. 'He'll not be out of bed tomorrow, if that's what you're thinking.' He turned a thick wrist to check the date on his watch. 'Let me see, Tuesday. You can call me Thursday morning for a progress report, and not before.'

'Yes, Doctor,' I said meekly. 'Thank you, and thank you for coming.'

'It's what we're here for.' A smile suddenly lightened his heavy face. 'You get a good night's sleep now.'

'Can I talk to him first?'

'No, you cannot,' he barked. 'He's sleeping under sedation. You can see him in the morning.'

We got beds at the superintendent's place, and at daylight next morning I crept into the hospital and found the room where Dad lay with a drip in his arm. His upper body was bare, and above the sheet, which was folded at his waist, I could see a shadow, like a faint stain, where the bruising was coming out. His face no longer looked as stark as it had, and I guessed rehydration accounted for that, but the greyness was still there. Even if his spleen was intact, they hadn't ruled out some degree of internal injury, the sister had said. I remembered him cantering away on Pigeon that day and wondered if he would ever swing into a saddle again.

As if he had sensed my presence, his lids stirred and opened. He saw me and his eyes moved to take in the strange room and the plastic tubing attached to his arm. I leaned forward in the straight-backed chair.

'Dad, how do you feel?'

'Bloody awful,' he croaked. He was working his mouth and I saw they had taken his teeth out. They were wrapped in a tissue on the locker along with a plastic cup and a bowl.

'Gi's my teeth,' he said, 'and a drink.' The cup, which had a press-on lid with a bent straw through it, contained water. 'That's better.' He sighed when he'd finished. 'I tell you, girl, there were times I didn't think I'd make it this far.'

'I know – me either. And I wanted to tell you I was sorry.' My chin trembled and I knuckled a tear away. 'Seppe's gone, Dad. Don't let's fight about it any more.'

'All right, girl. Least said.' His voice was fainter, his eyes closing. I could see he was in pain.

I bent quickly to kiss him. 'Just hang on, I'll find somebody.' But Sister Black was already on the way, carrying the injection in a cloth-covered kidney dish.

Later, when the sun was fully up, the doctor and pilot rode out on the back of a ute with Dad on a stretcher between them, and loaded him into the plane. It took off into the smoky sky, and when it was no more than a sparkle in the blue, Patrick and I drove home, to water the garden, care for the animals, and wait for news.

Dad was slow in mending. His liver had been split in the fall. It would repair itself, the doctor said testily, as if that were something everyone ought to know for themselves, but his body was badly bruised and it would be at least a fortnight before he was out of hospital. Mustering was effectively ended. I had sent a telegram to Sian about the accident, and while he fitted hospital visits around his work, Judith and Patrick took the plant across to Horse Gorge and let it go.

Next time we drove to the mission to collect the mail, instead of calling on the superintendent and his wife, who received all visitors to Doomadgee, Patrick and I went round to Isabelle's house. She opened the door, beaming, a baby on her hip and two older children peering round her skirts. We just wanted to thank her and Rob for their help with Dad, I told her, but she brushed the words aside.

'Come in, the kettle's on. I'll call some of the others. They'd love to meet you.'

There was a party line linking the white workers' residences at the mission – two rings for the nurses' accommodation, three for the school teacher, four for the office girls. By the time the tea was made, all those she had called had arrived bearing plates of biscuits and cake – Helen and Pearl and Jan, Lionel and Fred and Rob himself – all excited at the prospect of meeting strangers. For the white missionaries living there, Doomadgee was as good as a closed community. It was run by the Brethren Church, which discouraged contact with outsiders, few of whom ever got past the superintendent and his wife.

Isabelle was frank about it. 'Next time you come,' she said, 'don't go to the Hockeys, come and have a cuppa with me.' Helen, who was deputy head of the school, echoed the invitation. I thanked them sincerely – I saw few enough fresh faces myself, and none of them female. It was good to have women only fifty miles away whom I could visit. I would, I assured them, come often.

'You can start when your father gets out of hospital,' Isabelle said. 'I'll meet him off the plane when he flies out and you can pick him up here. All I need is the date.'

༄

Beau, the sick skewbald, died the day Dad got back. Driving out through the new paddock on our way to the mission, Judith and I saw the crows flapping about, and bumped across the spinifex to the edge of the swamp, where we found him lying dead in the grass.

We didn't tell Dad. We were so shocked by his appearance when he got off the plane that we could find little news to recount. His colour was bad and he seemed to have aged ten years. He looked, Helen said for our private ears, as though he'd had the stuffing knocked out of him. I knew what she meant. He seemed physically to have shrunk.

Judith drove home as carefully as if he were made of glass. She pulled up at the double gates, and when Patrick came out we saw his face register shock at the sight of Dad. Age had finally ambushed him, and from that day on we all thought of him as old.

EIGHTEEN

It showered right through January, including the day that Sian was married. When I looked up from the wireless where I was waiting to send our congratulatory telegram, there was a perfect double rainbow arching through a misty sky above the eastern range. None of us had met Leoni yet, for soon after the engagement she had been posted to the hospital at Charters Towers, and there was no question of any of us affording the fares to Brisbane to attend the wedding.

We pored over the photographs when they came: Sian, dapper in an unaccustomed suit, with his hair cut too short and his bride on his arm. Leoni had pretty hair, brown like her eyes, and looked lovely in her veil and gown. She was slightly shorter than Sian, with her head tilted to the camera in one shot, then bent sideways in the next, the veil streaming away and the heels of her shoes showing under the flattened dress.

'Must have been awfully windy,' Judith said. Then, 'Oh, yuk! Look at the hat.'

It was her going-away outfit – a yellow suit, white gloves and shoes, and a round white shape perched right on top of her head. 'Looks a bit like a pudding basin, doesn't it? She is pretty, though, even in that. Well, I guess we'll meet her some time this year.'

We didn't go to Mt Isa often, usually making no more than two annual trips for rations and fuel, which we carted out in 44-gallon drums. It was a swag-and-tuckerbox job to get there because all manner of breakdowns and dry bogs awaited the traveller in the dry season, while in summer early rain could bring down the creeks and turn the track to quag.

February brought storms but no proper monsoon, and the wireless chatter reflected the district's unease. Some areas of the country had received no rain for twelve months. We had feed in the horse paddocks at the house, but the creek had not even run. The waterhole was little more than half full, and driving to the mission for the mail, something one would not normally contemplate in February, even the dry cattle we saw were low in condition.

March brought no more rain. By the end of the month, the green had gone from the swamp grasses and the humidity from the air. The winds veered to the south, the strident cry of the cuckoo ceased, and the Wet, such as it was, was over. There were still three payments to make on the property, and though Dad hadn't left the house all summer, the rest of us had. We knew how poor the pasture was likely to be across the Gulf and that cattle prices would fall as a result.

236

Everyone able to do so would sell early, but that didn't include us.

'We've got to get that paddock up,' Patrick said. 'By the time we run a sale mob down in a season like this, they'll be bony as milking cows. Maybe we should forget mustering this year and hit the road again, drove a coupla mobs to get the payment in and a bit extra to keep going on.'

'We can't just leave the place for six months,' Judith said. 'There's the chooks and the calves and the garden, and anyway you'd just be signalling, "Help yourselves" to Basil and his mates. They'd be back like a pack of dogs into a poultry run the minute we were over the boundary.'

'Well, we have to do something. It'd be best if Dad did go droving,' I said, thinking it out. 'He certainly shouldn't be racing around in a stock camp and working wild cattle in a yard, but just poking along. Because we're not going to be able to make him quit, he'll fly into a rage if you even suggest it. So if two of us went and two stayed, we could be earning money and keeping the poddy-dodgers out of it, too.' I knew neither of them wanted to be responsible for Dad's health so I volunteered myself. 'I'd go with him, but one of you has got to stop here and look after things.'

'We'll have to put some black boys on. And you could take a dozen extra horses in the plant, twenty even,' Judith said with sudden inspiration. 'Get 'em away from the poison. Even if they were never saddled all season, it'd be worth it if it kept 'em alive.'

'So all we need now, then,' Patrick said, 'is a mob.' And within a week, almost as if it had been prearranged, Dad limped out into the garden, where I was digging vegetable beds, with a telegram he had just taken down.

'Look at this. Almost too good to pass up. Eddity Station's looking for a drover – they've got fifteen hundred steers to go down into the basalt country round Hughendon.'

We left in mid-April, travelling the plant south through Gregory, where Maccadams Plain was nothing but grey stubble and the river swished tiredly by beneath the bridge. It had had no more than a two-foot rise in it all summer, they said at the pub. The new hall was finished. It had been built in front of the police station and was twice the size of the old one, with a supper room down one side and wide double doors at the front. The country looked worn and dry, and everyone we met had a gloomy prognosis for the year.

At Nardoo, while Dad was talking to the men, I went across to visit Brenda, one of the Webber wives. She came quickly down the steps on sight of me, saying gaily, 'Well, come on. I want to hear every detail. Have you got your ring with you?'

I stared at her.

'Your engagement, silly! To this handsome geologist you've been keeping hidden. So how did you meet him and what –?'

'Where'd you hear that?' I scarcely recognised my own voice, and Brenda stopped in mid-sentence.

'Why . . .' she floundered. 'I believe . . . at Gregory. Wilma Foster told me . . .'

'Well, it's not true. I am not engaged, and you can tell her from me to mind her own damn business in future.'

'Right.' Brenda's colour was now as high as mine. 'Look, I'm sorry. Let's have a cuppa and forget it. Where are you heading anyway?'

'Over Normanton way.' I followed her inside, praying my face would cool. 'A station I've never been to, so it will make a bit of a change.'

We chatted over tea until Dad beeped twice on the horn to let me know he was ready to leave. The black boys would have the horses at the Twenty Mile and be looking for the camp by now, I thought. Tomorrow we'd turn left for Talawanta, another place we had worked at, but after that the new country would begin.

Eddity was south of Normanton and east of the Flinders River, a neat complex of sheds and outbuildings set around the shaded homestead. A bit of a creek fringed with gudda-percha scrub ran behind it, and there was a fenced compound full of steel posts and wire, and a set of heavy timber cattle yards. It was Flinders-grass country, open plains alternating with lightly timbered flats, and river channels running the length of the property.

We had Jervis and Michael from the mission with us again, and Dick, our old horse-tailer, and as large a plant as Judith could talk Dad into taking. When she and Patrick had mustered them out of Horse Gorge, they found another six dead: Beverly, Stormbird, Pigeon, Token's dam Trinket, Sungirl, and Dad's big skewbald Simon. They had also made a discovery about the poison – although the feed was light on in the valley, the bright green leaves and yellow flowers of the rattlepod were everywhere.

'It must come up on the first rain,' Judith had said. 'That's why so many of them are showing symptoms of the poison – they eat it because there's not much grass around, and don't touch it other times. If we could just get a decent Wet to make a body of feed, I'd bet they'd be safe.'

But for now, at any rate, the horses were browsing on Flinders while we camped on the creek below the homestead, waiting on the station men. They were drafting the working horses in a flurry of racing limbs and tossing heads, and trying out the wildest in the yard. They couldn't get started, Les Bolton the head stockman told us, until the road across the Twelve Mile plain had been graded, because the blacksoil was so pugged up by cattle it would rattle the camp caravan to bits.

In the meantime ringers and jackeroos swung the gates and lined the rails of the yard while Les dropped his drafting stick on tossing manes, calling, 'Bush gate,' or, 'He's yours, Mick.' Or Joe, as the case might be.

When each man had his half-dozen, all but the quietest were roughed in the yard to save grief later when they had to be saddled and ridden in the open. The brown gelding they called Wheelbarrow was given to a lanky blackfella with the front name of Scoob. Holding the reins he rolled his eyes resignedly.

'He been put me, I t'ink, this fella.'

'Oh, get on with it, man,' Les snapped. A good rider, by his own account, he was contemptuous of those less capable, and in particular lorded his skill over Nick and Jamie, the jackeroos. Jamie, the older of the two, could ride a pigroot, but Nick, a flat-footed, studious-looking lad with glasses, was hopeless.

Scoob's prophecy proved correct. The brown horse exploded under him, arching his back and spinning, dropping one shoulder as he came down. His rider sailed out of the saddle and hit the ground flat on his belly with a force to make me wince. Wheelbarrow stopped dead as soon as he felt him go and just stood there, blowing softly at the trailing reins.

'Buckjumper, is he?' I asked Barney the mechanic, who stood beside me at the rails. He had been a ringer before he switched jobs.

'Yeah.' His voice was hard. 'Bolton does this ev'ry time. Likes ter top-note himself, so he picks the poor riders an' shows 'em up. Young Nick there, you watch, he'll tell him ter take the ride, then when the 'orse has chucked 'im, he gets on it himself.'

Les was already looking at Nick. 'You could stand some practice, Goggles, Gawd knows! Get someone to hold yer specs and give him a try. Unless anybody else fancies him?'

Nobody did. And Nick, who I had expected to obey rather than refuse the unfairly offered challenge, surprised me. He had gone red, and then pale, the muscles of his jaw knotting. He said scornfully, 'You know I can't ride him. Why should I risk getting hurt just so you can look good?'

It fairly took Les aback. Nick might have been working in the stock camp, but as a jackeroo he was a company man whom Les had no power to sack. His eyes narrowed and he said, 'Well, if you ain't got the guts, I guess it's down ter me.' Then Jervis, bouncing over the rails like a tubby black ball, squeaked in his high voice, 'I'll ride him, Boss,' and seizing the fallen reins hopped aboard.

Wheelbarrow, who must have had many easy victories, got the lathering of his life. Jervis, with his short legs, plump body and moon face, didn't look a rider but he certainly was. He spurred the horse every time it landed and coo-eed every time it rose. When he stepped off, grinning through the dust, with the brown gelding heaving in a lather of sweat, the ringers gave him a cheer, which Les didn't join in. He snarled, 'Seein' you fancy yerself, tell old

Mac I said you can work him for the station.' Plainly he didn't relish the prospect of sharing his leather crown.

The original plan had been for us to do a couple of weeks' paddock work at Eddity, getting the steers mustered and dipped for the road, but it didn't turn out that way. We had scarcely got started in early May when it rained, and no short-lived storms either, but a steady downpour, resulting from a tropical low driven inland off the coast. It went on for days, running rivers, filling dams, and making impassable barriers of the blacksoil plains. The wireless at the Cleanskin outstation, where we had hutted up for the duration, echoed the graziers' relief with stories of four inches here, five there, creeks over their banks, and a fuel tanker tipped over in a bog on the Burketown road. Judith sent a telegram reporting eight inches at home, and we registered ten in the outstation gauge.

We were sharing the ramshackle old building with Alec Smerden, the elderly caretaker, having earlier pulled a tarpaulin over the truck and let the horses go in the Cleanskin horse paddock. They turned their rumps to the driving rain, miserable as drowning cats, while the water ran over the black clay underfoot and the river rose and work went out the window. I still had to cook, but at least there was a stove and enough dry space to stack the logs that Dick split for me.

When the rain stopped and the clouds cleared to pale wintry skies, we pulled the tarp off the truck and aired damp hats and coats, but the ground was still some days off drying. In the paddock the horses flung gouts of mud behind them as they galloped into the trough, and the stars looked brittle and icy-cold in the night sky. The river was up, cutting us off from the station, but a week after the rain stopped I saw somebody slogging up through the grey trunks of the coolibah heading for the outstation.

It was Barney, the mechanic. He'd pulled himself across the river on the flying-fox – a forty-four cut lengthwise and suspended from a cable some fifteen feet above the water. The pulleys were rusty and needed oiling, but it was the last few yards, pulling the drum up the sagging cable while holding it against his own weight, that had been the hardest, he said.

'Damn near had me arms outa their sockets.'

'You had a reason for doing it?' Dad looked up from his pipe.

'Yeah. Bolton and Scoob're back the other side. They want old Alec to drive the landrover down and tow 'em across. Scoob's gunna take the horses over to Leeson's yard – camp's gorn out there, y'see.'

We all rode down in the vehicle, glad to get out after the days spent cooped up. The ground was still greasy and the tyres spun thick layers of mud off their treads. You could see the green shoot coming through the feed, and the air was fresh and cool, bringing the distance close. It was a blue, blowy day with an edge to the wind. The river surface sparkled coldly in the thin sunshine and I pulled my jacket tighter round my neck. It was only mid-May but in the shade it felt like June already.

Les shouted something we couldn't hear above the river. It didn't matter. Scoob was already squatting in the flying-fox, and it didn't take a genius to work out that we had to attach the wire coiled at the base of the anchor tree on our bank to the vehicle.

Barney made it fast to the tow-bar, then vaulted up to stand behind the cab. 'Righto, Alec.' His voice was loud above the purring motor.

Alec drove like a maniac. The landrover bucked away, whipping the first fifty feet of wire off the coil as the flying-fox started to move.

'Take it steady!' Dad bawled over the revving engine.

Then Les was waving his arms and the flying-fox stood suddenly on its tail, flipping its pulleys off the cable as the wire on the far bank snagged a log. Even then, Alec didn't stop. We yelled, and Barney beat on the cab roof until the vehicle skidded to a halt. Then it ran back a few feet, allowing the flying-fox to slide down the cable to its lowest point.

Scoob had been flung out when it tipped up. He'd managed, somehow, to grab the pitching barrel and hung for a moment beneath it, pedalling his legs, before dropping about twelve feet into the river. His hat came off and spun away on the current, bobbing like a cork. The water was so cold it hurt just to look at it. Dick and Jervis started to run down the bank, and Barney catapulted off the vehicle and went after him.

Dad said, 'Jesus! Is that old fool Alec deaf, or just plain crazy?' But he didn't expect an answer. Scoob's head broke the surface and he began to thrash his arms. He was a good way downstream, but Dick had almost caught up. He clutched at the drowned foliage of a tree, then worked his way along it, and Barney and Dick pulled him up the slippery bank. One of his boots was gone, dragged off in the mud, and the skin of his face and hands looked shrivelled and grey with cold. His teeth were chattering so much he couldn't speak.

The head stockman seemed in no hurry to follow after Scoob. Barney had wandered back by this time and was looking with lively interest at the far bank.

'Bolton gunna risk it, I wonder?' But even as he spoke, Les was pulling off hat, shirt and boots and giving a hitch to his belt. He swam across, angling upstream, his arms flashing rhythmically through the grey water. 'Wouldn't yer just know he'd be a regular fish,' my companion muttered disgustedly when the head stock-man stood on the bank squeezing at his jeans.

'Cheer up,' I said. I didn't like the man much myself, but as he turned his head to say something to Dad, I saw that his wet hair no longer concealed the bare spot his hat had always hidden. 'Look, he's going bald.'

Later, after both men had dried off, they left, riding in borrowed saddles, with Scoob's bare black foot sticking incongruously through one stirrup. They'd have the mob together in less than a week now the country was drying out, Les assured Dad, because most of the steers were already paddocked when the rain started. There was a couple of days' work in mustering the channels for them, another day in the yard to draft and dip them, and they would be ready to hand over on the twenty-ninth.

⁓

It was a six-week trip, and with the green spreading daily through the grass and Dad riding again, I was suddenly glad to be making it with him. It would be the final one, I thought, and how better to be doing it for the last time than over a fresh route, with an abundance of green feed?

Dad seemed to be handling the riding well enough, but he tired more easily than he had, and there were times when he would come over shaky and grey-looking and have to sit down. I worried about him and the possible consequences for the station if he died before Patrick was ready to take over.

The mob got away on time but to an awkward start, because on the morning of the second day we had to leave the vehicles behind and take to the packs. A swampy hollow backed by a creek, both of them filled with milky-grey water, blocked the way. Cattle were bogging to the hocks crossing it, so the truck would never make it through. Better to leave it, Dad decided, and get one of the station men to drive it round by the top road and meet up with us in a couple of days.

I groaned. I hated grubbing about with packs but could not deny the sense of it, because there was really nothing else to be done. There'd be no shelter, no table, and I'd have to cook in billies and do without my spacious tuckerbox, but we could scarcely pull the mob up and wait for the road to dry. Time lost on the road was money lost. How often had I heard Dad say that?

We camped on a broken plain that first night, and the mob settled like champions and were gone again by dawn, moving into the new day with their mile-eating stride. They were all Brahmans, the new breed that was gradually infiltrating the Gulf – tall, sleek-coated cattle with swinging dewlaps and floppy ears.

The following day, late in the afternoon, Sian turned up with Leoni in a borrowed four-wheel drive, arriving just as we pulled up the plant on the open flat I had chosen for the night-camp. I stared at him, half dismayed, as he brought her proudly over to where I stood hanging onto a couple of horses, my hair a tangle under my hat, and my shirt like something you'd wiped the floor with. That was the other thing about packs – the grease that kept the leather pliable attracted dust. You couldn't touch them without getting filthy.

After the introductions, Sian borrowed Dick's mare, Tangerine, to ride back to the cattle which were about a mile behind us.

'You'll be right, love, I'll leave you here with Kerry and you can get to know each other,' he said.

'But, Sian . . .' Leoni protested faintly. I knew how she felt and I wanted to kick him. He had never had any more sense than a cabbage. I didn't want to be stuck with a clean and dainty sister-in-law in her ironed blouse and cotton pants any more than she wanted to stay. What I wanted was twenty minutes alone to bathe and change my clothes and get the knots out of my hair. But sundown was coming and the men had to be fed, so I grabbed the closest packhorse, which happened to be Locket, and was reaching to unbuckle the metre straps on her load when Leoni spoke behind me.

'What can I do to help?'

'Er,' I said. 'Nothing, thanks.' Locket jerked back, snorting. 'She's a bit touchy. Why don't you wait over there in the shade? Packs are awfully dirty.'

'Oh, I don't mind.' She smiled brightly, and before I could suck in a breath to bellow, 'Don't!' she stepped straight behind the mare and began worrying away with her manicured nails at the straps on the off-side of the pack. After my heartbeat had subsided, I said, 'Leoni, don't walk behind the horses, and particularly not this horse, ever again, okay?' I said it very slowly so she couldn't misunderstand.

'Oh, I'm not frightened of them.' She smiled at me. 'Sian said they wouldn't hurt me.' Sian, I thought crossly, was an idiot.

When the cattle were settled on camp, he did the dogwatch. Later, when Dick had ridden out, he ate, squatting on his heels the way he always had, talking while he cleaned his plate, with Leoni perched on a rolled swag beside him. He was full of talk, about his job and the house block they were saving to buy, until Dad interrupted him.

'Some of us want to sleep. Whyn't you drive your sister round to Eddity so she can pick up the truck? 's'bout forty mile, but the longer we leave it, the further away we'll be.'

'Righto,' Sian said. 'Reckon they'd sell me a bit of fuel?'

'There's a drum on the truck,' Dad grunted. 'Use that.' He toed his swag open and sank onto it, boots and all, and closed his eyes.

It was a long, slow drive to the station. The road was still wet in places, and twice I got out and broke a green bush to mark the side tracks around a boggy spot. The gates, when we came to them, looked strange in the headlight, and shadowy bushes loomed like waving men. Once a night hawk, swooping into the headlights' beam, smacked against the windscreen in a splay of broken wings. Leoni shrieked but the body was already gone, sliding down the glass to be whirled away in the rushing night. The air, coming cold through the window beside me, smelt of damp earth and rotting vegetation, of cattle and hot engines. The stars were very bright, and far over, thin as a nail paring, a silver slip of moon hung above the timber line.

'Won't do us much good on the trip,' I said. The horse-paddock gate came up in the headlights and Sian, pulling up, looked across at me over Leoni's sleeping head. 'No, still waning. The old fella's showing his age, and a good bit extra.'

'I know. It's the accident. It's just about finished him for work. That's partly why we're taking this mob – well, we need the money, too, but it's also keeping him out of the stock camp. Not that we told him that, of course.'

'But can you manage without him? Patrick's just a kid still. Maybe you'd all be better off getting out, selling the place, I mean.'

I looked at him. 'We won't sell. We haven't come this far to give up now.' I got out to open the gate.

It was nearly three in the morning when I nosed the truck gingerly into the camp by the glow of the parking lights. The cattle never stirred. Jervis, on the far side of the mob, was singing something about the glory seat as I pushed the fire together and fell into bed. Sian and Leoni had headed home from Eddity. He had twenty-four hours before his next shift started, but mine began in two and a half. I pulled the blankets up to my ears and was instantly asleep.

NINETEEN

The first ten days of the trip passed uneventfully. The route was wonderful because the rain had fallen all along the way, and the sappy green feed sparkled in the mild sunlight. The steers came onto the camp full, to stand or lie like statues chewing their cuds with gusty sighs. If it was to be our last trip, I thought, then we had a quiet mob and a better season to remember it by. Dad was tired each night but seemed fine otherwise.

We had crossed the Saxby River and were following it south, though at times the route diverged so that the mob watered at dams or bores. We would have to cross the river once more after we passed Lyrian Downs, and here the truck had again to go around because the Saxby still ran and only the higher, gravel crossing was trafficable.

'How far is it?' I asked. 'The round trip?'

'Sixty miles, say.' Dad measured it on the map with his thumb. 'About that. The crossing might be dicey. It depends how the gravel's stood up to the flooding. Perhaps I'd better take the truck. You and Michael and Jervis go along with the cattle. Sling a pack on old Legs for a dinner-horse, and I'll be waiting over the river when you get there.'

It suited me. I had been bogged, misdirected and had broken down along unmarked stock routes so often that I could have qualified for *The Guinness Book of Records*. It would be a holiday to ride with the cattle instead.

'Here's the stage,' Dad said and sketched it right there in the dirt at his feet. 'Dead simple. Follow the trails till you've crossed two paddocks, then turn down the fence till you hit the river. The channel will most likely be a swim, so don't crowd 'em on the bank. Then you head straight out through the timber to the open country. We'll camp there.'

'Seems simple enough.'

'See you don't lose 'em on me.' He heaved himself up, holding his hip, and I swung the coffee billy for the watches.

We were moving next morning by daybreak, the plant horses feeding alongside the cattle. It was bitterly cold. I wore a greatcoat over my jacket, knowing I could add it to Legs' load when the day warmed up. I had cut sandwiches for the four of us, rather than just packing bread and meat, and added a billy and the filled neck-bags to give us water for tea. There were tea-leaves and sugar in the packbags and both Dick and Jervis were smokers, so there was no need to bother about matches.

The sun rose, glinting on bit-bars and buckles, and spinning leaves, and my heart rose with it. It was a pleasure to be astride a good horse in the peace of the morning with the whole golden day stretching ahead. The steers, red and grey, brindle and yellow, moved steadily forward, eating up the miles, silent save for the rip of tearing grass and the tread of hooves. Out on the wing of the mob, Michael was whistling, the sound counterpointed by the intermittent jangle of horsebells.

We made our dinner-camp in a patch of scrub halfway across the second paddock. I had cut too many sandwiches, and faintly irritated by the waste, rewrapped the three leftover ones and stowed them in the packbag. Keeping the bread supply up was my main preoccupation on the road.

'Ho, well.' Dick's spur rowels jingled as he stood and stretched. I took the hint.

'Yep. Better make a move.' The others were already up, and little knots of steers starting to feed out from the shade. We reached the next fence and turned down it, with the shadows falling back to the east, and as the day grew on and the air began to cool, came at length to the river.

Dick went over first with the horses. He led Legs across, the grey's crooked neck and coffin head looming over his own mount, a flighty creamy pony called Trigger. He didn't like the water, but Dick picked a wandering course and managed to avoid the deepest parts. The cattle weren't so fussy. With Jervis on the lead, they started over, drinking as they crossed, to plunge up the far bank with streaming flanks and high-cocked tails. The sun was low behind the coolibahs as we drove through the river timber and no more than an orange afterglow when we reached the red flats of scalded claypan that should have been the night-camp.

It was deserted. A long open stretch of country fringed with the green of whitewood, box and bauhinia and, clumped between, the white-starred bushes of flowering conkaberry. It was an ideal cattle-camp, but there was no sign of Dad or the truck.

Dick hobbled up while we settled the mob down then one by one rode in to swap our saddlers for night-horses. I got a fire started in the lee of a conkaberry thicket, and Dick rode back to the river to fill the billy and neck-bags. We'd have tea to drink at least, but it looked like being a long, cold night.

The leftover sandwiches, shared between the four of us, amounted to no more than a taste. But it was better than we'd have for break-fast, I thought, unless Dad turned up first. He had to be bogged or broken down, because I couldn't let myself believe that anything – an accident, a sudden collapse – had happened to him. I had lit a fire, which we kept feeding, but it was still too cold to sleep on the hard red earth so I lay watching the sky and worrying. I wondered how Patrick and Judith were managing at home, and thought about Sian in his flat in town, with other couples living cheek by jowl on either side of him, and remembered what he had said about selling. We would never do that, though. And lastly, as I did every night, I thought about Seppe, wondering what he was doing now and if he was happy. It did no good, but in this matter I couldn't seem to help myself.

Mine was the dawn watch, but there was no need to call Dick at the end of it. I heard Tassle's feet thudding away through the timber and by daylight, because there was nothing to wait for, we had fresh horses saddled and were moving again. There was no track to follow, only the deep-trodden trails of the stock route, covered now in grass. My stomach was grindingly empty, and when Jervis made a joke about catching a goanna, I said, 'I tell you true, mate, the boss not back by dinner-camp all you fellas better catch lizards, and one for me, too.'

Luckily it didn't come to that. Dad drove up just before noon, lurching out of the cab, drawn and weary, his boots and jeans streaked with clay. The truck was covered in it, too. Great gouts of mud splashed the load, and the chassis was smeared end to end, as were the headlights, bonnet, and the spare hobbles buckled along the side rails. There was just an arc of windscreen left where the wipers had been working. You'd never know, I thought looking at it, that the truck was red, because all you could see was mud.

Dad looked tired to death. He said, 'Cattle okay?'

'They are,' I told him, 'but we're starving. Where was the bog?'

'Oh, 'tween the river and the main road. The jack packed up in the end and I walked out to the main road. I was lucky, coupla blokes came along in a Toyota and pulled me out. Then I did a tyre and had to go back to Lyrian to borrow a jack. The cook there told me Kennedy's been shot.' He was scraping a fire together as he talked, and I turned from the table where I was slicing bread to stare at him.

'Well, of course he was, five or six years ago. What's that got to do with anything?'

'Not the president of America, one of his brothers – Roger, or Robert.' His eyes were scanning the settling mob. 'They're a gun-happy bunch over there. But just shows, there're worse jobs than droving.'

We went on down south-east into colder country, through red dawns and starry nights, past Mt Brown and Lara Downs, with the miles slipping away under the swinging stride of the steers. Every couple of days I drove ahead to the different homesteads, to fill the water tanks and give notice of our coming to the landholders. This was sheep country, and the people and their attitudes were different. Often I had to give my message through a latched screen door and was only rarely asked inside.

Richmond, or at least the rail line running through it, marked the end of the tick belt, so we had to dip both the mob and the horses. Dad wouldn't put the plant through the plunge dip, it was too easy for horses to break their legs in the long concrete bath. They panicked and reared in the crush, unlike cattle, which jumped doggedly to their fate. We would have to spray them then, the stockie said, even if it took an extra day.

We were camped on the common next to the yards, which were right at the edge of town, and that afternoon, while the spraying was underway, a man drove into the camp. We'd had our share of sightseers gawking slowly past, for fifteen hundred head was a big mob for the inside country, where everything was moved in trucks.

Dad left the rails to speak to him, and from the far side of the truck I heard the stranger say, 'I see you have a jillaroo in the camp.'

'That's no jillaroo, she's my daughter,' Dad said. 'Why? What d'you want?'

He was a local businessman, he said, and his girl Shona, who had just finished school, was mad to go droving. She had talked of

255

nothing else since the steers arrived in town. Of course he wouldn't consider it, until he had realised there was already a woman in the droving camp who, perhaps, wouldn't mind chaperoning her? If Dad would just take her along for a week? She could come home on the train from anywhere down the line. No need for wages. Let her make herself useful for her keep.

'Has she got a swag, or something to sleep in?' Dad asked, adding, 'I suppose she can ride?'

'Oh yes, owns her own horse, rides all over the country. We'll fix her up with some bedding then, and I'll run her over in the morning. This is her lucky day.'

'The question is, will it be ours?' I asked once he'd gone, and Dad looked at me in surprise.

'It's only a week. Lighten up, for God's sake! A troop o' bagpipers wouldn't trouble this mob, let alone one kid.'

She arrived next morning as I was packing the truck. The cattle had already gone, to her obvious disappointment.

'Oh, I wanted to ride with them.' She pouted. Her face was round, with childish contours still, and she had pretty shoulder-length hair, golden as ripe wheat.

'You've got to be up before daylight for that,' I told her. 'Chuck us up your saddle. Your dad said you were seventeen.'

'Yes. How old are you?'

'I'm twenty-three.' Her mouth fell open and she stood, the sun in her hair, staring up at me.

'But you look quite young.'

'Thanks,' I said dryly. 'What do you want to go droving for? It's hard work, you know.'

'But it's so romantic! We learned about it in school. There's a poem –'

'"For the drover's life holds pleasures that the townsfolk never know." That one, you mean?'

She nodded.

'Did you know it was written by a lawyer? I don't suppose he ever went droving in his life.'

'But he knew all about it,' she argued stubbornly, '"cos he wrote the poem, didn't he?'

Shona irritated me beyond measure. She was as blithe and carefree as a butterfly, leaving tasks half done and forgetting what she was told almost as soon as you had finished saying it. She seemed incredibly childish to me. I thought I had never been so young, and then, with a twinge of guilt, wondered if I envied her because of it, whether it was this that was at the root of my irritation. She was as friendly as a puppy, wanting to play with everyone, and in the end, on the fourth day out of Richmond, I dumped the bread dough into the camp oven and went across to where she was sitting on her swag in the shade of the truck. Dick hadn't turned up yet with the plant, and the cattle were miles back. Rubbing at the flakes of dough on my hands, I took the plunge.

'Shona, you've got to stop romping around with the men the way you do.'

'Oh, they don't mind.' She was filing her nails, and lifted her hand to her mouth to blow on them. 'They never say they do, anyway. And they aren't tired like you said, or how come I couldn't catch Michael yesterday?'

'When I said that, I was hoping you'd take the hint, but you didn't, so I have to tell you straight out. They don't say anything because they're too embarrassed. You put them in an impossible position. How are they going to be rude to you and say what they think when you're a white girl? Any white bloke who'd been working all day and didn't want to be pestered would tell you to get lost pretty quick, I can tell you.'

She flushed and sat up, her eyes flashing. 'You're just being horrible because they're black. I don't care about that stuff. They're my friends. Just because they're different —'

'Shona,' I said, because her voice was climbing, 'just listen to me! Aboriginals are under the Act. That means by law there are lots of things they're not allowed to do. They know that, and they have to get along as best they can with the whites. Some whites cheat them, some treat them like children — they can't do what they want like we can. None of them have it easy, so if you like them you should try and give them respect. And that means not carrying on like you do. It can be dangerous for them, you see. What if some redneck saw you somewhere with Michael and went and beat him up, just to teach him not to mess with white girls? Do you think he'd be believed if he said it was all your idea?'

'I guess not.'

For the first time since we'd met, she was actually listening. Her soft face was thoughtful and she had forgotten her nail file.

'Well, it's something a girl has to think about if she works out here. There're lots of coloured men in the camps, some of them black as pots, others not much darker than me, and also plenty of white men who won't like you liking them.'

'I'll remember that,' Shona said, adding naïvely, 'you know, you're nice, really – I didn't think you were at first. And pretty when you smile.'

'What, even though I'm so old?' But I was touched by the compliment.

'Yes.' She seemed to puzzle over it. 'It's funny, because the rest of the time you just look sad.'

'That's definitely old age,' I said, and got up quickly to check on the bread.

There was scrub beyond Richmond which, after a couple of days, had turned into broken plains with nameless river channels wandering through them. At Darrowdale they were spraying nagoora burr, which grew shoulder-high to a horse, as thick as it could stick along both banks. The steers with their smooth coats shed the burrs readily, but not the horses. Their heels and mane hair seemed always to carry a forest of spikes to catch unwary fingers hobbling and bridling in the dark.

The tractor had trundled off by the time I had selected a camp. I backed the truck into wilga shade a couple of hundred yards from the channels, with half a mile of open plain for the night-camp. Shona rode in then from the feeding steers, which were a dark smudge on the horizon. She rarely put in a full day's riding, and Dad considered her too unreliable to have on watch. As a result she was never tired, and now she mooched about the camp, then sat on her swag and sighed.

'What can I do?'

I looked up from the magazine I was reading. 'Have a bath. You won't get a better opportunity. Wash your clothes while you're at it.'

'How am I going to do that?'

'Go down the river and jump in. Take some soap and a bucket for your clothes. Go on. Nobody's going to see you and you can't get lost, it's just through the burr there.'

She trudged off, bright hair flopping on the shoulders of her leather jacket, and I went back to my magazine. Time got away. Dick, who was sleeping under the truck, muttered something and rolled on his side, and when I next looked up a pair of emus were stalking by, only a stone's throw off, their bristly heads twisted sideways to stare at the camp.

Then Shona screamed. I jumped to my feet and ran to the edge of the burr in time to see her careering out of the channel clad only in her jacket and crash into the nagoora thicket. Barefoot and yelling her head off, she limped out towards me, then burst into tears.

I put my hands on my hips. 'What on earth's the matter? I thought you were being murdered.' She had burrs sticking to the flannel lining on the bottom and flaps of her jacket, burrs in her hair and scratches all over her legs.

'There was someone there – in the bushes,' she hiccuped, 'watching me. He started to yell – so I ran – I thought he'd catch me – What are you laughing at?'

'It was a bird, you twit. A cocky, for a bet. Look, why would anyone be lurking about in a bush on the off chance that somebody, some day, was going to pop along for a bath? Where are your clothes?'

'I – don't know. I must've dropped them.'

'Well, you'd better find them and pull the burrs out so you can get dressed. It's getting late, and the men will be along soon with the cattle.'

I turned to go, saw her face and turned back resignedly. 'Okay, hurry up then, and I'll wait for you here. And I'd advise you not to tell anyone or you'll never live it down.'

It was on the very next camp that we met the vanguard of the rat plague. There were rats everywhere in their hundreds of thousands, gnawing the roots and seeds of the grasses like a plague of locusts. It was a common occurrence in the open country following exceptionally good seasons. They swarmed in the blacksoil, vanishing underground during the day and coming out to forage at night. Riding my watch I could hear their scuttling progress and high-pitched squeaking, and sometimes catch the glow of red eyes reflected from fire-shine or carbide light. They chewed boots and swag wraps and saddles left on the ground. The tuckerbox had to be kept shut, and our meat, which Dick normally spread on bushes to air overnight, was now hung from a wire strung between trees. Jervis' hat had its crown chewed out one night, and any time I woke, I could hear the snorting and uneasy stamping of the horses at the night-horse tree. I had seen a plague before round the Julia Creek country, but that had been small compared to this. The land itself seemed to heave with rats. It was something to remember our last trip by, I thought. As was the doleful look on Jervis' black face as he inspected his ruined hat, and the sight of the grey mare we called Lindy Lou suddenly flattening her ears and striking down hard to crush a squeaking rodent – I hadn't known horses would do that.

We were very close by then to delivery. The last couple of days were spent following the bitumen, the steers, docile and sleek (they had picked up condition on the road) swinging their heads to watch the traffic pass. We delivered to the agents at the trucking yards in Hughenden, and that same afternoon drove Shona and her clumsy swag down to the station and bought her ticket. She hugged me warmly, and looking at her open, laughing face with its sunburned nose, I wished her well in my heart. Her hair was all lengths where I'd cut the burrs out.

'Good luck,' I called as she waved gaily from the carriage window.

'I'll be droving next year. Unless I get married instead.' The boy at the service station across the road had kissed her behind the pumps, she'd told me the previous night, but she hadn't decided yet if she'd marry him.

'Well, she's no loss to the road,' Dad said as the train pulled out. 'Remind me of her next time I'm agreeing to something silly.'

'She's only young.' I sighed and he raised his brows.

'You've changed your tune, haven't you?'

~~

We trucked the horses back to Mt Isa. There had been a telegram waiting for us at the agents' – the offer of another trip, this time with cattle Eddity had bought. A thousand head of cows from Vanwell Park, with a starting date in ten days' time. The train would save the horses' legs, and if Dick and Michael travelled in the guard's van, they could walk them out from the Isa in less than a week.

It seemed at first that we'd take almost that long to load the horses. The train didn't arrive till sundown, but even under flood-lights it was difficult getting them up the narrow crush into the dark cavern of the wagons. They didn't like the way their hooves echoed on the boards, or having to duck their heads to get in. Legs threw himself over in the crush and had to have his forequarters physically dragged from under the welded steel rails. When at last we had him in the wagon and the doors shut, the engine driver said, 'And about bloody time, too.' He was an hour behind schedule, he grumbled, as if that were more important than the horse.

Dad, Jervis and I walked back to camp then, watching the lights prick on like glow-worms across the town. It was strange to see them, and to imagine the lives of all those other people: agents, chemists, housewives, teachers, and people from the paper shop and the bakery and the bank. Their lives seemed alien to me, and I watched them curiously for a moment before turning aside to push the fire together and start tea.

TWENTY

Vanwell Park was north of the Isa, a scrubby run in ridgy country thick with turpentine and wattle. There were snappy gums on the slopes, spinifex, and gullies of broken stone, and down on the softer ground round Ringbolt bore, where we took delivery of the mob, miles of silver-leaf box.

A young stock and station agent called Tom Wallace was there, overseeing things for the new owners. He came across to the camp and introduced himself, a big, fair young man with a hearty manner and the sort of flat-crowned hat that agents wore. He had it all arranged, he said. The bulk of the mob – they were spayed cows – were in the holding paddock and there were a couple of hundred in the yard. They'd been added to make up the numbers and had been drafted and had their weaner calves taken off just that morning. We could hear them bawling from the camp, a continuous roar of sound.

Dad took his pipe out of his mouth, stared in the direction of the noise, then back at the agent. 'You're sending that lot with me? And you expect me to hold 'em in this scrub, and their calves taken off this morning?'

Tom Wallace lifted his brows, puzzled. 'Well, of course, they're thirsty now but once they've had a drink, Mac, they'll settle down and forget about their young 'uns.'

'Jesus,' Dad said in a wondering sort of tone. 'You oughta be bagging rice, son, not buying cattle. Don't you know when a nursing cow's had a drink that's just when she looks for her calf to suckle it? But you want me to poke 'em into the mob and drive 'em away. Simple as that. They'll give us hell in the scrub and hell on the camp. I dunno why I ever agreed to touch this mob.'

It was a sentiment he was to repeat often over the next few days. We went out through the tip of the Wagaboonyah Range, red, hole-filled country where lancewood grew in straight-stemmed profusion, then on past the Thornton and Seymour rivers, old, known ground to us. The first mob we had ever droved had been from Thorntonia, and Dick had grown up there amid the scrubby hills. They had a proper big devil in the ground, he reckoned, which was probably as good an explanation as any for the wildness of the station herd.

There were mineral salts in the soil, too, because every claybank we passed saw the cows rushing at it, ten and twelve of them down on their knees at a time, licking and shoving to get at the soil. There were hollows in the banks when they'd finished, and their muzzles were covered with red. They chewed voraciously at the bones of any carcass they came across, even green bones with bits of hide and flesh still clinging to them. They needed the supplements that cattle-lick provided, Dad said, and told me to wire a message to Eddity asking for a truck to be sent over with mineral blocks, and salt, to feed out on the night-camps.

We passed Police Creek and the Lily Hole turnoff and pulled up for half a day at The Knobbies. We were out of the hills by then, on the Gregory River, and I had calculated that we would be home by late September. I was worried about Dad. He had lifted his saddle that morning to swing it onto Silver's back, and collapsed instead, with the saddle on top of him. I had rushed over, my heart in my mouth, as he got shakily onto his feet, swearing that it was no more than a dizzy spell. But his face looked sickly under the tan.

'Sit down. And eat something,' I said.

While he was doing so Dick quietly saddled the mare for him, while Michael and Jervis let the cattle off camp. Dad had ridden out shortly afterwards, but he was still shaky at dinner-camp. He lay down by the front wheel of the vehicle when he rode in and would take nothing but a pannikin of tea. After lunch he went off with the others to water the mob, and immediately that was done rode back to camp and lay beneath the truck, dozing in his swag, his scuffed boots sticking out under the table.

Late in the afternoon I made some tea and opened a tin of fruit to see if he would fancy it. He ate a little but without much appetite.

'You want me to contact the station and get them to send somebody across?' I asked. 'Or should I call home and get Patrick to come down?'

'I'll be right.' He ate another peach slice as if to prove it.

But I was in no mood to be put off. 'You don't look right, Dad. You're as clammy as a frog. If you're too crook to go on, it would be better to say so now and hand the mob over before we have a smash.'

'Give us some more tea, will you?' He held out his pannikin. 'And don't fuss. I said I'm all right. A man just gets old, and it catches up with him.'

I wanted to say that I knew plenty of people his age and none of them were falling down weak, but I bit my tongue. It was the first time he had ever even hinted at physical weakness. It was true that he no longer rode colts, and at home he worked the tail instead of the lead, or poked along behind with the horses, but we had never said to him, and he had never admitted, that this was because he was old and no longer up to galloping. It was one thing for us to know it, I thought, but quite another to have him lying there spent and weak finding it out for himself.

'Okay, then.' I patted his leg, picked up the remaining, untouched peaches and tipped them into the creamed rice I was cooking.

That night we split his watch between us so he'd have a full night's rest, and it seemed to do him good, even though he sat uncharacteristically late by the fire next morning, drinking a second pannikin of tea while the men took the cattle off camp.

The Eddity manager sent the truck of lick across with Nick and Jamie, the two jackeroos. They were supposed to wait for the mob at Gregory, but having arrived early in the day got bored and drove upriver to meet us. They gave us the news during dinner-camp: the cook's little terrier had got its leg broken in a dog trap, Barney had pulled out after a row with Les

Bolton, and Scoob had ridden Wheelbarrow. The horse had humped up once, then trotted away like a regular lady's hack. 'That's Jervis' doing,' I said. Then Dad consulted his watch and told Jamie to follow me down to the night-camp where he could spread out the bagged salt.

'Just cut the bags and dump them. It won't hit the ground with this lot.'

I had to get fuel at the Gregory pub, so I showed the boys the camp on the common, then drove back to the bowser to fill up. That done, Jamie gave me a hand to cart wood from the timberline, and no sooner was the fire lit than the cattle were there, even though it was early, rushing from bag to bag as they found the salt spread across the night-camp.

'You won't have to watch them tonight,' Nick said. 'Look at 'em. Like they were glued there.'

Dad came riding up just then and overheard. 'Oh, they'll clean it up before dark. Few bags of salt won't go far with a thousand head, but it'll steady their craving a bit.'

'Ah, but we chucked the blocks out, too,' Jamie said. 'The more they eat of it, the less you'll have to carry on with you. Just plain sense, isn't it?'

'Jesus!' Dad looked appalled. 'Yer did what?' Bay Suzie leapt as the spurs hit her, then he was racing at the nearest clump of cattle, which scattered, still chewing from his approach. He jumped down, and even from the distance I could see dismay in every line of his body. 'Bring the truck,' he bellowed at Jamie, who hastened apprehensively to obey.

We loaded all forty-five of the blocks again. More than half of them had had their tops licked out and the corners chewed off. Three or four, incredibly, were almost completely eaten.

'Jesus!' Dad gasped, sagging against the truck tray. 'They'll be dropping like flies.' He stabbed a finger at a rounded cake of lick and glared at the two jackeroos. 'Where'd you get these blocks from? They're over a third urea, you bloody fools. Two ounces o' that stuff straight can kill a bullock. Why didn't yer bring the ones I asked for? Even then you wouldn't feed 'em straight off. Not to cattle with a craving like these have got.'

'It's what was in the shed,' Nick blurted out. 'The boss said it'd do. Will it really kill them, Mac?'

'You can lay money on it,' Dad said.

He was right. At daylight there were twenty-three dead on the camp.

I packed the tuckerbox up after breakfast, then got the snig-chain out, and Dick and I towed them away, carcass after bloated carcass, far back into the scrub at the edge of the common. Dad looked exhausted but he was furious too. He had sent the blocks back to Eddity with the two jackeroos and a scribbled note for the manager.

'What did you say in the letter?' I asked when the truck had driven off.

'Nothing I wouldn't have told the bloody fool to his face if he was here.' Dad grunted. 'But mainly that we're pulling out. I said we'd hang on here with the cows till he can find someone else. Remfrey's over at the pub and his plant's just behind him – I told him that, too. So we shouldn't be waiting long.'

The news was welcome in a way, but it left me troubled. 'We've never quit on a job before.'

'We've never had that happen to us either. Twenty-three dead. Jesus!' He shook his head. 'Well, from here we can be home in a week. Time enough to get a bit o' work done before the hot weather hits.'

It would cause talk, I thought, pulling out like that. They'd say the deaths were Dad's fault, and that was why Remfrey (if he took the cows on) had the mob. I knew Dad would have realised this, so he must truly have had a sickener of things for it not to weigh with him. He prided himself on his reputation on the road and his knowledge of cattle.

Two days later, it was all settled. Eddity had engaged Vic Remfrey to finish the trip, and Dad had got Michael and Jervis a lift back to the mission. Then, Dick, Dad and I took the plant home. When on the last day I reached the Three Mile gate with the horses, Patrick was sitting under the big beefwood tree there stolidly chewing his lunch. Muscatel came whinnying out of the scrub to the horses, followed by Pirouette and Gleam, all three flaunting their tails and kicking up their heels.

'What are you doing?' I asked by way of greeting, and Patrick picked the Donald strainers out of the dirt.

'Mending the fence.' There was a half-coil of wire on the gatepost and old Quartpot tied behind him in the shade.

'If you've finished, you can give us a hand with this lot then. Dad's gone to Doomadgee to take Dick back and pick up the mail.'

'Where'd you camp last night? Didn't expect you back for ages yet.'

'At the Dry Swamps, still a bit of water left there. Dad had a barney with the fella at Eddity, chucked the mob up.'

I told him about it as we rode in, looking around at the dear familiarity of the country, the swamps still carrying a tinge of green, and the station hole reaching almost to the road crossing. It lay motionless under the blue sky, mirroring leaf and branch of the paperbarks and the jewelled dart of a kingfisher's flight. When the horses pushed in to drink, the ripples rocked out from their legs, giving scalloped outlines to their reflections.

Red and Larry met us halfway down the horse paddock, and Judith, hearing the bells coming, had walked across to the yard to swing the gates wide.

'You're back early. Thought you weren't delivering till the end of the month,' she said. 'How's Dad?'

'Gone to the mission with Dick.'

'Hope he gets the mail, then. We haven't had any for three weeks.' She caught Opal and began stripping the hobbles off her.

Afterwards, when we had taken the plant back across the creek to the spell paddock, we slipped off our bareback mounts and carried the bridles back home. It hadn't changed much. It was still an ugly iron shed but coloured washing flapped on the line, and the lawn beneath it was vivid green. The great mass of creepers shading the verandah was in flower, as were the chrysanthemums by the back door.

'I had carnations, too,' Judith said. 'And carrots this long. Everything took off after the rain, just look at your trees.'

I had noticed their growth. I looked around, seeing the hens beyond the garden fence, the black cat with her forepaws tucked under her body in the doorway, and the pink flush on the tips of the bauhinia bush at the gate.

'The bauhinia's shooting. Surely it isn't going to rain again? What have you been doing?'

'Making a road,' Patrick said. 'I've got a line blazed for the holding paddock up in Goat Pocket Valley, but we can't get the material in without a road, so we've been making one. So far you can get the tractor along it okay, but there's a coupla steep pinches we might have to winch the old blitz up.'

'Never mind that now.' Judith was making tea. 'How come you're home anyway? I thought the trip –'

'I know. Dad quit at Gregory and Remfrey took the cows on.'

I told them about it from the beginning, about Tom Wallace and the newly weaned calves, the cattle's craving for minerals and what it had led to. 'Must be lousy, phosphorous-deficient land, that Vanwell Park. They were chewing up bones so green they stank. Dad said right at the beginning he wished he hadn't touched the mob – I thought it was just talk because of that smartalecky agent, but looking back I reckon he meant it. He hasn't been so well lately, not sleeping, getting off his horse deadbeat, that sort of thing. He passed out one morning too – he should see a doctor, but I suppose there's as much chance of talking him into that as . . . as . . .'

'Having him turn vegetarian?' Judith said.

'Something like that.'

Patrick went off to mend a tyre, and I buttered another piece of bread.

'I don't know what we're going to do about Dad. He was angry when he quit, but you know, I think he was – well, not glad but relieved, to have the excuse. The work's just too much for him. He seemed okay with the first mob but the cows worried him. Fretted at his nerves. I think that's why he collapsed.'

Judith sighed. 'Well, he's not going to sit home and go into voluntary retirement, is he? What was the country like down Hughenden way?'

'Lovely. You've never seen such feed.'

I told her about the trip, and picking up Shona in Richmond and her run-in with the burrs.

'She sounds a right dill.' Judith was unimpressed, and I thought, with sudden insight, that there was very little frivolity in either of our natures. We had, perhaps, been too busy, or had always carried too much responsibility to have room for superficial things. And thinking about it, I realised that it was true of most of the women I knew: a frivolous bushwoman was a contradiction in terms. Most of those women had a ready sense of humour, but they were practical to the bone. It was as if, for all of us, life were a droving job, something you rolled up your sleeves and got on with, and those who fiddled about with unrelated matters, or sat down to despair en route would never make it through to the final stage.

We built the holding paddock that summer, hauling the material over the travesty of a track that Patrick had gouged across the ranges. He had only had the old Ferguson tractor to work with, so the track looped about like knotted string, seeking the easiest going over the rocks and the thinnest patches of scrub. He made twenty-three miles of road in this fashion, as direct as the topography of the land allowed, because Patrick had a wonderful eye for country. He had already picked out future sites for dams, which we would need, he said, when the station was boundary fenced.

'Jesus, boy! You're getting a bit ahead of yourself,' Dad said, but Patrick didn't see it that way.

'It's got to happen, otherwise we're never going to improve the cattle. There's no point buying bulls until we clean the scrubbers out, and that'll never happen till we're fenced.'

'One thing at a time,' Dad said.

Patrick, however, disagreed. 'That's the old way of doing things, and it's not gunna work much longer. The cattle are starting to go into saleyards now, and ours aren't gunna stack up too well against places like Planet and Gregory where the herds have been paddocked for years.'

'This way o' doing things has worked well enough for the last sixty.'

'When it was all open range,' Patrick said. 'Well, now it isn't. It's like saying you can still manage with a horse and cart when everyone else has trucks. As soon as the last payment is made, we want to be thinking about more fencing.'

I thought of all the other things we needed, the foremost being an airstrip, something that had been on my mind ever since Sian's accident two years before. And in the strange way that things happen, the very next day, while the others were out getting a killer, the manager of Redbank Mine, which was situated over the border and well north of us, arrived. The company was planning an aerial survey, he told me, and he was looking for a place to site an airstrip somewhere south of the Nicholson on Bowthorn country. Would that be a problem?

'You've got to be kidding,' I said. 'Except for a grader I can't think of anything we need more. Come on in. You can show me on the map while the kettle's boiling.'

TWENTY-ONE

There wasn't much rain before Christmas that year, so we were able to attend both the speech night at the mission school and the teachers' break-up party. Getting to Doomadgee was not always easy in summer, though, because there was a lot of low-lying ti-tree country between us, making literally miles of swamp, as well as two large creek crossings and the Nicholson River. Still, it was worth the risk of getting stuck because, disregarding the weather, which of course you could never do, driving to Gregory for the Country Women's Association party or the New Year dance was out of the question. That amounted to a round trip of two hundred and forty miles, which was by our way of reckoning distance a ten-hour drive.

'A full-blown ball wouldn't be worth that.' Judith was clear about it.

'No.' I had never danced with Seppe, so there could be no memories to hurt me, but I still didn't want to go. It would be better to watch the drama of the school concert and join the barbecue afterwards with the teachers. We had made many friends at the mission, particularly among the young school teachers, all of whom were adept at creating their own entertainment. And the school concert, often unintentionally, figured high on the list.

This one was no different. Only the three of us went, swooping at tremendous speed along the windy road through the Accident swamps to get over the wet crust before the weight of the vehicle broke through it. The river was running a shallow stream across the main channel, and when Patrick pulled up on the edge of it we heard, in the sudden quiet as the engine died, the distant rumble of the falls. The sun was setting behind us, and in the darkening sky ahead a long flight of flying-foxes rose and fell above the river timber. We washed at the water's edge and changed our clothes – the only way to arrive clean – then swished through the river's flow and up the bank, our headlights tunnelling the dark.

The school was a raised building, so the concert was held under it on the wide expanse of concreted floor. The manual arts class had created the stage, and the teachers had rigged curtains at either end, more to delineate the area and serve as wings than with any thought of opening and closing them. There was a huge audience. Entertainment was as much a rarity for the Aboriginal population, which numbered about seven hundred, as it was for us. Everyone was there, from barefoot old grannies to babes-in-arms.

Sitting with Helen and Isabelle at one end of the long row of backless benches, I let my eyes wander over the mass of seated people, picking out the men who had worked for us. I caught the eye of an enormous woman seated cross-legged on the ground in a dress like a tent. When she waved and gave me a dazzling smile, I recognised Big Sally from Lawn Hill.

The first act proved a non-starter for the year ones. They were dressed as rabbits, with cardboard ears and cottonwool tails, and having been coaxed onstage by their young teacher were greeted with such an uninhibited roar of mirth that they fled. Jan mustered them again and they reappeared in a huddle, but the audience could not contain themselves and this time the little black rabbits went for good – under the stage, into the wings, out into the dark. Jan whirled on the laughing, clapping crowd. 'I think you're all very rude,' she cried, and ran off in tears.

There was an abashed silence. Someone went after her, another teacher picked up his guitar and began a clap-along chorus, and the show went on. I had never, I thought, really appreciated how shy the bush Aboriginals were. Even with an audience of largely their own people, the hula dancers in year five could not be persuaded to face them. They gyrated obstinately with their backs turned, bowing to the vacant night when they finished, presenting twenty grass-skirted backsides to the cheering crowd.

Helen rolled her eyes in despair. 'I don't know if it's farce or tragedy. No matter how you plan ...'

Perhaps wisely, they had left the nativity play to the year sevens, but even this fell apart, for Mary, settled onstage with a washing tub lined with spinifex to represent a straw-filled manger, had forgotten baby Jesus. Somebody tossed the doll from behind the wings but one of its legs came off in mid-throw, and the young mother, faced with two flying objects, caught neither. Baby Jesus hit the third king, who yelled and dropped his plastic canister of river water, which was masquerading as myrrh. It doused the makeshift powerboard and there was a bang, a brief blue flash, and the lights went out.

'Thank goodness for that!' Helen murmured in the warm darkness, amid long, wailed 'oooohhs' of disappointment from the uncritical audience. 'I don't think I could have stood much more.'

Driving home afterwards, we discussed the concert and the barbecue that had followed it.

'Did you see Isabelle's son in the corroboree scene?' I asked. 'He certainly looked comical, a painted white boy alongside all those painted black ones. The people thought so too, they were pointing and laughing. He wasn't bad, though.'

'I liked the bit —' Judith began, and was cut off when Patrick suddenly stood on the brakes and killed the lights.

'Hang on,' he yelled, then swerved violently and steered us wildly into the timber.

'What —?' I twisted to peer back and caught a brief glimpse in the starlight of something bulky and dark, lumbering off with lowered head into the scrub.

'Buffalo.' Patrick sounded terse. 'Lying in the road. We'd have had a long walk home, if we'd hit him.'

'Supposing we still could,' I said.

It wasn't buffalo country, but every year a few big old bulls that had lost their place in the herds to younger challengers wandered into the Gulf Country from the Territory. We had encountered three so far, but never quite as close as that. The memory of it kept us wakeful for the rest of the two-hour journey home.

～

Christmas 1968 was a quiet affair, just the four of us, with the distant timber line melting into mirages, and the heat making the tin roof crackle. We were back on the soak again, water our greatest pre-occupation, with the pump constantly stopping and starting. To get a break from it, we packed up the Toyota on Christmas Day and drove across the range to Elizabeth Creek, where the water was clear and deep in the big gorge hole. The precipitous road down the face of the cliff no longer worried me, and I couldn't think why it ever had. We built a fire in the shade of the paperbarks edging the hole and ate our Christmas dinner there, then swam and fished through the heat of the day. The clouds bounced up over the range in mid-afternoon, big white ones towering into the burning blue, and when they had covered the sun, Judith and I climbed the gorge wall.

'You're mad,' Dad said, settling back under a tree with a book. I tipped my head up to study the sandstone wall, which was scored with cracks and broken ledges. It looked easy enough, and the view from the top would be spectacular.

We found a bowerbird's playground under a conkaberry bush at the mouth of the gorge. The corridor of woven grass in its centre was surrounded by bits of shell, white pebbles and fragments of bleached bone.

'Look!' Judith held up a teaspoon tarnished from long exposure. 'Who in the world, d'you suppose . . .?'

'Very genteel poddy-dodgers?' I had never seen a teaspoon in stock camp cutlery. 'Must've come from a mining camp when BHP was prospecting round here through the fifties. Hang on.' I felt in the pocket of my jeans for the lids of the soft-drink bottles we had emptied with our meal. 'I'll leave him these. He'll think it's Christmas.'

'Be right, won't he? Come on, are we going to climb this cliff or not?'

We went up carefully because the leather soles of our boots were slippery, grabbing with our hands at the bare roots that spread like tentacles over the sandstone from trees growing right atop the cliff. The bright green foliage of emu-apple gave way to the squat grey shrubs of dead-finish and the occasional cluster of vine. Then there was only the last stretch of rock, and when we had hoisted ourselves up onto our stomachs and wriggled over, we were on the top, where the thin coating of pebbly soil grew spinifex and a scatter of snappy-gum trees.

'What a view, eh?' I turned slowly clockwise, taking in the opposing wall, the thin trail that was the track down the cliffside, the lower gorge – no more than a watery gleam between timber – then layer upon layer of range shadowed in lavender and purple under the cloud-laden sky. There was a storm falling to the west, I saw, like a black curtain drawn over that part of the range.

'We should do this more often. Every Christmas, say.' I waved my hand to encompass it all. 'All the things you worry about – Dad's health, the water supply, stuff like that – they make you forget that this is here.'

'Nobody is stopping us – coming back, I mean,' Judith said.

'It's made a nice Christmas day, even if I never thought you'd be here for it.'

It was the first time in all the months since he had left that she had alluded to Seppe.

'Well, I am.' I looked at her. 'And I will be, at least until I get a better offer than that.' I nodded at the panorama before us. 'Do you think you could live in the city now?'

Judith didn't hesitate. 'Not likely.' She knew it wasn't an idle question. 'Is that what he wanted?'

'Yes.'

Perhaps one day I would feel able to talk about it, I thought, but not yet. 'Look,' I pointed, 'the cloud's moving. Let's go down before the sun comes out again. I put the Christmas cake in – we can have some for smoko before we pack up.'

⁓

It rained throughout February and March, heavy, constant rain that thundered on the roof and sheeted over its unguttered edges. The creek rose, the frogs chorused nightly in the swamps, the insects multiplied, and, when it was over, the feed was belly-high to a horse and rippled like a green sea in the April winds.

The stock camp – Judith, Patrick and Dad – went out in May, for the first time with the gear on a vehicle rather than the packs. It meant that they could not only carry the portable radio for emergencies, but also get Dad home quicker if he was ill. And the probability was that he would be. He had come down with a kidney complaint over summer, and had twice put his back out welding up gates for the new yard we were building. Patrick had taken over the job, and Dad had done little more then, for the rest of the summer, than sit on the verandah working hide and, occasionally, limping over to the yard to find fault with the way things were going there.

The morning they left, I watched them out of sight, then wandered back from the saddle shed and worked in the garden for a while, overseen by old Larry who lay chin on paws at the back gate. There was no need to chain him now because he was too old to follow a horseman away. Then I took a broom to the store shelves, stacking and dusting the cartons of goods and knocking down the mud nests that the wasps were constantly building there.

It was midday by then. I switched the wireless on to catch the noon traffic list, then made the tea and went to find a book to read while I ate my sandwich. Running my hand along the shelf, my fingers came to rest on *A Passage to India*. Memory stirred at the title. I pulled it out and turned to the fly-leaf, and there it was, the address of the correspondence school in Brisbane. I had always intended to make use of it one day, and that day, I realised, had arrived. The concept of studying was no longer a vague ambition but something I really wanted to do.

Forgetting lunch, I got out the pad and sat down to write away for an enrolment form.

﹏

By July, when Neil Armstrong landed on the moon, Dad and the others were droving our sale cattle down to the Lawn Hill yards to be trucked away and I was writing weekly assignments, studying Hardy and *Macbeth* and trying to discover what a split infinitive actually was. I listened to what I could pick up of the broadcast from Houston, and that night went out to stare at the moon above the carbeans. It looked as it always had, a yellowy-silver disc patched with shadows clearly discernible to the naked eye – a real drover's moon. Yet men had walked there. The realisation bemused me almost as much as the knowledge that I was soon to be an aunt. Leoni was pregnant, Sian had written. It seemed only a handful of years since we had all been children ourselves and now, in a few months, we would become uncles and aunts to a new generation.

Sian's daughter, Wendy, was born a couple of days before the lightning balls started the fire at Shady camp, which burnt out the valley. It was one of those fierce dry storms of early summer when the skies split apart and the ranges seem to leap before the forces unleashed from the heavens.

Patrick had been dragging the verges of the new airstrip with the Ferguson tractor when the balls hit, whizzing like blazing projectiles through the standing scrub. There had been an instant conflagration, which he tried unsuccessfully to combat by clearing ahead of it with the tractor. He had staked a front tyre almost immediately and then there was nothing for it but to abandon the tractor in the centre of the airstrip and hoof it the six miles home.

It was sundown before he got back, with the west glowing like a furnace behind him. Bushfires were an annual summer event. They mostly burned themselves out, doing little damage, and even benefited the country by thinning the scrub and clearing out the old season's dead growth. But this fire was different. It was heading straight down the valley towards the paddocks where the working horses ran. If we could not save the feed, we would have to return the plant to Horse Gorge where, last year, twenty-eight of the workers had died from poison.

'It'll burn itself out,' Dad said as we ate dinner. 'When it gets outa the scrub onto the sand flats, it'll run outa steam.' He dismissed the subject by starting another. 'I see George Butcher's got Wentworth on the market. It's in the paper.'

'Yeah? Well, I'm not waiting to find out if it stops or not,' Patrick said. 'There's feed enough to carry it even on the flats.' We finished the meal quickly, loaded shovels and drinking water onto the Toyota, and left Dad with the dishes. There was too much walking involved in firefighting for him, even if he were to deem it necessary, but Red, thinking he was missing out on something, leapt aboard just as we pulled away.

Patrick heard the thump as the dog landed in the tray-bed. He stuck his head out the window, bellowing, 'Go home! G'wan, you great galoot! Go home!' but Red never took any notice of Patrick anyway. He stayed where he was, a black shape against the stars, his ears and tongue blown back by the wind.

There was still too much breeze to backburn, so we drove to the airstrip and tried to improve on the break that Patrick had begun there. Across the front the flames had died to a crawl. They marked the outer edges of the burn, where the ruby eyes of smouldering logs winked from total blackness. There was enough light to see the eddies of pale smoke rising and the tortured silhouettes of crisped leaves on branches whose bark had burnt off.

'Should be able to hold her now,' Patrick said.

We got the shovels and began work along the face, smothering the creeping flames. Red snuffled and pounced amid the spinifex, chasing lizards and grasshoppers. Animals were safe enough, they could move before a fire – even an echidna, which was pretty slow, could bury itself – but insects, reptiles and nestlings were fair game.

We worked steadily in the fitful glow, shovelling sand, kicking smouldering sticks back onto burnt ground. Then, ahead of us, the fire reached the spinifex. Fed by the wax-coated stems, new life poured into the flames. Suddenly they were eight and ten feet high, the heat of them like an open furnace.

Arms up to shield our faces, we stumbled back, and then the fire was in the wattle, which blazed into white incandescent beauty. The sap burned in little blue spurts through the whiteness, and banging like a string of crackers, the wattle branches exploded, showering coals like shooting stars.

'It's like that fella with guns to the right of him, guns to the left of him – remember?' Judith said. 'We're getting surrounded here.'

'Cannons, you mean. Tennyson.' The poem was in one of my study books. 'Let's get out of it.'

We fell back, and then back again as the night wore on. The vegetation was mostly spinifex, and no matter how many creeping grass flames we could smother there was no holding the spinifex. Its clumpy growth covered the soil thigh-deep in places, and when a patch like that caught all you could do was run.

By midnight we were in the creek watching the banks burn. The loose bark on the gums flamed; and the shrubby growth around their feet, the rusty-coloured grasses and old leaves and dead wood all roared together. By the glow above it, which paled the stars,

I could see bright leaf embers and flecks of floating ash – and Red scrabbling and biting at something in the sand.

'Leave it!' Judith hauled him off, then stooped to pick up a terrapin the size of a dinner plate. 'Talk about optimism! Fancy him trying to beat a fire! I'll take him home with us.'

The terrapin was playing dead, everything pulled in under his shell. With Judith balancing it upside down on her palm, we shouldered our shovels and trudged back to the airstrip to collect the vehicle, because it was no good continuing until the wind either dropped or changed.

'Once it gets outa that damn spinifex, we might have a chance,' Patrick said. He had a hole burnt in his shirt from an exploding ember, and my legs felt as if they had walked ten miles. Red lined up with the rest of us at the water bottle. I pushed the crown of my hat in and filled it for him, then we threw the shovels up the back and drove home.

The light was out, but Larry stood stiffly in front of the gates, whiskery muzzle grey in the headlights. It was late, past midnight by the stars. I put my hand down to feel for the terrapin's shell under the seat and screamed when it bit me.

'What the hell –?' Patrick switched the cab light on, then grabbed the terrapin and pulled it off me. Its beady eyes shone in the weak light and I could see blood, like a black thread, down the side of my fingernail. It had no teeth but its bony jaws gripped like a vice.

Mindful of her hands, Judith dropped it over the garden fence where it could find its own way to the creek, then we trooped wearily inside, pausing for a moment on the back verandah to look to the west. Patrick clicked his tongue and I knew what he meant.

The valley was ablaze from range to range. The fire was miles away, but it seemed so immediate that I almost expected to hear the crackle of the flames. I listened but there was nothing save the sough of the wind soft against my face and the wailing of curlews along the creek. There was a world of desolation in the sound and I felt the hairs brush up on my arm. As if, I thought fancifully, they recognised the glow for what it was and cried their plaint to the listening night.

TWENTY-TWO

We went back the next night, driving through roiling smoke onto the blackened earth where it would be safe to leave the vehicle. The fire had been burning steadily down the valley all day, but we couldn't go out before nightfall. Firefighting was the most exhausting work I knew, without doing it in forty degrees of heat. And the hot air produced willy-winds that drove across the burns, sucking up embers and flaming leaves that created new blazes wherever they fell.

'How are we going to do it?' Judith asked when we were on the scene. It was as bright as day along the fire front, though the stars were out behind us. I could see the colour of the man's handkerchief she wore pulled across her nose and mouth, and the gleam of the stirrup-patterned buckle on her plaited hatband.

Patrick, as usual, had a plan. We only had to turn it, he said.

Nobody ever tried to put out open-range fires – you would have needed a hundred volunteers for that. Instead you saved your paddocks if you could, using whatever man- or woman-power the station had. We would start on the northern side of the road where the front was burning slowest and work our way across the valley towards the range behind the creek. If conditions were right when we got there, we would backburn from the northern bank of the creek. If not, we would try to turn it into the ranges where it could burn itself out.

'Or keep going till it gets to Elizabeth and cleans up the brood mares' feed,' Judith said.

'It might.' Patrick picked up his shovel. 'We'd have time to turn it again, though, once we've got it away from the paddocks here. Well, talking won't fix anything. Let's go.'

It was back-breaking toil. We worked spread out in a line within sight of each other, shovelling earth on the flames, scraping and digging to clear a break, whacking the back of the blade over break-away blazes, resting when we must, then shovelling again. The smoke made our eyes smart and tear, and Judith got a coughing fit that had her retching. But gradually the blackness grew behind us. Every so often, the crackle of flames flared to a sudden roar as the fire hit a thicker patch of fuel, then we'd all run to the trouble spot and work furiously together to prevent it getting away from us.

When we reached the creek, my knees were giving out. I lay gasping in the sand, listening to the thunder of my heart, which was louder even than the flames, while Judith raked the bank clear of flammable material. There were drifts of leaves in the creek bottom which could carry the flames across. We had stopped the lower end of the fire but that was only half the job. It had already crossed the creek higher up.

Behind us the valley lay dark under a skimpy moon, with only the red eyes of burning logs and stumps to break the blackness. We sprinted up along the southern bank to get at the flames eating through the long grass there, thrashing at them with green boughs while the heat scorched our faces, until finally we had them out. Beyond that was a gravel ridge with only a sparse growth of spinifex, and then the steeper face of the range. It was mostly rock and witchetty bush, with a crown of scrub and a thin carpet of spinifex over all. You couldn't get a shovel into the rock, so we beat at the creeping fire with the flat of our blades. It was slow but effective, until the wind came.

It came from behind us, laden with the acrid stink of ash and charred timber, and had the force of a ten-knot gale. We were halfway up the range when it hit, and my mouth dropped open.

'Dear God!' The words, spoken or thought – I couldn't tell – hung in my mind as the crown of scrub seemed to sway forward then explode. The sky was scarlet, shot through with fierce yellow flames, and the night roared like a beast in agony as the fire raced along the ridge faster than a man could ride.

We stood and watched it go, hurtling through the night like a burning train, curving slightly east from its southerly line, heading straight for the spell paddock. It would have taken an ocean to stop it.

'Jee-zus,' Patrick said slowly. 'It must be doing sixty miles an hour.' Flakes of burning ash and bits of lighted sticks rained down. He stomped on one that flared into flame at his feet, then shouldered his shovel. 'That's that then. The paddock's gone. There's nothing more we can do so we might as well quit.'

It was a good two miles back to the vehicle. We trudged it in dispirited silence, and once home fell exhausted into our beds.

I woke in the grey light of dawn to the smell of burning and the gentle fall of ash. Everything stank of fire. Across the horse paddock, smoke wreathed like blue mist between the trunks of the ti-tree and silver-leaf, and the surface of the waterhole was scummed with ash.

Even as I watched, a tree fell on the far creek-bank, swaying downwards with a mighty thump, its butt gnawed through by flames.

We breakfasted in gloomy silence.

Dad said, 'Scrub country's made to burn. I told yer you'd do no good with the fire,' which wasn't strictly true.

Judith was immediately angry. 'It's not a matter of being right or not, it's about what the horses are going to eat, apart from poison.'

Dad buttered his toast. 'We could always sell out.'

'It mightn't all have burned,' I began, before his words registered. 'What?'

Patrick was already rising from the table. 'I'll ride out and check. We mightn't even have a paddock left the way that fire was going last night. If we haven't, I suppose we'd better get the packs out and shift 'em.'

He picked up his bridle, and a short time later I saw him saddling Gingham and vanishing with her over the creek-bank at the back of the house.

I went to fill the calico tuckerbags we used with the packs and forgot Dad's remark about selling.

Patrick was back before mid-morning, a silly, unbelieving grin on his face. 'You just wouldn't credit it!' he said jubilantly. 'Every post is standing, and we haven't lost a yard o' feed.'

'How come?' Judith asked blankly.

Patrick shrugged, opening his hands. 'It burnt to the end of the ridge and just run outa steam, I guess. There's a big heap o' broken sandstone there, nothing much for the flames to catch. It went down the slope a bit and fizzled out, and on the flat country it got to within a yard o' the fence and stopped.'

'Why?' I stared at him, perplexed. 'I mean, what stopped it? Something must have, surely?'

'A horse-pad. How d'you like that? Must've been just creeping then, no wind, so nothing to carry it across. Anyway, it's out.'

I unpacked the tucker I had been putting up, and then, because it was plane day at the mission, Dad and I drove across to pick up the mail. I left him at the office, waiting for the bags to be sorted, and went round to Isabelle's place, but found only her ten-year-old son. His mum had gone to the hospital, he said, because someone was having a baby. So I went looking for Helen instead.

The deputy principal shared a flat that had been built onto one side of a large meeting hall, with a screened verandah along one end. She was there, working at a cane table, with a coffee cup beside her. A big woman in her late thirties with long brown hair, she had lived at the mission for nearly twenty years.

'Thanks.' I took the coffee she made me with my left hand, looking at her books. 'Are you studying too, Helen? University?

I thought you had to go to lectures and stuff, actually attend. I mean, to get a degree?'

'Not with an external course. They send lecture notes out. I'm doing an arts degree. You could too, you know.'

'Me?' I stared at her and laughed. 'I didn't even do high school.'

'You're doing it now, aren't you? Get yourself two good senior passes and you can apply for entrance as a mature-age student. Look, it's all in the handbook here. Take it home and read it. You could do it. Anybody can be as educated as they want to be.'

'You sound just like my father.'

She poked a biro into her hair. 'He's a smart man, then. When do you sit exams?'

'Next year. I've started a second subject, so I'll sit both then. Here at the mission school, actually.'

'That means you've got twelve months to think about it.' She cleared the cups away and picked up a folder of notes. 'Bring the handbook back when you've finished with it, won't you?'

Among the letters that day was a fat buff envelope addressed to Dad. He opened it when we got home, and when the evening meal was over, spread the papers on the table for us all to read. It was a sale prospectus for Wentworth Station, containing a description and a two-page listing of the stock and plant included in the sale. Wentworth was a large property lying to the north of Bowthorn, with the Territory border as its western boundary and its northern one the coastline.

I skimmed the pages, neither the price nor the number of cattle really registering, my mind already made up. I pushed them away. 'What's this, then?'

Dad was filling his pipe. He poked the stem of it at the papers, now in Judith's hands, and said, 'That's where we ought to be. Now, if we bought that place, with the herd numbers old George is showing there, we could –'

'No.'

'You haven't thought about it, girl. They've got flat country with roads already pushed through, permanent waters, yards that'll hold stock. If you'll just –'

'No.' I shook my head. 'I'm not interested in selling.'

'Me either,' Judith said. 'We're just starting to get this place into shape. What's the point of racing off to begin again somewhere else?'

'The point? Jesus!' Dad slammed his hand down on the table, making the pressure light jump. 'The point is to better your situation. You could keep horses up there, for one thing. They don't have poison in that country.'

'Because it's coastal,' Judith said. 'That means sour feed, tidal creeks, man-eating crocs – give me the rattlepod any day. How much stock do they lose to crocs and floods? That's a fifty-inch rainfall area on the coast.'

'Every property has its drawbacks,' Dad said. 'It mightn't be perfect, but it's twice the size o' Bowthorn, for starters. What d'you think, son?'

Patrick put the papers down and shook his head. 'We'll have this place paid off next year. I say we stop here and work it. The poison's a problem, but you just got through saying every property's got something wrong with it. Wentworth's too far out, for one thing.'

'Too far?' Dad looked incredulous. 'How can any place be too far? You want to live in town, or what?'

'Every mile from market adds to yer cost,' Patrick said mildly. 'Comes to that, we're already too far out here.'

'Christ on a camel!' Dad sounded disgusted. 'Anyone'd think you were forty. I've never seen such a conservative bunch as you lot. You've got the chance to grab something better and you worry about freight.'

The light hissed and flared as we listened, unmoved, to his tirade on missed opportunities and the many times his ideas had triumphed over our caution, but I think he realised, even as he spoke, that this time we meant it. He grumped off to bed at last, leaving us sitting there.

Judith folded the papers up and stuck them under the lamp. 'He's getting restless,' she said. 'We've been here three years, that's nearly a record for us.'

'It's more than that.' I felt sad for him, but no more inclined to sell up because of it. 'He just wants to run things again. I mean, he drives the camp vehicle and does a bit of cooking, and that's about it. A green kid could do as much. I suppose he thought if he could talk us into buying he'd be making decisions, mapping new country. He'd feel back in charge.'

'You're probably right,' Judith said. 'I wish ...' But she didn't complete the sentence, and next day I found the screwed up prospectus in the woodbox. I lit the fire with it, and though Dad was morose for a week, he didn't broach the subject of selling again.

The rest of summer was spent putting in a power plant and building a shed to house it. Only the generator was new. We used the old diesel motor off the boring plant and built the shed, which was circular, out of creek stones held together with a mortar of crushed termites' nests. It set like concrete and was every bit as durable. The floor and engine block were done with cement, but the rafters were cut from lancewood and the roof made from inch-thick slabs of bark stripped from giant river paperbarks.

Patrick had taken himself to Doomadgee to see the electrical contractor working there, and came back equipped with the necessary knowledge to install the plant and wire the place.

Dad, who wouldn't touch it himself, was edgy. 'That's two hundred and forty volts, son. You want to know what you're doing.'

'I do.' Patrick spoke briefly. He hadn't finished fourth-year primary school but there was genius in his fingers. They could build or repair anything from a faulty pressure lamp to an internal combustion engine, and when the generator arrived in late January, he demonstrated that he understood electric circuitry quite as well as anything else he undertook.

The old tin shed we called the house was wired by then, so the first time the diesel coughed into life we were all waiting, somewhat uneasily, in the kitchen where the switchboard had been installed. And soon Patrick's hat bobbed into view in the window.

'Okay,' he said, 'turn it on.'

I pulled the switch he had shown me and the shadowy corners of the long building sprang suddenly clear as light blazed over them. No loud bangs or smoke accompanied the action, and nothing burst into flame. I breathed again, hearing the engine settle into a slow, metronomic beat, and then we were grinning delightedly at one another as the full import of this new acquisition burst upon us.

'We can get a coldroom,' I said. 'And a washing machine.' We already had a motor-driven one with a choking exhaust that made it a penance to use.

'Fans for summer,' Judith added. 'And no more lamps!' Hands on hips, she looked about her. 'Us, with electricity. Whoever would have thought it?'

That month was not only the start of a new decade, the seventies, but for us a new era as well.

There was heavy rain in February and March, but by April the country was drying out and it was colt-branding time again. Judith and Patrick went off to the Elizabeth Creek country to get the stallion's mob back, and taking a rare day off from study, I went fishing with the dogs.

It was pleasant down by the creek. I chose a sun-sprinkled section of bank away from the taller tussocks where the mosquitoes lurked, and threw in my line. Angling, for me, was more about uninter-rupted thinking time than catching fish.

I pondered assignments and the course notes I was reading while taking in the moving patterns of light and shade on the water, the ripple that was a fish rising, and the antics of the beetly things that scurried around on the surface. Larry, stiff and bony, lay in the dappled shade but Red plunged about, ears up and tail wagging. He was in and out of the water, snuffling after the tiny darting angler fish until I growled at him. 'Quit it, will you? You'll scare 'em all off.' Then the line jerked and went out with a rush that set him barking with excitement.

It was a big catfish. I hauled it in until it lay flapping in the shallows, not like a fish at all with its smooth gunmetal skin and long whiskers, the spine on its back erect as it struggled. I wound the line short and swung the fish up the bank, and Red gave a great happy *whuff* and grabbed it just as I yelled. The spine pierced straight through the roof of his mouth. He let out a scream and shook his head, and the fish went flying, all slime and tail, with the sunlight winking on the wet line and the silvery hook through its lip.

Red kept screaming and scrabbling at his jaws. I could sympathise, a catfish spine was instant agony. He bundled about, shaking and howling, while Larry watched like an old grey judge, his front paws crossed and head a little to one side. I bent to pat Red but he shot past me yelping, heading for home. Larry yawned happily, tail stirring, then lowered his head onto his paws. Red was top dog these days, and Larry had had to get used to it.

The brood mares returned, fat-rumped and glossy-hided, some with young foals, others with yearling colts running on them. Old Queeia was as black and shiny as an enamel pot. She was an ugly, long-headed mare, but the quickest thing I had ever ridden, and was now the mother of a big bay colt. Her black ears lopped and she snorted at us, shuffling sideways to keep us away from him.

'Oh, look at Teena's filly!' I watched the foal springing about the yard on delicate limbs, dainty as a gazelle.

'Pretty, eh?' Judith eyed her. 'Going to be a grey.'

I nodded. You could tell by the look of her tufty coat that the colour would change.

'What's the liver-chestnut there? Big filly with the star.' Dad pointed and I snapped my fingers trying to remember.

'That's ... oh ... Blondie, isn't it?' I looked at Judith.

'Yes. Token's foal, so she's old Trinket's line. Dead quiet, just like her grand-dam.'

It was more than you could say for the colts. They skittered about, snorting, crowding the corner of the yards while the mares were drafted off. The stallion, Decimal Currency, was already working himself into a lather in another yard, and from time to time, as we carried out the branding and gelding, his imperious whinny blasted across the maze of rails and gates separating him from his harem.

When we had finished them all, Judith opened the side gate and let the mares trot out into the big receiving yard with its twenty-foot cap-rail cut from a single bloodwood trunk.

'We could call her Honour,' she yelled, as Teena's filly danced past. 'Let the stallion out, will you?'

I was closest. I climbed over the rails and jumped down into the loose sand his restless hooves had churned. The horse's body was black with sweat and the great muscles of his neck and chest gleamed as though oiled. He dipped his head, snorting, and swung into a canter, tail bannering behind him, then his front foot skidded on the turn and he drove straight into the gatepost and broke his neck.

I heard a crack, overlaid by the thunking noise of his head smashing into the post, and saw the dust rise as he fell. He was dead before he hit the ground. It was as quick as that, and as he died, down by the gate, Teena swung her head over her foal's back and whinnied to him, ears pricked above soft dark eyes, the sound coming high and clear under the bright April sky.

TWENTY-THREE

In May, when the cattle work started, Judith and Patrick mustered first along the Accident, because the short days gave them an opportunity to work the newly broken colts. Dad rode out with them twice, just to hold the coaching mob – the quiet cattle they took with them to run the wilder stuff into.

Next day the four of us drafted and branded in the station yards, with Dad tending to the fire and the irons while the rest of us handled the gates and ropes. He could no longer spring for the rails or get out of the way when a beast charged, so we preferred to have him outside the yard.

The drafted cattle consisted of big steers and a few dry cows – every herd had its barren females – which were sold off as fats. Patrick ran them through the cooling yard, where they moved about, testing the rails, sunlight glinting on their burnished hides. There was a wild set to their heads but paddocking would settle them down. Tomorrow, Patrick said, he and Judith would start across to Goat Pocket with them, and get them safely behind the wire there.

'We'll take the packs, so two's enough for the job,' he told Dad. 'Maybe you two could get the rest of 'em out when we've gone.'

'After we get a killer,' I reminded them. So we killed next morning, and hung and salted the meat. Then I got our saddlers up from the paddock. Dad had Silver, who wore a matronly look because she was in foal to poor dead Decimal, and I put my gear on Charlie. Larry walked halfway to the yards behind us, then lay down, cocking his knobby old head to watch us go. Red was on the chain, howling mournfully at being left, the noise fading behind us as we rode.

It was a golden May morning, with the drying feed bending before the breeze in ripples of colour and the air dense with the scent of early wattle. There were ducks on Boring Plant swamp. They flapped, whistling into the air as we passed, and Dad, tossing a stick at a pair of calves bunting each other in play, reined alongside me.

'You know, girl,' he said, 'I rode out on a morning just like this, years back, at Anson's paddock. You were with me, or maybe it was your sister. Anyroad, whoever it was was learning to tail horses. I don't suppose you remember?'

'I remember Anson's. Mulga country, with a big dam. Patrick used to go yabbying there.'

'That's the place. You were all just kids then.' His eyes moved over the little mob of cattle, the big, cock-horned cow in the lead

302

and the calves playing on the tail, the fresh brands clear on their glossy hides.

'We've come a fair piece since those days. Had some good horses, too.' Sitting awkwardly in the saddle with his bad leg stuck out, he patted Silver's neck. 'This old girl's the last of 'em that I'll ride.'

I looked across at him. 'What d'you mean, the last? What are you talking about?'

'I'll be leaving. You don't need me here. A man's a nonentity in the business, nothing but a wood-and-water joey.' He spoke mildly but there was a hardness in his gaze, as if his age and infirmities were somehow attributable to us.

'Dad . . .' But there was nothing to add. I would not assault his pride with words. The facts were that he could not work, nor would he stay idle, and it had never been in his nature to take second place. 'What will you do?'

'I've been offered a job by one o' the agencies, flogging cattle-lick and fencing round the stations. Quite a big area o' country – Normanton across to Croydon, down to Julia Creek. You don't have to worry about me. I shan't starve.'

'But you can't just walk out and begin all over again! The station –'

'O' course not. I'd need a vehicle for starters. No, if you're all agreeable, I'll take the rest o' the payments coming in from the sale o' Yeldham. They run another, what, six years, counting this one. That'll set me up.'

'And where would you live?'

He shrugged. 'Find a flat somewhere, some bush town. I'll see when I get that far.' He reined the grey mare into the shade of a beefwood. 'This'll do 'em. They'll find their own way from here.'

We sat and watched the cattle draw away from us until all but one young cow, which had stopped to suckle her calf, had melted into the scrub. It was very quiet, just the background noise of flies and birds, and the wind like ghost feet passing in the grass.

I watched Dad's hands pressing down on Silver's neck as he eased his hip and felt keenly unhappy for him, but at the same time, and not without guilt, I was relieved by his decision to go. His health and age were a burden on my mind, as was his discontent, which led him to constant faultfinding. He had not been easy to live with for the past couple of years.

He looked up, and pulling his quart pot from its cradle, gave it to me. 'Slip down and get us a drink, will you?'

We were sitting our saddles on the banks of Halfway Hole, so I reined Charlie onto the pad leading down through the bull grass to the rocks and water below. Gums overhung the hole, shading the surface to an inky blackness, and Charlie, stiffening his front legs as he slid down the bank, made little whiffling snorts of unease.

'Get on with it!' I touched him with the spurs and he gave a mighty blast and whirled about so fast he almost unseated me. Something streaked in a low dive from the rocks to the water's edge, then my hand hit the bank that Charlie had barged into and Dad's quart pot followed the little croc into the waterhole.

The water was waist-deep where it had fallen, so I wound up wet through, though all but my jeans had dried by the time we got back to the yard. It was midday by then, the shadows short on the hoof-tracked ground. Beyond the yard crows flapped and quarrelled about the killer's carcass, which we had towed across the swamp, and a score of kite hawks perched like bloated statues in the trees above it.

Dad swung himself heavily down and unlatched his Bates' gear.

'I'll do it.' I pulled the saddle off Silver and slung it across the rail in the shed, putting my own behind it.

Dad slipped the bridle off the mare, scratching behind her ears where the sweat itched, then let her go with a pat. 'She'll foal in spring,' he said, watching her walk away. Then Larry came halting out from under the pack rail to join us. 'Poor old fella.' Dad squatted, something that was no longer easy for him to do, and the dog came slowly to him. He gently pulled the tattered ears through his big fingers and when he had done Larry licked his hand. The dog gave a little shiver and a great sigh and flopped forward and died with his head across Dad's boot, his whiskery muzzle just brushing the ground.

I sank down beside him, feeling as if my legs had been kicked from under me. Death's blue film had already covered the warm intelligence of his eyes. I touched the broad ridge above them and looked at Dad. 'Just like that?'

'He had a fair crack o' the whip.' Dad was gruff. He stroked the limp body, then pulled the collar from round Larry's neck and hung it in the shed. We took the old dog out behind the yards and left him there in the grass for the birds to find.

Turning away, I had a memory out of childhood of all of us – Sian and Patrick, Judith and me – standing round the body of the first horse ever to die on us. Larry had been a pup then, all feet and head, and I had been about twelve.

'Remember when Bora died? And we actually wanted to bury him? Sian had the shovel all ready.'

'I do.' Dad slanted a look at me. 'Proper newchums you were back then. You've learned a bit since.'

Yes. Animals died, that's what we learned. The best, the worst, the ones you loved the most – and today it was Larry's turn. I put the kettle on for tea and we sat on the verandah to drink it, talking of inconsequential things but feeling the emptiness a dog's death leaves.

～

It was the end of June before Dad actually went. He had been down to Townsville by then to buy a suitable vehicle, but there was business with the bank and the solicitor regarding the deeding over of his share of the property to us. We had talked the matter over privately between us, all three agreeing that his decision was for the best.

'If there was just something he could do about the place,' Judith said. 'He could have the office with my blessing, but he hates book-work. It's why he pushed it onto me in the first place.'

Dad, having made his intentions clear, did not enlarge upon them. It wasn't his way. When he packed up, he left his spurs and whip and saddle, but took his swag and the old tin trunk he'd carried droving. He left his dog, too. 'Be a nuisance, travelling,' he said, looking down at Red. We made our goodbyes, and he took a last look round at the sheds and yards drowsing in the quiet morning, then got into the vehicle and drove off, the dust pluming high and straight behind him.

'Well,' I patted the whining dog at my side, 'that's that, Red. You'll just have to make do with me.'

Life on the station went on just the same without him. He wrote from time to time and occasionally called me on the wireless from whichever property he was visiting. The days continued to wind past into weeks, which in turn became months. But I was studying so hard I scarcely noticed his absence or the passing of time. In July, the sale cattle went off to the Lawn Hill yards again, and when Judith and Patrick returned, it was with the story of a horning that had occurred while they were down there.

'He was a townie,' Judith said. 'A friend of the Kahls, staying in the big house with them. Just out for the weekend with his family, and it was old Kahl who brought him down to the yards, to see how it's done, I s'pose. Only he insisted on making like a cowboy and getting in with the cattle. We'd just finished loading our lot and the truck was pulling out when we heard all this bellowing. It was Kahl – the man's got a voice like a bull – and he was yelling, 'Get up the rails, Al! He's behind yer! Get up the rails!' She paused. 'So instead of jumping for his life, what does Al do but stop for a look. It was a big, speary-horned bullock and it got him in the buttock. The doctor came out and picked him up just after lunch.'

In August the two of them were back out mustering and Dad had settled into a flat in Mt Isa, where he was to live for the next five years. I had memorised all the major speeches in *Macbeth* before Judith and Patrick returned but was in despair over my studies since, try as I would, none of the papers were ever marked higher than a six or a seven, and there were few helpful comments about the cause of the low marks. 'Spelling!' was sometimes written in red ink across a page, or 'Keep to the point, please' along the margin of an essay. It took a month for the corrected work to come back, and I now dreaded opening the returned envelopes.

'If only I knew what they were marking it out of,' I told Judith. 'I mean, if it's twenty there's no point in sitting the exam. I got a five for the history assignment on the Roman senate – that's only 25 per cent. And if they mark out of ten, well, it's still not much better, is it? I'd need at least eight just to scrape in.'

'Have you ever thought it might be out of seven?' Judith pulled off her boots and wriggled her toes.

'Don't be daft. Whoever heard of . . .? It was always twenty, or ten at school.'

'Well, you could write and ask.'

I stared at her. 'No I can't. It's bad enough messing up the work. I'm not going to admit I don't even know *that*.'

She stood up. 'Okay. I'm having a shower. You sit here and worry if you want, but I know what I'd be doing. When are the exams anyway?'

'In November.'

'So why don't you ask Helen? Show her one of your papers and maybe she can tell you what, if anything, is wrong.'

'D'you know, I never even thought of that.' I jumped up. 'You're a genius.'

'I'm not,' she said, 'I've just got commonsense. You could use a bit sometimes.'

We had already had the mail that month, so in September I went across to Doomadgee with Patrick, taking two corrected papers with me. I had to wait until school finished, then nipped across to the meeting hall, catching Helen just as she pushed the gate open.

'I won't stay,' I said hastily after my greeting. 'I expect you want to study. It's just – I wondered if you could take a quick look at something?'

'Of course. Come inside. How're your studies coming along?'

'Terrible. With the marks I'm getting there's no way I'll pass. But my teacher doesn't tell me anything, except that I can't spell, and I know that. I thought maybe you ...'

'Let's have a look.' She dumped the books she was carrying and ran her eye down the coversheet of my papers, then flipped quickly through the stapled pages, reading the red-inked comments. 'Well,' she looked quizzically at me, 'what's the problem?'

'The marks. That one's seven, and the other one's only a six. I've never got any better, I even had a five in the last lot. I didn't worry last year. I thought I'd improve, but how can I pass with that?'

She snorted, saying dryly, 'Oh, easily, I imagine. The system you're rated on makes four a pass. So five is a credit, six a distinction, and these sevens you're so worried about equal a high distinction.'

'They do?' I was stunned for a moment, then felt myself redden. 'I thought they were marking them out of twenty, or ten at the best – I'm such a fool. But a relieved one. I'll go now, and thank you, Helen, thank you.'

The euphoria of learning that I wasn't the dunce I had feared lasted through September but ebbed as October arrived. Towards the end of the month, Patrick and Judith brought the plant in for the last time and pulled the shoes off them in the yard. Half the horses went into the spell paddock, and the rest they took across to Horse Gorge and let go. Squeaky, the black cat, had another batch of kittens, and the humidity suddenly became so high that every bauhinia on the sand flats decked itself in scarlet tips. I worried that it would rain and put off the exam. And then I worried that it wouldn't.

'You'll be fine,' Judith said, but I was sick with nerves.

The dreaded day finally came. I went, remembering nothing of the drive across to the mission, and sat in isolation and wrote about English literature. Afterwards, drinking tea with Helen, I couldn't recall a single line of it. I drove home knowing I must return for the second history exam scheduled for later in the week, and when that was over I moved through weeks of regret, wishing I had tried harder or prepared more. And when finally the results of the first exam came in the mail I took up the envelope and couldn't open it. I stood there by the table for ages, just staring at it, afraid to tear it open and find out that I had failed. It seemed a long way back to where it all began – my mind skipped through the years, remembering Padre Brian and his books, and before that the dictionary I'd bought, and Dad in that camp on Riversleigh saying anyone could educate themselves.

In those days I had only wanted a home. And now, after years of work, I had one – not just a roof over my head, but a place to belong. It had to be the more difficult achievement, I thought, therefore if one could be accomplished why not the other? Taking a breath I slid my thumb under the flap and opened the letter.

'Well?' Judith demanded impatiently, and dazedly I passed it to her.

'High Distinction. I can't believe it! I'm going to do that uni course. It'll take years to finish. And then . . .'

I could see it, somewhere far in the future, as distant a prospect as the clouds that, glimpsed over dry lands, would someday patch them with green.

'Well?' She was grinning at me, waiting.

'Then I'm going to be a writer.'

EPILOGUE

Today Bowthorn is still home to the three of us. Things are very different now though – brick homesteads have replaced the old tin shed, and phones the wireless. We finally succeeded in getting a bore, and watering the garden is no longer a worry. There are gravel roads across the station, which has diversified into tourism, bringing throngs of travellers to our gates. All three of us still work the property, which Patrick manages. Judith runs the tourist camp in the centre of the station, and during school holidays Patrick's two children join the mustering team.

Sian is fruit farming these days in south-east Queensland. He has three grown children and still makes an annual pilgrimage to the bush with tuckerbox and swag. He became a grandfather in 2000 when Wendy's daughter was born. Dad knew all five of his grandchildren but not his great-granddaughter, for he died in

1992 in Charters Towers, his final camping place. He was eighty-five.

And me? I still garden and cook for the station, run the homestead tourist accommodation, and write. At the track's end where home begins I'm lucky enough to have it all – the special place I wanted and the career I chose, just as I dreamed all those years ago.

ACKNOWLEDGMENTS

For her encouragement, skill and sound advice I am deeply indebted to my friend and literary agent, Jane Arms, without whom this book would not have been written. Thanks are also due, and in no small measure, for the painstaking work of Penguin editor Meredith Rose, and to the many readers of *Pieces of Blue* who wrote and rang to ask, What happened next?